SPIRIT
COMMUNICATION

*A comprehensive guide to the
extraordinary world of mediums,
psychics and the afterlife*

ROY STEMMAN

D1465117

700039133021

PIATKUS

First published in Great Britain in 2005 by Piatkus Books Ltd
This paperback edition published in 2010 by Piatkus
Reprinted 2011 (twice)

A CIP catalogue record for this book
is available from the British Library.

ISBN 978-0-7499-4111-6

Text design by Briony Chappell
Edited by Krystyna Mayer

Typeset by Phoenix Photosetting, Chatham, Kent
Printed in the UK by CPI Mackays, Chatham ME5 8TD

Piatkus
An imprint of
Little, Brown Book Group
100 Victoria Embankment
London EC4Y 0DY

An Hachette UK Company
www.hachette.co.uk

www.piatkus.co.uk

Contents

Acknowledgements

The author would like to thank The Spiritual Truth Foundation who made a significant contribution to the publication of *Spirit Communication*.

The Foundation was established for the promotion and advancement of the religion and religious philosophy of Spiritualism. It finances the publication of books whose contents deserve a wider audience than that represented by the Spiritualist movement. It supports the publication of the series of books on the spirit teachings of Silver Birch and reprinting of out-of-print classics on spiritual knowledge and phenomena. The charity also alleviates poverty among Spiritualists.

For more information about The Spiritual Truth Foundation, or to make a bequest, please contact The Spiritual Truth Foundation, 15 Broom Hall, Oxshott, Surrey, KT22 0JZ.

Foreword

Spirit communication has been an integral part of most cultures from their earliest days, with the special gifts of oracles, shamans, witches, seers, mystics, prophets or psychics helping to guide and direct individuals and groups. Just over a century and a half ago, however, it seemed that the veil that separates this world from the next was lifted a little more, to allow greater contact between the two. Gifted individuals declared that a new age was dawning; loud raps and knockings responded to questions with a simple yes/no code, indicating contact with an unseen intelligence; and the religion of Spiritualism was born in the United States, quickly spreading around the world.

Spiritualism's humble birthplace was the tiny hamlet of Hydesville, just outside New York City, and its first, relatively modest manifestation consisted of strange knockings in the home of the Fox family, which began on 31 March 1848. Disturbed by these inexplicable sounds, John Fox, his wife and his two daughters Margaret and Kate soon discovered that they could communicate with the spirit responsible, who used a code to rap out his answers. He claimed to be a peddler who was murdered in the house and, indeed, human remains were later discovered buried in the cellar.

Hundreds of people witnessed the phenomenon: the raps were often so loud that many individuals gathered outside were able to hear them. Several committees were formed to investigate the phenomenon, and their tests included asking questions *mentally* to which the spirit gave replies. The raps followed the Fox sisters when they visited other places, and the talent seems to have spread quickly to others. Before long, Margaret, Kate and their older sister Leah were giving private sittings.

Within three years, there were an estimated one hundred mediums offering their services in New York and between 50 and 60 private circles had been established in Philadelphia. The first experimental organisation, the New York Circle, was also formed to test the powers of mediums claiming to be able to communicate with the spirit world.

Spiritualism had arrived but its birth was not without complications. By April 1855, the *North American Review* reported there were nearly two million Spiritualists in the United States. More powerful mediums than the Fox sisters had appeared and incredible stories circulated about heavy objects levitating, spirit voices speaking and even full-form materialisations of the dead appearing and speaking to their loved ones.

With Spiritualism's rapid growth and startling phenomena, which challenged both orthodox religion and science, it was inevitable that it attracted many detractors wishing it a short life. Their wish was almost granted, with the 'confession' of fraud – later retracted – by the Fox sisters in 1880. By then, however, there were enough serious-minded and influential people willing to testify to the truth of Spiritualism for it to survive the embarrassing behaviour of the movement's founders.

It took no time at all for Spiritualism to cross the Atlantic. It arrived in the form of Mrs W.R. Hayden, the first visiting medium, whose arrival in Britain in 1852 was greeted with derision by the press. Despite this, she convinced a number of intellectuals, among them veteran socialist Robert Owen, that the spirit world could communicate with them.

It wasn't long before Britain was experiencing an epidemic of table-turning and producing its own mediums, of whom Scottish-born Daniel Dunglas Home, who had moved to the United States at the age of nine in 1842, was one of the most spectacular, producing a wide range of manifestations in good light. The first investigator to be satisfied that he had mediumistic powers was a Professor George Bush, a distinguished theologian and Oriental scholar. Home returned to England in 1855 and was soon travelling throughout Europe, demonstrating his powers to heads of state, famous intellectuals and royalty, including Napoleon III, the King of Bavaria, the King of Naples and the Queen of Holland.

It is hardly surprising, then, that when Prince Albert died in 1861, Queen Victoria, like millions of others, turned to Spiritualism for comfort and reassurance that her beloved husband lived on and would be waiting for a reunion with her in the spirit world. She had sittings with several mediums and many Spiritualists believe that John Brown, her ghillie, was also a powerful medium through whom Albert regularly communicated with the Queen.

Despite attacks from narrow-minded religious zealots and closed-minded sceptics, Spiritualism still thrives globally, in different forms. It does so because, despite ridicule and criticism, it continues to provide evidence of spirit communication that many people regard as indisputable. Moreover the appearance and development of new mediums, who are continuing its tradition of providing a psychic bridge between this world and the next, are ensuring that its future is assured.

Spirit communication and Spiritualism are huge subjects and it would be impossible for a single volume to do justice to the past 150 years of its history. Fortunately, I do not need to do this, since there are already two excellent books that tell part of the story and to which this book should be seen as a companion volume.

The first of these books is *The History of Spiritualism* by Sir Arthur Conan Doyle. Born in Edinburgh in 1859, Sir Arthur was a physician whose passion for writing led to the creation of the world-famous fictional detective Sherlock Holmes. The cautious author spent 20 years studying and researching Spiritualism before proclaiming his acceptance of spirit communication. Having done so, he became one of Spiritualism's most enthusiastic advocates, embarking in 1916 on lecture tours to many countries to spread the word. The 150th anniversary of his birth was celebrated by Spiritualists in 2009.

Sir Arthur was assisted in producing *The History of Spiritualism* by W. Leslie Curnow, whose extensive knowledge of the

Spiritualist movement makes a vital contribution to the book. Its pages record the extraordinary contact with the spirit world experienced by Emanuel Swedenborg in the mid-1700s, the special powers of Andrew Jackson Davis, who predicted the coming of Spiritualism, and the incredible story of the movement's humble beginnings in the home of the Fox family at Hydesville in 1848.

The book covers the highlights of Spiritualism's first 75 years, introducing us to remarkable mediums such as Daniel Dunglas Home, the American brothers Horatio and William Eddy, slate-writing medium Henry Slade, Italian physical medium Eusapia Palladino and Boston physician's wife Margery Crandon, to name but a few of those whose mediumistic gifts convinced thousands that they could speak to the dead. We learn of sceptics such as Judge Edmonds and Dr Robert Hare, a professor of chemistry, who were not only forced to change their minds by the evidence they encountered, but also developed their own mediumship.

Eminent researchers such as Dr Alfred Russel Wallace, Sir William Barrett, Sir Oliver Lodge and Sir William Crookes add their testimonies that survival of death is beyond doubt and communication with the dead can occur through a variety of mediumistic phenomena, including trance, automatic writing, spirit photography, direct voice communication and materialisation.

Sir Arthur Conan Doyle's book was published four years before his death. Inevitably, with his passing, his widow and sons received numerous claims from around the globe that the world's most famous Spiritualist had a message for them. They made it clear that only those who believed they had irrefutable proof that they were in touch with the spirit of Sir Arthur should trouble them. One communication that provided that proof is recounted in Maurice Barbanell's book *This Is Spiritualism* and concerns medium Mrs Caird Miller. Days after he died, Sir Arthur gave her his ex-directory phone number, produced a spirit photograph of himself and materialised the key to his study on her pillow.

Maurice Barbanell was the founder and editor of *Psychic News*, a weekly Spiritualist newspaper, and later edited *Psychic World*. He therefore had unrivalled access to the very best mediums. Although *This Is Spiritualism* is not a historical record of the movement in the early part of the twentieth century, is does provide us with an exceptional, journalistic account of his personal spirit communications. He reported, for instance:

- That the disembodied spirit voices of his wife Sylvia's dead brother and grandmother spoke to them in daylight, in the presence of American medium Ann Keiser.
- How he arranged a reunion in Estelle Roberts' seance room between the spirit of Sir Henry Segrave, who was killed attempting to break the world water speed record on Lake Windermere, and his widow.
- Of thriller writer Edgar Wallace's spirit return on a photograph taken under test conditions.
- How well-known British industrialist Sir Vincent Caillard materialised at a Louisa Bolt seance and gave his signature, which was later shown to be identical to his earthly autograph.

Sir Arthur Conan Doyle's book was first published in 1926 and Maurice Barbanell's in 1959. The good news is that both are still in print, thanks to the Spiritual Truth Foundation, one of whose two principal charitable aims is to spread spirit truths by keeping important books in print or publishing new ones. (It has also supported this book's publication.)

Barbanell noted that Spiritualism had changed since the early days portrayed by Sir Arthur, with much less physical phenomena in evidence. In the 45 years since Barbanell completed his book, that dearth of physical evidence continues. But other phenomena have appeared that may yet prove to be as convincing as the early raps and levitations that so excited the Victorians.

We live in rapidly changing times, with science and technology seemingly taking precedence and organised religion experiencing dwindling numbers. Yet spirit communication continues to play a vital role in many people's lives.

I first encountered Spiritualism as a teenager, after reading a newspaper's serialisation of one of Air Chief Marshall Lord Dowding's books about spirit communications that he received from airmen killed during the Second World War. He recounted how, while in charge of Fighter Command and masterminding the Battle of Britain, he was also attending regular seances at which some of those who had been killed in action returned and asked him to contact their families with messages.

Intrigued, I began reading other books and, by a series of coincidences – some would call it fate – found myself writing about the subject as a freelance reporter for *Psychic News*. Soon I was a permanent staff member of the Spiritualist newspaper, assisting editor Maurice Barbanell in its weekly production, and remaining in that post for eight years. This gave me an unrivalled opportunity to meet and discuss spiritual matters with prominent UK Spiritualists – including Lord Dowding – and to witness the best mediums in action.

I sat in physical circles where direct voice and materialisations were said to be produced, received a psychic portrait of a dead friend, conducted experiments with leading mediums as well as a famous psychic photographer, spent a night in a house with a poltergeist, listened to the wisdom of spirit guides and witnessed numerous remarkable spiritual healings, as well as benefiting from healing myself.

I also became a council member of the Spiritualist Association of Great Britain, which gave me a useful insight into the workings of a major Spiritualist enterprise that continues to attract visitors from around the world to its Belgravia headquarters in the centre of London. After Maurice Barbanell's passing, my association with *Psychic News* was renewed and I joined its board, first as a director and then as chairman.

Some people assume that the moment you become a Spiritualist you lose your critical faculties. In fact, the opposite is usually true. Having been convinced of the reality of spirit communication, I also recognised the need for scientific investigation – an early interest in conjuring having shown me how easy it is to deceive people. For many years, I have been a member and supporter of the Society for Psychical Research – whose founders, incidentally, included several Spiritualists.

My interests also extend beyond mainstream Spiritualism, particularly in the area of reincarnation, and I have investigated many cases that have convinced me that some souls do return from the spirit world to live another life on Earth – perhaps even we all do. My investigations included a research trip to Lebanon, accompanied by a TV crew, to talk to the Druze community living in and around Beirut. Rebirth is the cornerstone of their religious belief and I encountered some truly astonishing stories.

The question I have been asking for the past 40 years is: what happens when we die? Spiritualism says it has the answer to this question, and I believe that when you reach the end of this book you will conclude that a far greater abundance of evidence and testimony to spirit communication exists than you ever imagined. You will also discover that the experiences and phenomena of the last half century are as colourful, exciting, thought-provoking and convincing as Spiritualism's first one hundred years.

It will then be time to seek your own experiences.

Chapter 1

My Introduction to Spiritualism

The image of a medium in a darkened room, calling 'Is there any-body there?' to invisible spirits, is one you are likely to see only in old films or plays. Today, spirit communication is performed in the full glare of spotlights on the stages of some of the world's biggest venues, or is beamed from television studios via satellites to millions of viewers around the globe.

Darkened seance rooms are still said to be necessary for the production of some physical phenomena, such as direct voice and materialisation, and I examine this aspect of Spiritualism in a later chapter. But it is mental mediumship – in which the medium's conscious mind is impressed by the spirits of the dead – that most exponents demonstrate, and it can be performed in almost any surroundings.

American mediums such as John Edward, James Van Praagh and Sylvia Browne, and British mediums Tony Stockwell, Sally Morgan, Derek Acorah and Colin Fry, appear to be as comfortable communicating with spirits in front of TV cameras as they would be in their own homes. The medium of television has introduced the possibility of spirit communication through human mediums to millions of people who would almost certainly not otherwise have gone in search of a Spiritualist meeting, at least until they suffered a bereavement. Now they can ponder its implications without leaving their armchairs.

The first Spiritualist meeting I attended, in 1959, was a weekly

1

London event run by a cockney medium, Joe Benjamin, whose style and humour made for a very entertaining evening, regardless of whether one received a spirit message or not. Unaware of this, I confess I walked up and down outside the Alliance Hall, near Victoria, several times before I plucked up the courage to go inside. I imagined all sorts of spooky happenings, but eventually took the plunge. Besides, I had a job to do: I was there to report on the meeting for *Psychic News*. It was the start of a quest that has continued for over 40 years, during which time I have been privileged to see top mediums in action and witness a variety of remarkable phenomena. Not all the mediums I encountered convinced me that they were in touch with spirits. But many have left me with no alternative but to accept the reality of life after death. Here I share that evidence with you as I examine the many different forms of spirit communication.

Laughing at death

Joe Benjamin's performance was outstanding and, for me, a revelation. Spiritualist meetings, I discovered, are not morbid affairs. The medium paced the platform, pointed to audience members and told them about people only he could see and hear, but whose names and descriptions were clearly recognised. Every so often, he would pause as if listening to someone whispering in his ear, then give a name or a date of special significance.

Sometimes, the people receiving these communications were so overcome with emotion that tears streamed down their cheeks as they nodded acceptance. Those close enough to witness this reaction were equally moved. But however poignant and emotional the content of a message, Benjamin always had a quip or a joke that would lighten the atmosphere.

'I told a lady last week that I had a gentleman in spirit who was telling me he had died of music on the brain,' he would tell the audience. '"That's right," she replied. "A piano fell on his head."'

By the time the laughter had subsided, Joe Benjamin had already started giving the next spirit message. There was no denying that for the majority of those present, the meeting was a very comforting experience.

Is it real?

Could I take this demonstration at face value, I wondered? Was the medium really talking to spirits, or were there other explanations? Few people who attend such a Spiritualist meeting for the first time come away totally convinced, and I was no exception. Even some of today's top mediums admit that they had doubts in the early days of their enquiry into Spiritualism. I certainly had mine, and as I journeyed home my mind was full of questions and theories. Before I could accept something as momentous and life changing as spirit communication, I needed to be sure that Joe Benjamin was not getting his information in some other way.

Could he have been a fraud? If this was the case, the cost of researching the information or paying someone else to do this would not even cover the admission charge at his small, weekly public meetings. A variation of this theory is that the recipients of a medium's messages are known to him. I deal with these and other allegations of fraud later (*see pages 167–76*). In the case of Joe Benjamin I soon satisfied myself that they did not apply – as indeed has been the case with the other prominent mediums I have encountered since.

A more plausible explanation – and the one most often put forward by sceptics – is that mediums are simply doing 'cold readings'. This is a technique of providing general information to which most people will respond positively, combined with close scrutiny of body language or verbal responses to carefully worded questions. The information elicited is then fed back to the person getting the message, who is convinced that the medium obtained it paranormally.

There are no doubt countless 'psychic readers' who employ these methods to make money out of gullible people. However, when you watch the best mediums demonstrating spirit communication, the information given is often so specific and remarkable that the 'cold reading' explanation has to be discarded.

As a reporter of public demonstrations of mediumship in those early days, my role was not only to record the mediums' statements but also to speak to as many of the recipients as possible when a meeting ended. In doing so, I uncovered some remarkable stories about why particular messages were so significant. This is where television does a better job, in some respects, than a public Spiritualist meeting, because after each message the information is analysed and discussed with the recipients, and shared with the viewing audience. The problem with TV mediumship, however, is that we have no way of knowing how much wrong information might have been left out in the editing in order to provide us with a more convincing programme.

Clairvoyance and clairaudience

Having satisfied myself that mediums could obtain information paranormally, I began learning more about the way in which they 'tuned in' to the dead. I discovered that mental mediums commonly used three psychic abilities to facilitate spirit communication: clairvoyance, clairaudience and clairsentience. These words all derive from the French and mean 'clear seeing', 'clear hearing' and 'clear sensing'. For some mediums, one of these psychic abilities dominates, so they are described as either a clairvoyant or a clairaudent, but in reality most use all three psychic senses.

This is how John Edward, the New York-based medium whose *Crossing Over* TV programme has a huge following, explains spirit communication in his book *One Last Time*:

Like other psychics and mediums, I hear sounds, see images, and – most difficult to explain – feel thoughts and sensations that are put into my mind and body by spirits on the Other Side ... In some cases, I can give a good reading simply by passing on what I'm hearing, seeing and feeling. But in most instances, I must interpret the information so that the meaning is understood. I call the entire process 'psychic sign language'. What I've been able to do in the years since I started this work is to become more fluent in understanding the symbols, making it easier for me to validate the presence of spirits.

Compare this with the words of Doris Collins, one of Britain's top mediums and healers, whose famous sitters included comedians Peter Sellers, Michael Bentine and Frankie Howerd, taken from her book *The Power Within*:

I operate by sense, sight, feeling and hearing and my knowledge comes from one or more of these faculties. It is not sufficient, however, just to see clairvoyantly. I have also to interpret what I am seeing. Those in the spirit world who wish to reach us often convey messages through symbols that they think will be easily understood.

The clairvoyant faculty provides the medium with images; clairaudience produces sounds, such as names; and clairsentience allows a medium to sense emotion, pain or illness. John Edward, incidentally, refers to two other psychic faculties: clairalience (clear smelling) and clairambience (clear tasting). He also says that it is his own inner voice – 'my mind's voice' – that he hears during a spirit communication, although he also occasionally hears a male or female voice, and even his mother's voice, talking to him.

A novel way to communicate

Finding the best image or symbol with which to convey information to a medium is clearly a major problem for spirit communicators, as the following story, recounted to me by Rosamund Lehmann, one of Britain's great twentieth-century romantic novelists and author of, among others, *Dusty Answer* and *Weather in the Streets*, demonstrates well. Rosamund was grief-stricken when her 23-year-old married daughter Sally, who was living in Java, died from polio in 1958. Having heard of friends' psychic experiences, she decided to attend a public demonstration of Ena Twigg's mediumship at the College of Psychic Studies in west London.

Ena Twigg

Rosamund Lehmann attended unannounced and was shocked when Ena Twigg began her demonstration with the words, 'I must come to this lady in the front. There's a very beautiful spirit building up behind you. She's writing the letter "S" around your head. Do you understand?'

Rosamund Lehmann murmured an acknowledgement.

'She hasn't been over very long,' the medium continued. 'My! This is a very strange message, one of the strangest I ... Why is she talking about the War God? She is saying Wotan, Wotan the War God... She is saying she does wish the War God would believe she is alive... Can you understand?'

At first, this meant nothing to the novelist.

'Oh! Now she's saying I haven't got the name quite right. She is laughing. She says you will understand. Do you understand?'

Suddenly, Rosamund Lehmann comprehended. It was impressive evidence from a complete stranger that her daughter was still alive. Her first husband, Sally's father, was Wogan Philipps. Sally, apparently, had replaced the 'g' with a 't' in Wogan as the only means of conveying the name.

When I interviewed the novelist about that first spirit communication, she recalled that at the end of the demonstration she joined a group of people eager to speak to the medium. 'Eventually I was able to say how wonderful the message had been, adding, "Would you like to know how extraordinary it was?"

"No, my dear," Ena Twigg replied. "I'm glad if it helps you.'"

Impressed with the medium's powers, Rosamund Lehmann arranged a private sitting with her. Sally communicated again, this time entrancing the medium and saying, 'Wasn't it clever of me, Mummy, to get his name through? I couldn't find the name in the medium's mind so I thought of doing it like this. Wasn't it clever of me?'

'My husband and I had been separated since 1941,' the novelist told me, 'and I wasn't thinking about him. Of course, I knew he was heartbroken at Sally's death, but I also knew there was no question of his sharing my beliefs, experiences and investigations. And I had never remotely connected him with the War God. If the name had been picked out of *my* subconscious it would have been his correct name, not Wotan.'

Despite Sally's explanation, I must say that I know of many cases of mediums giving foreign names that mean nothing to them, and are presumably not in their subconscious, but which are recognised by recipients.

Rosamund Lehmann received many more spirit communications from Sally through Ena Twigg, other mediums and her own mediumship, which she describes in her book *The Swan in the Evening*.

Spiritualism and the Church

I believed when I embarked on my investigation of Spiritualism that the Church was totally against spirit communication. That was certainly true of some clergy, whose outspoken comments on the subject grabbed headlines in local newspapers as they campaigned to get Spiritualist meetings banned. My thoughts were also influenced by the knowledge that the Church of England had suppressed the findings of a two-year commission of inquiry into Spiritualism, during which its members had seances with mediums. The majority found in favour of Spiritualism, but their report, submitted in 1939, was not officially released at the time – though it was leaked and published by *Psychic News*.

As I delved deeper, I discovered that throughout its history Spiritualism has always had supporters from within the Church – and to my surprise, I soon found I was having far more dealings with the Church and its leaders than I had expected. They included Dr Mervyn Stockwood, Bishop of Southwark – a South London diocese of two-and-a-half million people – who kindly wrote the preface to my very first book, *Medium Rare: the Psychic Life of Ena Twigg*.

'Knowing Ena Twigg as I do, I am not surprised by Roy Stemman's accounts,' he wrote. 'Not only have I complete confidence in her integrity, but I have been present on many occasions when things have happened which cannot be explained, so it would seem, by the ordinary means of perception.'

He ended with these words: 'As a Bishop I would not want to subscribe to all the views expressed in this book, but I am in wholehearted agreement with its main purpose, which is to invite readers to examine the possibility of a realm of existence which is greater than that to which we are normally accustomed, an existence which includes but transcends the grave.'

What led a Church of England bishop to speak so positively about mediumship at a time when many of his colleagues were still outspoken against Spiritualism? The bishop agreed to be interviewed for the book, as well as to write the preface for it, so I kept an appointment with him at the House of Lords, where he had taken prayers before the House sat, then listened while their noble lords discussed matters ranging from germ warfare to the salary scales of speech therapists. Question Time over, he rose from the government benches and made his way to the high-ceilinged, wood-panelled Bishops' Room to discuss spirit communication with me.

'I have had experiences with Ena Twigg where these theories [telepathy and reading the subconscious mind] cannot apply,' he told me. 'For instance, I never knew my father. I was born in 1913 and he was killed in 1916 so he was virtually unknown to me. Yet I have had encounters with him, through Ena Twigg's mediumship, where he has referred to all sorts of people whose names meant nothing to me at all. It was only after I had checked with people who *did* know, that I found such people had existed and that he had known them.'

I was fascinated to learn that there were times when the Bishop of Southwark realised that spirit communication was the only way for some people – Christians and those of other faiths – to come to terms with the loss of loved ones.

'I have sent them to Ena Twigg, and indeed to other mediums as well, and they have received that degree of assurance that gives them hope; that makes them believe that death is not the end; that their loved ones are alive and communication is possible. I would not send them to just *any* medium. Some are the biggest crooks I have encountered; utter rascals, who exploit grief. But you get this in all religions. Even the Church of England, I have no doubt, has unworthy parsons who bring no credit whatsoever on their alleged vocation.... . On the other hand there are mediums who are people of integrity. I believe Ena Twigg is one of them. I have explicit trust in her credentials.'

The irony was that only twenty years earlier, in 1951, the British Parliament had passed the Fraudulent Mediums' Act, which gave Spiritualists religious freedom. Before that legislation was passed, Ena Twigg and thousands of other mediums were liable to prosecution under the Witchcraft Act of 1735 every time they held a seance.

Guidance from beyond

Proving life after death is the main purpose of mediumship, but offering guidance on earthly matters often goes hand in hand with providing such evidence. Purists dismiss this as fortune-telling and discourage mediums from discussing future events. When, however, spirit communicators have the ability to glimpse the future, and want to convey what they see, they usually pass it on, for what it is worth. The message may be about nothing more significant than a change of house or job, but at times it can be a matter of life and death.

Doris Stokes, one of Britain's most famous mediums in the 1970s and 1980s, recounts an astonishing personal experience of receiving such guidance in her book *Voices in My Ear*. It concerns Yorkshire medium Walter Brookes, who was an impressive public demonstrator and the first one to give her a spirit message – from her father Sam – when she was investigating Spiritualism. Later, she and her husband John got to know Walter well. One day during a casual conversation with Walter, he told her she would have to go into hospital in July, where she would be told she was going to die. Aged 33 and feeling extremely well, she was surprised but sceptical, despite knowing how good a medium her friend was. He then insisted that she write down the name Mrs Marrow, who was the person she must ask for when that situation arose. This information, he added, was coming from her dead father. Her husband John Stokes was equally sceptical, yet he jotted it down on a piece of paper and placed it in his wallet.

Doris Stokes remained in good health until she awoke one night in July with excruciating stomach pain. She was rushed to hospital, where an ectopic pregnancy was diagnosed. The egg had fertilised in the Fallopian tube instead of in the womb. 'I'm sorry, Mr Stokes,' the consultant said. 'Your wife is dying.'

Recalling Walter Brookes' spirit message from his wife's father, John Stokes took the name he had been given from his wallet and asked the consultant if he knew a Mrs Marrow. He was told she was a gynaecologist working at Nottingham Hospital. At his insistence, despite the seriousness of his wife's condition, Doris Stokes was transferred by ambulance to Nottingham and put under Mrs Marrow's care, and made a gradual but complete recovery. Thanks to spirit intervention her life was saved and she went on to become a top medium in her own right, demonstrating in Britain and abroad at huge public meetings, including sell-out shows at the London Palladium – the first time a medium had taken over that famous venue for a Spiritualist meeting.

However difficult it may be for us to accept that those in the spirit world can sometimes see what the future has in store for us, there are plenty of excellent examples of mediums communicating such information. Fiona Golfar, editor at large of the fashion magazine *Vogue*, described with awe a telephone conversation she had years ago with Derbyshire medium Rita Rogers. Fiona was then a new wife, a new mother and living in a new house. A lot of things were happening to her and, she told writer Justine Picardie, she felt she needed guidance.[1] Two friends told her how helpful medium Rita Rogers had been, so she rang her. She recounted:

> I was in London and she was at home in Derbyshire, but she told me everything – from the smallest details, like the fact I was phoning her from a red room – to very important stuff, like saying that my brother needed to be tested for diabetes, and that I would have a daughter within a year. True enough, my brother was diagnosed as diabetic two months later, and I had a baby girl.

Princess Diana's Spiritualist beliefs

Years later, on 12 August 1997, Rita Rogers became one of Britain's most famous mediums when a Harrods helicopter landed in a field next to her house in a working-class district of Chesterfield, Derbyshire, and out stepped Diana, Princess of Wales, and Dodi Fayed. The princess had been consulting Rita Rogers for four years before that visit and had been comforted after her father's death. The high-profile visit, caught on camera by locals and published in the tabloid press, made Diana's visits to a Spiritualist medium world news. Just over two weeks later, the princess and her lover were dead, killed in a car crash in Paris.

Rita Rogers has said that during that fateful visit to her home in August 1997, she warned Dodi he would be in an accident. But, she told Jane Kelly: 'I didn't know that Diana would be with him. When she called me from Paris [at 4 pm on Saturday, 30 August 1997, a few hours before she died], it all came back, and I told her to come home immediately, in daylight. That was the last thing I said to her.'[2]

Some have criticised Rita Rogers for not warning the couple what fate had in store for them, but that assumes that mediums or their spirit guides know *everything* there is to know about the past, present and future. Even if they did, however, perhaps there are some things we are not meant to know. My own view, which I share with most Spiritualists, is that there is a blueprint – a purpose – to our lives, but that we also have free will. We must make right or wrong decisions in our lives, and should not depend on mediums or the spirit world to tell us what to do or what not to do. After all, they could be wrong.

That's something else I learned early on. Mediums are not infallible. Having said that, when the great mental mediums of the 1960s, 1970s and 1980s – such as Stanley Poulton, Norah Blackwood, Ena Twigg and Gordon Higginson – were certain about the accuracy of what they were receiving, they would happily convey it to the recipient, and it was usually proved that their information was correct. Their clairvoyant, clairaudient and clairsentient faculties had developed to such a level that they were even able to fill the huge Royal Albert Hall in London, year after year, at Spiritualism's annual Service of Remembrance, close to Armistice Day. When they were not participating in public propaganda meetings, they toured the UK, appearing at some of the estimated 700 Spiritualist churches.

My first sitting

Impressed though I was with the early public demonstrations of mediumship I observed in churches and halls, I was still not totally convinced that spirit communication was the only explanation for the phenomena I was witnessing. Clairvoyance and clairaudience were apparently forms of telepathy between a medium's mind and the minds of spirits of the dead. Perhaps mediums were misinterpreting the source of what they were seeing and hearing. Could they be picking up the thoughts and desires of people in their audiences? To help me reach a conclusion, I decided that the time had come for me to have a private sitting: a one-to-one discourse with a medium.

My search for personal evidence of spirit communication took me to the door of Bertha Harris, in north-west London, at the end of the 1950s. Known affectionately as Battling Bertha, she was one of Britain's top mediums during the Second World War and was still producing remarkable results when I consulted her. I had booked the sitting over the telephone and given an assumed name, just to rule out the possibility that she could have done some research on me before we met, even though I knew that this was highly unlikely.

The sitting lasted two hours, beginning with an aura reading, moving on to events in my life and then providing evidence of survival after death. My father appeared to communicate, correctly indicating the cause of death and also the day of the week on which he died. The medium then took hold of the end of her long dress, wrapped it around her thumb and made a dabbing motion. She released the material, then clenched her right hand as if holding an implement, and made squiggly movements along the tabletop.

'I've no idea what I'm doing,' she told me. 'But he's showing me that he did this.'

I was taken aback. My father was a painter and decorator who loved creating wood-grain effects on plain walls. He would vary the effects, sometimes creating a walnut appearance by dabbing the freshly stained wall with a cloth wrapped around his thumb. In other rooms he used a steel comb, which he dragged over the surface in an undulating fashion to imitate the pattern of wood grain.

Throughout my sitting, I said as little as possible, deliberately confining my responses to a nod, or a 'Yes' or 'No'. There was little I needed to say because she was making statements rather than asking questions. So I acknowledged the significance of the actions she had demonstrated without explaining why.

Bertha Harris said, however, that her spirit helpers were telling her that I was very sceptical and later, when I thought about this evidence, I would decide that she had been reading my mind. So, they would try to give me some information that was unknown to me and I would need to check it.

She told me she was aware of the spirit of a journalist. Immediately, my sceptical mind kicked in. I was a teenager consulting a medium and making copious notes. It was not too difficult for Bertha Harris to have concluded that I was a journalist. My scepticism evaporated when she added: 'No, I'm sorry, he's not a journalist. He's the *father* of a journalist you work with. His name is Smith. I'm sorry it's such a common name but I can't change it. And he tells me you work in a large room with other people but his son is the only other man in the room.'

All of that was spot on. I was then an editorial assistant on a weekly trade magazine and the only other man on the team was the assistant editor, Arthur Smith, who was in his forties. But I was sure Bertha Harris was wrong, because Arthur often spoke of visiting his mother and father at the weekend.

'This man is telling me his initials are W.G. or W.J. – I can't quite hear if it's a J or a G – and that he died of a lung condition.'

I wrote this down on a piece of paper and casually asked Arthur during a pub lunch a few days later if his father was still alive. He looked a little shocked when I explained why I was asking, then responded, 'No, he died when I was three years old. His initials were W.G. I never really knew him and my mother remarried, so when I talk about my parents, it's actually my mother and stepfather. I believe my father died from a wound in his side. I'm seeing my mother this weekend. I'll ask her.'

The spirit communication was correct. W.G. Smith's death

certificate showed that the cause of his death was a lung condition – the result of inhaling mustard gas during the Second World War.

As far as I was aware, Bertha Harris and I were the only people in her dimly lit sitting room. There were no raps or knocks; no ghostly breezes or misty, ectoplasmic shapes – just a very elderly lady who could apparently see and hear the dead who were crowding the room eager to communicate with me.

It was my first sitting with a medium and it remains one of the best. It proved to me that telepathy could not explain some of the information I had been given and convinced me that Spiritualism was worthy of serious investigation. Four decades of study have reinforced that verdict.

1 *London Evening Standard*, 9 January 2004.
2 *Daily Mail Weekend*, 20 October 2001.

Chapter 2
When Spirits Take Over

Impressive though they are, there's no getting away from the fact that spirit messages from clairvoyants or clairaudients are conveyed through a go-between. How much better it would be if it was possible to speak to our dead loved ones more directly. Well, the good news is that, to a degree, trance mediumship satisfies that need. A well-developed trance medium allows his or her body to be taken over by spirits who can then control speech and carry on a normal conversation, just as they did when on Earth, about events and people of mutual interest.

Trance, whether self-induced or brought about by hypnosis or spirit entities, has featured prominently in the history of Spiritualism and psychic research. It is, however, a relatively rare form of mediumship in public, and when it is demonstrated it tends to be a single spirit guide who does the talking, giving descriptions of spirits and their messages. Private or home circles tend to be where the best evidence is produced and where one-to-one conversations take place.

Spiritualist terminology and definitions can be confusing at times – even to seasoned Spiritualists. But it is generally accepted that we each have a spirit guide who watches over us throughout our lives. Some prefer to use the term 'guardian angel'. This spiritual being is concerned about all aspects of our life. Individuals who develop mediumistic abilities are often channels for their guide. But they also have others in the next world whose interest is specifically in assisting with communication between the two worlds. They are sometimes called 'spirit controls' or 'controllers' and the personalities they present can range from serious adults to mischievous children. The spirit controls also act as 'doorkeepers' for trance mediums. Usually, the control is a go-between, relaying messages from the departed. But in special cases, they allow the spirit to take over the medium's body and speak directly to the sitter.

An impressive trance medium

One of Britain's top trance mediums during the war years was Lilian Bailey.

Lilian Bailey

By the time I met the chain-smoking medium at her home in Wembley, north-west London, she was in her late sixties and giving very few private sittings. With her white hair and a black patch over her left eye, she was an imposing figure with a remarkable presence. She happily talked to me about her trance mediumship and how frightened she had been when she was first 'taken over' by her spirit guide, William Hedley Wootton. 'I thought I was going to die,' she told me.

Lilian Bailey was reticent about talking of the many famous sitters who had been comforted by her mediumistic powers, but I knew they included Hollywood greats such as silent screen film star Mary Pickford, the actress Merle Oberon and the inimitable Mae West, as well as Canada's longest-serving prime minister, William Lyon Mackenzie King, and Chinese diplomat V.K. Wellington Koo and his wife during his time as Chinese Ambassador to Great Britain. The medium gave sittings in the Koos' London home. Koo was China's acting prime minister from 1926 to 1927 and also served as ambassador to France and the United States.

Royal seance

Nothing prepared me for the story that Lilian Bailey's son-in-law Gordon Adams, bookshop manager and company secretary at Psychic Press, publishers of *Psychic News*, confided in me after my first meeting with her. He revealed that a remarkable seance had taken place in 1953, not many years before I began investigating Spiritualism. I was sworn to secrecy and it was not until Lilian Bailey's death in October 1971 that I and others who knew the story were free to discuss it.

Lilian Bailey knew there were people who required her to perform under the strictest test conditions before they would be prepared to accept the evidence of their own eyes and ears, and she always did her best to satisfy those demands, within reason, Adams told me. So when she received a request from a stranger to give a seance at a house in Kensington, she agreed. A limousine took her to a well-appointed property, then she was taken on to another address. She was required to put on a blindfold during the journey so that there were no visual clues about the person or people she would be meeting. Again, she agreed.

She was eventually led into a room, where she sensed others were gathered, and was asked to conduct the seance still wearing the blindfold. This was not a great hindrance, since she often worked in a trance. Puzzled but philosophical about the lengths to which people went to test her mediumship, she eased herself into a chair and soon felt herself drifting off into a trance, allowing her main spirit helper Bill Wootton, and others in the next world, to take over her body and speak through her lips.

In what seemed to her like no time at all, she returned to normal consciousness and was told she could remove the blindfold. As her eyes grew accustomed to the light she surveyed the sitters. Sitting in a circle on gilt chairs were the Queen Mother, the Queen, Prince Philip, Princess Margaret, Princess Alexandra and the Duke of Kent.

This astonishing experience, which happened a year after the death of King George VI, had clearly been arranged in the hope of receiving a communication from the dead monarch, and it was almost certainly successful. However, since she was in trance, Lilian Bailey knew nothing of the conversations that took place between members of the British royal family and those from the spirit world who wished to speak to them. Unsurprisingly, none of those who participated has ever commented directly on the secret seance.

Royal biographer and *Daily Telegraph* court correspondent Ann Morrow included this story in her book, *The Queen Mother*. She had asked Gordon Adams if Lilian Bailey was unnerved when she removed her blindfold. He replied: 'My mother-in-law had dealings with all sorts of people, such as the Chinese leader Chiang Kai-shek and the King of Greece. So she did not feel intimidated by royalty; it was all in a day's work for her.'

The Queen Mother is reported to have continued to phone Lilian Bailey for some time after the seance and further private sittings took place. Eventually, when she came to terms with her loss and was clearly satisfied that the dead king continued to watch over her from the spirit world, she asked the medium to come to Clarence House one last time. Removing a piece of costume jewellery from the dress she was wearing, the Queen Mother pinned it on Lilian Bailey's shoulder, saying: 'You know we do not have many possessions, but I would like you to have this.' It expressed her gratitude for the comfort she received. Almost immediately, she returned to public life.

Since the royal family have not confirmed the story, can we be sure that this remarkable event actually took place? Those who knew Lilian Bailey – who was awarded an OBE for services in France during the First World War, when she served with the Queen Mary's Army Auxiliary Corps – are adamant that she would not have invented such a story to boost her reputation. She was already famous and, since the story was never published during her lifetime, it did not affect her standing among Spiritualists or the public. That may not satisfy sceptics.

More to the point is an observation made by Ann Morrow. In

writing her book, she received assistance from the Queen Mother and her private secretary Sir Martin Gilliat. They saw proofs of the book and raised no objection to the inclusion of the report on the royal seance. The story was repeated, again without objection, in Ann Morrow's *Without Equal: Her Majesty Queen Elizabeth, the Queen Mother*, published in July 2000 to mark her centenary.

A bird named Charlie

For some time before King George VI's death, he had received spirit communications passed on to him, through Lilian Bailey's mediumship, by a third party – Lionel Logue – and it is this connection that almost certainly led to the royal group seance. Logue was an Australian speech specialist whose remarkable talent enabled the King to overcome a serious stammer, after which they became intimate friends. In 1946, when his wife died, a grief-stricken Logue contemplated suicide. He turned for help to one of the country's most famous journalists, Hannen Swaffer, who was also a prominent Spiritualist.

A few days later, Swaffer invited Logue to his London flat to meet Lilian Bailey. The journalist told her nothing about his male guest and no name was given when they were introduced, but immediately she felt embarrassed, saying: 'I don't know why it is and I scarcely like to tell you, but George V is here. He asks me to thank you for what you did for his son.' Subsequently, Logue's dead wife communicated, controlling Lilian Bailey's body and wrapping her arms around her husband. She talked to him about changes he had made to the house and garden – things which no one else knew about. The medium's spirit guide Bill Wootton even told Logue that his pet name for his wife was Muggsy. Then he invited the speech therapist to ask any question.

'Does my wife want to say anything about the place where we first met?'

Bill Wootton responded with a puzzled expression. 'She is referring to a bird named Charlie. It is not a canary. It looks like a sparrow.'

Logue was overwhelmed. Charlie Sparrow was his best friend and it was at his twenty-first birthday party that he and his future wife met and fell in love. From then on Logue had regular seances with Lilian Bailey and on many occasions he spoke to King George VI about them, without meeting any hostility. 'My family are no strangers to Spiritualism,' he told Logue. This was certainly true, for Queen Victoria had held seances with several mediums after the death of Prince Albert. King George VI had expressed his gratitude to Logue by giving him a beautifully carved chair – the one in which he sat during his speech therapy sessions – and Logue, in turn, passed it on to Lilian Bailey. She used it for all the sittings given in her own home.

Though most trance mediums are also clairvoyant or clairaudient, their ability to slip into an altered state of consciousness in which spirits can communicate more directly with their loved ones provides us with some of the best evidence for life after death. Yet many trance mediums restrict communication to their spirit guide. Perhaps this reflects a worry about allowing unknown spirits to take over their physical bodies, though usually the guide or another helper acts as a 'doorkeeper' to prevent unpleasant entities invading the medium's mind.

Going into trance

Entering a trance can be very unsettling. Lilian Bailey at first resisted it because she was worried that if she were entranced when carrying her baby daughter Dorothy, she might drop her. The experience of Douglas Johnson, who became one of Britain's most sought-after mediums in the 1950s and 1960s, when he first went into trance at the age of 15 in a Spiritualist development circle, is typical:

Suddenly I felt as if I were going to faint. I knew that we weren't meant to break the circle (everyone was holding hands), and I thought this feeling would go off. The next thing I knew, I was given a glass of water by my host. I was very apologetic; I said I had never fainted before and I couldn't understand it. But he said, 'Have a look at your watch.' And to my astonishment it was three-quarters of an hour later. I was told I had gone into the trance state and someone had been speaking through me.... This frightened me very much, and I determined not to have anything to do with psychic things for an awful long time. I lived in fear it would come on at school or on a bus.

Eventually, as his other psychic gifts developed, Douglas Johnson did allow his spirit helpers to entrance him. In an interview with *Psychic* magazine, he explained:

I very often can hear for a while at first the voice that is speaking through me, although I can't stop speaking, and then I lapse into a deeper state of trance in which I hear nothing. Towards the end of the session, I seem gradually to come to, so I very often hear the end part.

His spirit guide Chiang has explained how trance works:

He says he does not enter directly into my body but that around each of us there is a field of force, something like a magnetic field, termed by some the 'aura'. Chiang says that he stands closely in this field of force and manipulates me rather like a puppet.

That, one suspects, is a rather oversimplified explanation for what must be a very complex process. Ivy Northage, who became one of England's most respected teaching mediums and the channel for Chan, has described how her spirit guide first took control of her:

It was as if I stepped behind myself and something came in front of me. I was fully conscious but with no control over my speech. It was as if something was making me speak. That was how Chan entered into our lives, with a few intermittent words spoken through me which I allowed because I had no idea what was happening or what I should do.

Years later, when she was a regular demonstrator on Spiritualist platforms, she always sensed when she was about to be entranced: 'It is very peculiar, the way Chan comes. It is as if he pulls an invisible hood over my head. As he does so, the conscious part of me seems to step behind it and he wears the hood.'

Our minds certainly have hidden depths and the book *Trance – the Natural History of Altered States of Mind*, by writer and broadcaster Brian Inglis, provides its readers with a very thorough examination of our current understanding of hypnosis, mesmerism, psychology, psychiatry and mediumistic trances. He includes the following quote about 'spirit' or 'secondary' controls from barrister Edward Cox's *What Am I?*:

I have heard an uneducated barman, when in a state of trance, maintain a dialogue with a party of philosophers on 'Reason and Foreknowledge, Will and Fate' and hold his own against them. A quarter of an hour afterwards, when released from the trance, he was unable to answer the simplest query on a philosophical subject.

Multiple personalities

There are many levels of trance, from a light 'overshadowing' during which the medium is fully aware of what is being said but not controlling it, to deep trance during which the medium's consciousness is oblivious to the proceedings. The belief is that the deeper the trance, the less likelihood there is of the medium's mind interfering with, or 'contaminating', the communication.

Some people believe that the spirit guides who speak through entranced mediums are not spirits at all but are the medium's secondary personalities – similar to those which manifest in multiple personality syndrome – and that the altered state of consciousness and dissociation from the medium's normal personality results in an enhancement of psychic powers. This may explain why most spirit guides offer little information about themselves in any detail.

This was a subject I was able to explore in some depth in 2003, during a visit to New York, when I visited the headquarters of the Parapsychology Foundation on East 71st Street. Its co-founder was the remarkable Irish-born medium Eileen J. Garrett, who died in 1970. Her daughter Eileen Coly and granddaughter Lisette Coly are both actively involved in continuing her work. As well as being an outstanding trance medium Eileen Garrett was also a strong supporter of parapsychology – more commonly known as psychical research – and willingly submitted to a multitude of tests conducted by paranormal investigators.

Eileen Garrett doubted that her two principal 'spirit guides', Uvani and Abdul Latif, who spoke through her in trance, were who they purported to be, suspecting instead that they were products of her subconscious. Uvani said he had been a soldier in India centuries ago and Abdul Latif claimed to be a twelfth-century physician from the court of Saladin.

Who are the guides?

Psychical researchers attempting to determine the truth spent many hours talking to the two trance personalities as well as to Eileen Garrett in her normal state, even using word association tests on all three of them. The results were inconclusive. One investigator came to the conclusion that Uvani was a split-off portion of the medium's unconscious mind, while another decided that Uvani and Abdul Latif were independent personalities. Uvani, incidentally, said that in order to communicate he did use a split-off portion of Eileen Garrett's mind, but that is very different from being a product of her mind.

In later life, Eileen Garrett wrote in her autobiography *Many*

Voices: 'I have never been able wholly to accept them as the spiritual dwellers on the threshold, which they seem to believe they are.'

I was surprised to learn that her daughter and granddaughter had rarely had the opportunity of hearing Eileen Garrett in trance because those sessions were always held in private. The first opportunity for the daughter Eileen Coly came when she was acting as secretary and a researcher (Martin Ebon) asked her to put some questions to her entranced mother on his behalf.

'Well, I did it,' she told me, 'and I was quite impressed that I was talking to this rather charming personality of Uvani who apparently gave the usual greeting, sitting up and paying attention. Then he said, "How may I help you?" Being completely practical, I said: "I don't know. I understood that you might have some kind of communication or message. Martin Ebon, whom you've met before, of course, suggested that I communicate with you." So, in his rather Indian-style, he didn't tell me very much.'

Lisette Coly burst out laughing and observed to her mother, 'You didn't ask very much!'

'Well, you know, I didn't have much ...,' Mrs Coly responded. 'If it was now, I'd say, "By the way, can you dig up my husband Bob for me?" So I said, "Thank you for your time. I'm sorry to intrude. All these years I've been aware of the help you've given people, so keep on doing it...." He was charming. I was very deferential and I wasn't going to waste his time and everybody else's. I liked him, which is quite something because I don't like everybody.'

What fascinated me was that whereas Eileen Garrett had doubts about the nature of her trance controls, her daughter was happily talking about Uvani as a separate entity.

'Because he *was* Uvani,' she explained. 'It was *not* Eileen Garrett, *not* my mother.... And yet, don't ask me if I really believe in the hereafter....'

I turned to the medium's granddaughter for a response.

'Are the controls real and is the survival hypothesis true?' Lisette asked, referring to the Spiritualist belief that mediumship provides proof that we all survive death. 'I just don't know. Isn't that a cop out? But at least I don't say that they are on the strength of seeing Eileen Garrett in trance. But I awfully hope so. I really hope so.'

Captain of airship R101 returns

Whatever the reality of the spirit guides, there seems to be no denying the identities of individual spirits who manage to speak through entranced mediums of Eileen Garrett's calibre. One of the most sensational cases of this kind involved the British R101 airship.

On 7 October 1930, soon after the death of Sir Arthur Conan Doyle, journalist Ian D. Coster arranged a trance sitting with Eileen Garrett in the hope of speaking to Sherlock Holmes' creator from beyond the grave. To his initial disappointment, the person who announced himself through the lips of the entranced medium was Flight Lieutenant H. Carmichael Irwin, captain of the huge R101 airship that had crashed on a hillside in Beauvais, France, a few days earlier. Irwin talked about his pre-flight concerns and gave a graphic description of the airship's last moments, including a wealth of technical detail that appeared to be confirmed when an official inquiry took place six months later.

Coster had a scoop on his hands, and so detailed were the spirit communications that Major Oliver Villiers of the Ministry of Civil Aviation participated in a seance with Eileen Garrett, during which Irwin and other crew members took over the medium's body and spoke through her. Many people regarded this as indisputable proof that we live after we die and that the dead can communicate with us.

With her customary caution, however, Eileen Garrett asked British psychic investigator Archie Jarman to check all the facts and look for alternative explanations. On Garrett's death in 1970, at the age of 77, Jarman – who had known her for almost 40 years – revealed that the medium and the Parapsychology Foundation had asked him to 'dig into the famous R101 airship case as deep as I could delve'. He had agreed to do so and pledged he would take neither fee nor expenses, so that whatever his investigation disclosed, it would be seen that he had worked 'without fear or favour'. Of his 80,000-word report, completed in 1963, he had this to say:

The completed saga, so often briefly mentioned, turned out to be a pretty massive affair. It took nearly six months and finally filled 55 pages of typescript and blueprints. It involved two trips to Beauvais, where the R101 crashed. There were conferences with aeronautical experts, such as the designer of the R101's heavy diesel engines (which were partly responsible for the fatal crash), and with the aging but active captain of the sister-ship, R100.

Technical witnesses were interrogated; ordnance maps scrutinised; Eileen's own aeronautical knowledge investigated (result, nil, she knew hardly enough to float a toy balloon). At close range I became familiar with meteorology, geodites, with prewar political manoeuvring and with a certain conspiracy at a ministry, with aerodynamics and with scandalous decisions which took nearly 50 brave men to their deaths.

It was the technical aspect of this case which makes it unique in psychic history – and I mean unique ... My opinion is that greater credulity is demanded to believe that Eileen obtained her obscure and specialised data by mundane means than to accept that, in some paranormal manner, she had contact with the remembering psyche of the 'dead' Captain Irwin to the moment of his incineration with his vast airship.

I later discovered that this apparently glowing account did not accurately represent what Archie Jarman believed. When I interviewed him at his Brighton home in 1980 it was obvious that he had serious doubts about just how evidential the R101 spirit communications were. He eventually agreed to put these into print for me, in the form of a book review for the magazine *Alpha*, of which

I was co-editor.[1] The opportunity arose when noted American author John Fuller wrote *The Airmen Who Would Not Die*, based on the Eileen Garrett R101 seances.

Possible rational explanations

Archie Jarman's review is a masterly summary of the negative and positive elements of the case, in which he asks whether the 'agitated voice' speaking through the medium was the 'true' spirit of Irwin, a secondary personality of Eileen Garrett or a 'mischievous spirit' posing as the dead captain; or whether Uvani was 'unconsciously reading the subliminal mind of Ian Coster' who, as a journalist, would have read all the news about the R101 tragedy.

'Expert opinion finally decreed,' Archie Jarman wrote, 'it was *not* the true Irwin,' but he did not suggest which of the alternative theories was the correct one.

It transpires that although Major Villiers had the firm impression that he was talking to the dead officers from the airship through the medium, other witnesses with greater knowledge of the R101 insisted that most of the technical information given at the seances was inaccurate.

For example, one of the statements made by Irwin through the medium was: 'I noticed that the gas-indicator was going up and down, which showed there was a leakage or escape...' Wing Commander R.S. Booth, who had flown the R101's sister airship, the R100, to Canada and back, observed: 'No such instruments were fitted.' It was also pointed out that Eileen Garrett had spoken at some length to Sir Sefton Brancker (who died in the crash) about inherent dangers, some ten days before the airship was due to sail. 'It would be strange if no part of this lodged in her subconscious,' Jarman noted. Because Jarman has offered contradictory verdicts on the R101 case, I prefer to treat his conclusions with caution.

Trance mediums who convinced scientists

Perhaps we are simply expecting too much from trance mediumship. Maybe the spirits of Irwin and the other crew members of the R101 *were* present in the seance room and trying to speak through Eileen Garrett, but the quality of those communications was inconsistent – perhaps it was as if they were speaking on a very bad telephone line, when words get misheard or misinterpreted.

What the R101 case demonstrates is how very difficult it is to assess, to *everyone's* satisfaction, the veracity of a spirit communication. The advantage of trance mediumship is that it provides evidence on a number of levels: the speech patterns and mannerisms of the communicator, the ability to converse about subjects with which he or she was connected during their earthly life and knowledge of people and intimate information that could not be known to anyone else.

Two of the finest twentieth-century trance mediums – Mrs Leonore Piper and Mrs Gladys Osborne Leonard – demonstrated these abilities for decades, willingly submitting to scientific tests that left the investigators satisfied that they had received communications from the spirit world.

Mrs Piper was born in Boston, USA, and her mediumship was discovered by eminent psychologist Professor William James, who spent 18 months investigating the spirit communications received through her. He declared himself 'as absolutely certain as I am of any personal fact in the world that she knows things in her trances which she cannot possibly have heard in her waking state'.

Mrs Piper was invited to England, where even tighter controls were imposed. She was followed everywhere. Anonymous sitters were presented to her. In one house where she stayed, even all the servants were changed before her arrival to be sure she could learn nothing from them. The famous physicist Sir Oliver Lodge was one of the investigators, and he declared, 'I have satisfied myself that much of the information she possesses in the trance state is not acquired by ordinary commonplace methods, but that she has some unusual means of acquiring information.' He added that no conceivable deception on Mrs Piper's part could explain the facts, adding that 'her attitude is not one of deception'.

But the biggest surprise was the reaction of a British investigator from the Society for Psychical Research, Dr Richard Hodgson. He had a reputation as a fraud-buster but was impressed by Mrs Piper's mediumship during investigations in Boston, though he refused to accept that it was spirits of the dead who were communicating through her. Later he conducted more experiments, which totally changed his mind. In his report of that work he wrote:

I cannot profess to have any doubt but that the 'chief communicators'... are veritably the personalities that they claim to be; that they have survived the change we call death, and that they have directly communicated with us whom we call living through Mrs Piper's entranced organism. Having tried the hypothesis of telepathy from the living for several years, and the 'spirit' hypothesis also for several years, I have no hesitation in affirming with the most absolute assurance that the 'spirit' hypothesis is justified by its fruits and the other hypothesis is not.

Having provided some of the most outstanding evidence for life after death ever recorded through trance mediumship, Mrs Leonore Piper died, aged 93, in 1950.

Britain had its own Mrs Piper in the form of trance medium Mrs Gladys Osborne Leonard, who was similarly tested by the scientists of the day. With the development of her trance abilities, the Lancaster-born medium abandoned a singing career and concentrated on providing evidence for life after death. During trance, she was controlled by her guide Feda, a Hindu girl who was said to have been married to the medium's great-great-grandfather, William Hamilton. 'Feda told me . . . that she had been watching over me since I was born, waiting for me to develop my psychic powers so that she could put me into a trance . . . I must confess that the idea of going into a trance did not appeal to me.' But there was work to be done and she agreed.

For 50 years Mrs Osborne Leonard – who died in 1968 aged 85 – was the most tested British medium. Like Mrs Piper, she convinced many people of the reality of spirit communication. Sir Oliver Lodge was able to speak to his dead son Raymond through her mediumship soon after he was killed in the First World War, and these communications play a prominent part in the scientist's book *Raymond, or Life After Death*.

Most of today's well-known mediums in Europe and the United States still use trance as a means of spirit communication, but they do so in private and seldom advertise the fact. That may be partly due to the belief that clairvoyance and clairaudience are just as effective as trance mediumship, and less demanding on the medium. As a result, however, very little has been done in the way of scientific research since the early part of the twentieth century. British psychical researcher W.H. Salter wrote in *Zoar* (1961):

A few years ago, when Mrs Leonard had restricted her activity as a medium, an exhaustive search was made in Great Britain for other trance mediums worth intensive study, with disappointing results. Reports from America indicate that things are no better there. Fortunately there is in the Proceedings of the SPR [Society for Psychical Research] an almost embarrassing wealth of material, on which the student can rely.

As a result, most modern reports of trance mediumship are anecdotal, but some are powerfully evidential. Writer and broadcaster Ingrid Tarrant, wife of presenter Chris Tarrant, host of *Who Wants to Be a Millionaire?* on UK TV, has revealed a remarkable visit she and a friend made to an unidentified English medium who lived in a council house. She told the *Daily Mail* newspaper, in October 2004, that during this sitting the medium started rocking slightly, rubbing his knees and talking in a guttural Norwegian accent.

I was astonished. I recognised the voice as my grandmother's who was from the West Coast of Norway, and whose arthritis was so bad that she constantly rubbed at her painful knees, just as he was doing.

Trance mediumship in recent times has also played a role in bringing murderers to justice (*see pages 63 and 65*).

Those fortunate enough to sit with mediums like Leonore Piper, Gladys Osborne Leonard, Eileen Garrett and Lilian Bailey discover that spirit communications given in trance can take the evidence of life after death to another level. There are, however, other forms of mediumship that can be just as convincing.

1 'The R101 Rises Again', *Alpha*, No. 6, January/February 1980.

Chapter 3

Automatism – Spirits in Control?

What's in a message?

One of the criticisms levelled at spirit messages is that their contents are mundane or banal. Nothing of any importance is communicated from the spirit world, say the critics. Having listened to many spirit messages from clairvoyants in my early days, I initially had some sympathy for the sceptics. As well as expressing love and support from the departed, the messages also had a tendency to discuss homes that needed decorating, cars that needed repairing or relationships that required more tender loving care. Such issues may sound trite, but Spiritualists point out that they are of the greatest concern to the recipients and reassure them that their loved ones know what is happening in their lives.

As well as reporting on public demonstrations of mediumship I had begun reading avidly about Spiritualism's history, discovering in the process that, like all generalisations, the claim that spirit messages are trivial was just not true. Some spirit communications are so remarkable and evidential that they have converted sceptical investigators into believers that the next world can contact us. Some of the best of these messages are produced through automatism – a form of mediumship in which the medium is usually conscious but has no conscious control over what is happening.

Ouija boards and planchettes

One of the most common demonstrations of automatism has been provided by the use of ouija boards and planchettes, which became popular more than a century ago and continue to puzzle and entertain the curious around the world to this day.

A planchette is a small, heart-shaped piece of wood fitted with two wheel castors and using the point of a pencil as its third support. When a hand is placed lightly on the planchette it eventually begins to move, producing a few badly scrawled words in some cases, and long and complex scripts in others.

A variation of the planchette is the ouija board, on which letters of the alphabet and numbers, as well as the words 'yes' and 'no', are displayed. The ouija board uses a planchette with three small wheels to act as a pointer, moving from letter to letter, spelling out messages or answering questions when one or more hands rest on it.

Though regarded by most Spiritualists today as little more than gimmicks that might also be dangerous – they could be psychologically disturbing or even attract mischievous or evil entities – planchettes and ouija boards have all played their part in Spiritualism's development.

Communications from Oscar Wilde

An Irish medium, Hester Dowden, who after her marriage became known as Mrs Travers-Smith, used a planchette to receive spirit communications, doing so wearing a blindfold for some of the sessions, so that she received no sensory clue to what was being received. Oscar Wilde is reported to have communicated at a series of seances at which Mrs Hester Travers-Smith was present, either as the automatist or – if someone else held the pencil – with her hand resting on that person's hand. At one of these sessions, with an unidentified male sitter holding the pencil (referred to as Mr V), the other two sitters were Miss Geraldine Cummins and Eric Dingwall, research officer of the Society for Psychical Research.

In the fascinating communication, which caused a sensation when it was published in *Oscar Wilde From Purgatory* (1924), Wilde turns the tables on his earthly contacts by questioning the existence of Eric Dingwall, who was known to be a sceptical psychical researcher:

> *Being dead is the most boring experience in life. That is, if one excepts being married or dining with a schoolmaster. Do you doubt my identity? I am not surprised, since sometimes I doubt it myself. I might retaliate by doubting yours. I have always admired the Society for Psychical Research. They are the most magnificent doubters in the world.*
>
> *They are never happy until they have explained away their spectres. And one suspects a genuine ghost would make them exquisitely uncomfortable. I have sometimes thought of founding an academy of celestial doubters ... which might be a sort of Society for Psychical Research among the living. No one under sixty would be admitted, and we should call ourselves the Society of Superannuated Shades. Our first object might well be to insist on investigating at once into the reality of the existence of, say, Mr Dingwall.*
>
> *Mr Dingwall, is he romance or reality? Is he fact or fiction? If it should be decided that he is fact, then, of course, we should strenuously doubt it. Fortunately there are no facts over here. On earth we could scarcely escape them.*

Patience Worth

Leading psychical researchers of the day studied her mediumistic abilities and she willingly co-operated in their experiments.

However, few of the readers of Patience Worth's epic novels, which enjoyed great literary success in the early part of the last century, were aware that they were written on a ouija board, and that 'Patience Worth' claimed to be the spirit of an Englishwoman who had lived in the seventeenth century, having been born in Dorset,

England, and been killed by Native Americans after moving to America. The messages were received by a housewife, Pearl Curran, whose schooling in St Louis, Missouri, had finished at the age of 14. Together with a friend, Mrs Hutchings, she had decided to play around with 'a talking board', as the ouija board was popularly known, in 1913, and after several sessions Patience Worth began communicating with the young women.

In time it was discovered that it was not necessary for both women to operate the ouija board; her messages could be produced by Pearl Curran alone but not by Mrs Hutchings. A prestigious volume of material was produced in this laborious way, including plays, six full-length books and 2,500 poems, which together totalled more than four million words, filling 29 volumes. The writings received critical acclaim, particularly *The Sorry Tale*, a 300-word story of the life of Jesus that took over two years to dictate through the ouija board. In time, Pearl Curran discovered that she could anticipate the letters the pointer would move to, and began reciting these, leaving the pointer to circle the board aimlessly. She dictated the communications by automatic speech from 1920 onwards.

Sceptics argue that this case simply demonstrates the tremendous creativity of the mind – creativity that for the most part is untapped. As in the case of other automatic communications, however, if this is indeed the explanation, how do we explain the *content*? If Patience Worth were simply a secondary personality of Pearl Curran, conjured up by her mind as a way of releasing her creative talents, then we need to explain why her subconscious was clearly superior to her conscious self.

After two years of study, an American Professor, Charles E. Long, came to the conclusion that Patience Worth's mentality was of a very high order, original and creative, and he was also surprised and impressed by her high moral and spiritual standards. 'Here is a subconscious self, far outstripping in power and range the primary consciousness,' he declared. That verdict, however, does not begin to explain how Pearl Curran's subconscious could write poems to order instantly, in response to a given subject. Nor does it throw light on the extraordinary use of language in one of her novels, *Telka*, about medieval England. A philologist who analysed the book found that it contained no words that came into use after the seventeenth century – which is what one would expect if Patience Worth really was a spirit communicator who had lived when she said she did, rather than being a secondary personality of a twenti-eth-century housewife. Because of that, *Telka* has been described as 'a philological miracle'.

Another striking phenomenon is associated with the Patience Worth case. On one occasion, a chapter of a book she was writing was lost. Two months later, she redictated it. Eventually, however, the original chapter was located, and when it was compared with the second version it was found to be exactly the same, word for word.

Glass and alphabet method

An even simpler technique than the planchette and ouija board methods involves the use of an upturned glass on a tabletop. Several people place their fingers on the glass, causing it to move to letters placed on the tabletop. It was this method of automatism that convinced Dr Reginald Hegy, a former ship's surgeon and founder member of the College of Physicians of South Africa, of the reality of spirit communication. I interviewed him in the 1960s, when he was visiting London, and his down-to-earth approach dispelled any lingering doubts I had about the use of automatism.

With a small group of friends, Dr Hegy had attempted to contact the next world using the glass and alphabet method. The results were outstanding, for they came not only in English but also in French, Hungarian and various provincial German dialects, all of which were languages unknown to the sitters. It took time to have them translated and checked, but they were proved right. What's more, many of the messages were from people who were not known to the group but who helpfully supplied names and addresses. All this demonstrated that the sitters' minds were not influencing the results.

'Among the hundreds of names, dates and other facts given, not one proved to be incorrect on investigation,' Dr Hegy told me. His research group did everything they could to overcome sceptics' objections about their method of communication. At some seances everyone who had contact with the glass was blindfolded, then the person who was making notes rearranged the letters of the alphabet on the table. Finally, the participants turned their heads away from the table, to ensure they could not glimpse anything from beneath their blindfolds. The messages were just as accurate, but were delivered even faster than normal. Dr Hegy described these spirit communications in detail in his book *A Witness Through the Centuries*.

Automatic writing

In time, such methods of contacting the next world began to be seen as unnecessary because mediums found that they could simply hold a pen or pencil in order to receive spirit messages. But again, we have to pose the question: where do the messages come from? Do they originate from the spirit world, through extrasensory perception (ESP) or from the sitter or medium's subconscious? The answer to this question differs from medium to medium, but I suspect that all three possibilities are sometimes involved in the process of producing automatic scripts.

There is no dispute about the phenomenon being a product of the subconscious: some psychologists have found that it gives them valuable insights into the minds of mentally disturbed patients. There is also evidence that it might be a useful way of 'tuning in' to or exteriorising extrasensory perceptions. Famous nineteenth-century editor W.T. Stead, who drowned in the *Titanic* disaster, was an accomplished automatic writing medium who as well as apparently receiving messages from the dead, also received communications from the living. He would ask mental questions about friends – without actually talking to them – and his hand would write the answers.

One example Stead cited concerned a woman with whom he had arranged a lunch engagement. Knowing she had been out of town for the weekend, he asked mentally whether she had returned to London. He received a long reply describing an unpleasant encounter with a man in a railway compartment. The man had sat close by her when other passengers had left, and had tried to kiss her. She had hit him with his umbrella, which broke. The train unexpectedly stopped and the man fled.

Stead sent his servant with a note of condolence to his friend's house, much to the woman's surprise. 'I had decided not to speak of it to anyone,' she wrote in reply. She confirmed all the details of the encounter contained in the automatic writing script, except for one error of fact. The umbrella belonged to her, not to the man. In exceptional circumstances the mind can, it seems, perform remarkable feats. In our search for evidence of spirit communication, we must ensure that such explanations – however unlikely they may seem – are ruled out.

The medium and the message

Geraldine Cummins, a professor's daughter, was Ireland's most accomplished automatist at the time I began my investigations into Spiritualism.

Geraldine Cummins

When I visited Geraldine Cummins in her Chelsea home in the early 1960s, I was delighted that she agreed to demonstrate her mediumship for me. A brief message of encouragement came through from her spirit control, Astor. Although I was disappointed not to receive something more personal or evidential, my own quest for evidence was as

---

nothing compared with the challenges the Cork-born medium had faced for 50 years or more. During this time she devoted herself to producing scripts that not only shed light on history but also provided impressive evidence for survival of death. Her book *The Road to Immortality*, which purports to consist of communications from the spirit of leading psychic investigator and co-founder of the Society for Psychical Research F.W.H. Myers, is a fine example of her work, as is *The Scripts of Cleophas*, which is said to supplement the Acts of the Apostles and the Epistles of St Paul. Impressive though these publications are, they do not constitute proof of communication with the spirit world, as Geraldine Cummins readily recognised. Her crowning glory, however, is in my opinion the Cummins-Willett scripts.

In 1957, W.H. Salter, honorary secretary of the Society for Psychical Research, wrote to Geraldine Cummins asking if she would take part in an experiment. She agreed to do so once she had returned to her home in County Cork, Eire. Two weeks later, he wrote again saying simply that a Major Henry Tennant hoped to receive a message from his mother. The result was 40 scripts, received over a two-year period, in which the mother discusses her life, her relationships with others and her involvement in psychic work.

Major Tennant's mother, it transpires, was also an automatic writing medium – Mrs Winifred Coombe Tennant – but her true identity was hidden from her psychic colleagues behind the pseudonym of 'Mrs Willett' because she wanted to keep her talent a secret. This is not surprising when one realises she was a Justice of the Peace and the first woman magistrate to sit on the Glamorganshire, Wales, County bench. She stood unsuccessfully for Parliament as a Liberal Party candidate in 1922, and was the first woman to be appointed by the British government as a delegate of the League of Nations Assembly. She died in 1956, a year before the request was sent to Geraldine Cummins.

The scripts were published in Geraldine Cummins' book *Swan on a Black Sea*, edited by Signe Toksvig, which has a long and masterly foreword by Professor C.D. Broad, Fellow of Trinity College, Cambridge, and a leading psychical researcher. After examining alternative explanations for the Mrs Willett scripts, he comments: 'I found them of great interest, and I believe that these automatic scripts are a very important addition to the vast mass of such material which *prima facie* suggest rather strongly that certain human beings have survived the deaths of their physical bodies...' Major Henry Tennant, who was initially sceptical, wrote to Geraldine Cummins after receiving the first communication to say: 'The more I study these scripts the more deeply I am impressed by them.' He found only one incorrect name, adding, 'every other name and reference is accurate, and to me very evidential and at times surprising. There was no tapping of my mind because much appears that I never knew.'

The moving pen

In the same year that Mrs Winifred Coombe Tennant passed to the next world, Gordon E. Burdick, who was serving in the Canadian Navy, stationed at Vancouver, also died. He was just a week away from visiting London, where he intended marrying his fiancée, Grace Rosher, an artist. Just over a year later, after writing a letter concerning an aunt, Miss Rosher wondered if she had time to write another before receiving a visitor for tea. But a voice urged her to keep her hand on the writing pad and she was astonished to see it beginning to write of its own volition. She was even more surprised to read the words, 'With love from Gordon'.

This was the start of regular automatic written communications from the man Miss Rosher planned to marry, as well as from other relatives and even one message – complete with signature – from the great physicist and psychical researcher Sir William Crookes. I visited Grace Rosher in 1961, soon after her book *Beyond the*

Horizon was published, and saw for myself the extraordinary phenomenon of her fountain pen, resting loosely on her hand, writing a legible message. 'When it first happened, I thought it was some sort of electric force in myself that was causing the pen to move,' she told me. But she was soon convinced that it was her fiancé's spirit hand that was controlling the pen.

Some sceptics argue that it is not difficult to produce this effect if you choose a pen with the correct balance. That may be so. I was also puzzled as to how Grace Rosher had discovered that the pen could do this. Resting a pen on your hand is a rather strange thing to do. But I have no reason to doubt her integrity. A handwriting expert, F.T. Hilliger, compared the automatic scripts with Gordon Burdick's earthly writing and confirmed that there was a strong similarity between the two. This led him to the conclusion that 'the writing reproduced by Grace Rosher was, if it were humanly possible, genuinely inspired by the personality of Gordon E. Burdick'. As for the content, it is difficult to evaluate when the communicator is the medium's loved one, for we must make allowances for the understandable desire on Grace Rosher's part to receive messages of comfort from her fiancé, and recognise the part her subconscious may have played in their production.

The world's most prolific writing medium

Of all the automatic writing mediums I have met, Francisco de Paula Candido Xavier was undoubtedly the most remarkable – certainly in terms of output. This poorly educated man, born in 1910 in Brazil, had a day job as a clerical worker with the Ministry of Agriculture in order to be able to give his mediumistic services free to the thousands who sought his help. He became known as the Pope of Spiritism – a form of Spiritualism that has grown rapidly in South America, among other places, and which is described more fully later (*see page 183*).

I interviewed 'Chico' Xavier in London in 1965 when, together with Dr Waldo Vieira – another automatist – they were on their way to the United States on a lecture tour. During the 75 years he devoted to spirit communication, 'Chico' Xavier published more than 400 spirit-inspired books. Most were religious in content, but there were also novels about the spirit world as well as works of philosophy and science.

Poetry From Beyond the Grave contains 259 poems written by 56 dead Brazilian poets. The widow of one of them tried to sue 'Chico' Xavier for royalties, but the court ruled that 'the [poet] is dead, and the dead have no rights'. This led the highbrow newspaper *Estado de São Paulo* to comment that if the poems were not actually written by the dead poets then Xavier should be sitting in the Brazilian Academy of Letters.

After moving to Uberaba in the state of Minas Gerais in 1959, 'Chico' Xavier established a thriving Spiritist community dedicated to helping those in need. Every week it distributed hundreds of baskets containing food to the poor of the region. All the profits from an estimated 25 million copies of his books were channelled into this charitable work.

'Chico' Xavier always said he would die when his country was rejoicing, and this is what happened. On Sunday, 30 June 2002, the day when Brazil's victory in the World Cup football championship resulted in the biggest celebration for years, the world's most prolific medium slipped peacefully into the next world. In the two days of his wake, 100,000 people filed past his body to say their farewells, and those who paid tribute to him included the Brazilian president and the country's Islamic, Jewish and Christian religious leaders. Brazil, incidentally, has an estimated 20 million Spiritists.

A medium dedicated to serve others

Another humanitarian medium in the same mould as 'Chico' Xavier is Divaldo Franco, who has dedicated his life to the enlightenment of others and to helping the less fortunate. The enlightenment comes, once again, through automatic writing. So far, he has produced 170 books communicated from beyond the grave, written by the likes of French novelist Victor Hugo, the Indian sage

Rabindranath Tagore and the Mexican nun and poet Juana Inés de la Cruz. He is also the founder of an outreach project, Mansão do Caminho, which has housed and provided for more than 30,000 children and their families since 1952. Above all, he is an orator who has proclaimed the truths of Spiritualism for over 50 years; even in 2004, at the age of 77, he was lecturing in the United States, one of 46 countries he has visited in his quest to make more people aware of spirit communication.

'Psychography'

Brazilians, incidentally, refer to automatic writing as 'psychography', a term first used by one of Britain's most prominent nineteenth-century mediums, the Rev Stainton Moses, who was also a Church of England minister. Stainton Moses displayed many forms of mediumship, including copious automatic writing, much of which was published in the books *Spirit Teachings* and *Spirit Identity*. Like many other automatists he busied himself with other activities while his hand was apparently writing under the control of spirits. Cautious about the source of the scripts, he wrote:

It is an interesting subject for speculation whether my own thoughts entered into the subject matter of the communications. I took extraordinary pains to prevent any such admixture. At first the writing was slow, and it was necessary for me to follow it with my eye, but even then the thoughts were not my thoughts. Very soon the messages assumed a character of which I had no doubt whatever that the thought was opposed to my own. But I cultivated the power of occupying my mind with other things during the time that the writing was going on, and was able to read an abstruse book and follow out a line of close reasoning while the message was written with unbroken regularity. Messages so written extended over many pages, and in their course there is no correction, no fault in composition and often a sustained vigour and beauty of style.

Ghostly writing

An automatic writing medium of a very different kind began to make a name for herself in the 1970s and I was delighted when she agreed to take part in an experiment I had devised. Margo Williams, from the Isle of Wight, together with her husband Wally, had visited many places where, they said, they had been able to release earthbound spirits and send them 'to the light'. The ghosts communicated with her by controlling her hand and giving the reason for their distress.

In 1979, Margo and Wally agreed to allow me to drive them to places in southern England, chosen by me and not divulged to them before they reached the destinations. In this way, I could be sure they had not had an opportunity to research the sites. My choice was dictated as much by historical interest as by any alleged hauntings. Typical of the communications received during this three-day experiment was the following, which Margo wrote in Farnham Parish Church, Surrey:

> *Canst thou hear me, Ann, Ann? It is thy husband John Lacey, who hast been searching for thee. Now through the ears of some stranger I can get this written. Ann, I hast searched for thee, up and down I wander. Where art thou Ann, my dearest? Can the one who hears this help me?*

I concluded after returning to various sites with Margo and Wally that these scripts did not provide evidence of spirit communication. There were few names or other details on which to base a conclusion. In the case of 'John Lacey', however, there *was* a wall plaque in the church recording that nearby lay the bodies of John Lacy (not Lacey) and his wife Agnes (not Ann), who died respectively in 1766 and 1784.

Had Margo Williams seen this plaque and consciously or subconsciously – and incorrectly – noted the information? It is highly likely that she had, since she and her husband looked around the church before she began writing. Or was her mind picking up information from somewhere else? All I could be certain of was that if these really were spirit communications, they fell far short of the level of evidence required to satisfy sceptics.

Automatic music writing

Francis Clive-Ross, editor of occult magazine *Tomorrow* and a staunch critic of Spiritualism, should have been familiar with some of the best mediumistic achievements when he threw down the gauntlet in 1963. He argued that little of significance had been communicated from beyond, whereas the 'welter of rubbish has been stupendous'. He added: 'According to Spiritualists the spirits of great composers also survive, and it should be a fairly simple matter to communicate some music.' Perhaps Beethoven could write a new symphony, he suggested. Wagner could produce a new opera. Or Puccini, Verdi, Donizetti, Gounod or Bellini could transmit an aria from the next world. He said:

> The great writers have been silent, so now let us see whether the great composers can do any better.... It need not be anything very elaborate; just one of the latest compositions by any of these composers from the spheres where, the Spiritualists tell us, they continue to work and 'progress'.

At the time, newly widowed Rosemary Brown was struggling in poverty to bring up her young son and daughter in South London, working in a school kitchen, and it is highly unlikely that she would have been aware of Clive-Ross's challenge in an obscure occult publication. Yet within a year, this natural psychic began writing well-developed music in the style of famous composers such as Liszt, Chopin, Bach, Beethoven and Rachmaninoff, resulting in the release of the record 'Rosemary Brown's Music' in 1970, with the medium playing the simpler pieces on one side, and renowned pianist Peter Katin playing the more complex compositions on the other. Her musical mediumship began, she explained, with the appearance of Liszt, who became her spiritual guide as she sat at her piano. 'I could stumble through an easy tune,' she wrote later, 'but this was like automatic playing. I began to play virtuoso-style pieces, and it grew from there.'

This automatic control of her hands was replaced with dictation by the dead composers who spoke English. Those speaking other languages – such as French, German or Polish – presented her with real problems. Yet one observer who saw her writing music while in contact with the spirit of a composer was amazed at the speed with which it was taken down. This devout Christian, who made little money from her gift, explained: 'It's very hard work, and I never know how it's going to sound until it is played.'

Pianist Hephzibah Menuhin said: 'I look at these manuscripts with immense respect. Each piece is distinctly in the composer's style.' Composer Richard Rodney Bennett was among her many admirers: 'A lot of people can improvise, but you couldn't fake music like this without years of training,' he declared. 'I couldn't have faked some of the Beethoven myself.'

According to musicologist Sir Donald Tovey, writing from beyond the grave through Rosemary Brown's hand, the purpose of these musical compositions was not to offer possible listening pleasure, 'it is the implications relevant to this phenomenon which we hope will stimulate sensible and sensitive interest'.

Rosemary Brown played the spirit-inspired compositions at London's Wigmore Hall and New York's City Hall, and two further recordings of these works were released before ill-health made it impossible for her to continue.

Among those who have paid tribute to Rosemary Brown and her spirit-dictated compositions are pianists John Lill and Peter Katin, composers Richard Rodney Bennett and Humphrey Searle, and Ian Parrott, Professor of Music at the University College of Wales, Aberystwyth, who wrote *The Music of Rosemary Brown*, a book about her mediumship. He singles out three compositions as particularly outstanding: 'Grübelei' (1969) from Liszt, 'Sonata movement' in C minor (1971) from Beethoven and 'Revenant' (1972) from Stravinsky. He does not believe that a clever faker would be able to produce such results.

George Bernard Shaw is also said to have dictated a new play through Rosemary Brown, called *Caesar's Return*, 23 years after his death. Performed at the Edinburgh Festival in 1978, Shaw is said to have made his presence felt during rehearsals by passing on instructions and additional lines of dialogue through the medium. Other, non-musical, communicators included Einstein, Jung and Bertrand Russell. Despite associating with such luminaries, Rosemary Brown remained modest and self-effacing, insisting that she was no more than a channel for spirits determined to prove the reality of an afterlife.

I have often wondered what Clive-Ross made of these musical and literary compositions. I suspect he remained adamantly sceptical, despite apparently having his challenge accepted by the spirits of long-dead composers as well as famous writers and thinkers.

Automatic painting

Some readers may wonder what the spirit world's response would have been if his challenge had been artistic, rather than musical. The answer would have been much the same, since automatic painting, though rare, has also been demonstrated over the years. One of the most talented exponents is Brazilian Luiz Antonio Gasparetto. Born in São Paulo in 1949, he has no artistic talent – until the spirits of famous artists control his hands. The son of a medium, he discovered his strange talent as a child and has been allowing over thirty famous artists to paint through his mediumship ever since. He takes no money for his demonstrations, but he does sell his paintings, putting the proceeds into a centre that provides food, counselling, healthcare and job training for the poor.

When Luiz Gasparetto visited Britain in March 1978 he was filmed by the BBC. As cameras recorded him for an hour and a quarter, the Brazilian medium completed 21 paintings while in a light trance – an average of one every three-and-a-half minutes. BBC TV's *Nationwide* programme cut this artistic extravaganza to 30 minutes, showing him using his hands, not brushes, to achieve paintings in the style of several artists. At times he was seen painting two pictures simultaneously, one the correct way up and the other upside down. He even used his feet to paint some of the canvases. Naturally, these results were achieved under the full glare of television lights. What is surprising is that, back in Brazil, he normally works in darkness, so the colours he uses and the compositions are invisible to him and others present until the lights go on. Among the artists said to work through him are Goya, Picasso, van Gogh, Renoir, Manet, Toulouse-Lautrec and Modigliani.

The BBC passed no judgement on the demonstration, leaving it to viewers to decide whether the non-artistic medium's subconscious was responsible, or if the spirits of deceased painters were demonstrating their survival of death. But I liked the observation of one commentator, Marcus McCausland, who has carried out paranormal research with healers and mediums: 'To be perfectly honest, I think either way it is marvellous. If this is what our subconscious will do, it's fabulous. If it's us being controlled, from beyond the grave, I think that's fabulous.'

There are, of course, artists who earn a very good living from painting in the style of the masters, sometimes doing so with such style that they fool experts, and sceptics will dismiss artistic mediumship on that basis, conveniently disregarding other aspects of the paintings, such as the speed with which they are usually created. But it is pertinent to wonder how forgers are able to paint in the style of great artists.

A year after Luiz Gasparetto demonstrated his amazing abilities in the UK, forger Tom Keating, together with art dealer David Lionel Evans, was due to appear at the Old Bailey charged with deception and conspiracy, but the trial was abandoned because of his ill-health. Keating was a talented artist capable of painting in the style of many artists. Giving evidence on 1 February 1979, before the trial was halted, Keating testified:

Sometimes my pastiches were so good I can say with all due modesty that I think there was some curious combination with the old master [Goya] himself. Some painters say it is Spiritualism. I am not a Spiritualist, but there were times when the master came down and took over the painting. It was terribly difficult to tell the difference between his work and my own. I have had that experience about twenty times in my life. It happened with Goya. That was so good I marked it in white lead so if it was X-rayed it would be seen that it was not a Goya.

Goya appears to have contributed to the spontaneous automatism – both automatic writing and drawing – which occurred during the remarkable poltergeist experiences of Matthew Manning. These first occurred when he was 11 in the early 1960s (*see page 221*) and returned more strongly when he was 15. Among the psychic talents the British teenager developed at that time was an ability to be controlled by a spirit entity who gave his name as Thomas Penn and wrote medical diagnoses for people whose birthdates were provided, including audience members of a David Frost television programme in 1974. Manning's hand was also seemingly controlled by artists who drew in their recognisable styles, yet the drawings produced were never identical to the ones on which they appeared to be based. One macabre picture – incorporating a hideously mutilated man transfixed to a tree by a long arrow, an owl, a dead mouse and the heads of two drowning men in a pool – was signed by Goya, with a few lines written in French. An expert on Goya identified seven separate features from the artist's work in the Manning picture. A number of other art specialists have testified to the quality of drawings apparently transmitted through Manning by Aubrey Beardsley and Henri Matisse, among others. Manning has since written several books about his experiences and the manifestations that have surrounded him, the latest being *One Foot in the Stars*[1].

Though many of the researchers who have investigated Manning may have concluded that he was demonstrating extraordinary powers of extrasensory perception (ESP), his own verdict is that he was in touch with the surviving consciousness of the individuals who communicated through him.

Spirit communication or the influence of the subconscious?

As we have seen, one of the greatest challenges for psychical researchers analysing all this evidence is to separate what appears to be pure spirit communication from other material that may emanate from a medium's subconscious. Maybe it is not easy to differentiate. In the Cummins-Willett scripts (*see page 40*), the spirit communicator Mrs Willett refers to Geraldine Cummins' 'subliminal mind, which is called Astor'. If we take this description at face value, it suggests that Astor – the medium's spirit control – is not a real person. However, in other automatic scripts produced through the same medium, the dead South African philosopher Ambrose Pratt refers to Astor as 'both a secondary personality of Miss Cummins and an individual who once lived on Earth'.

This may seem like a contradiction, but it has support from other spiritual sources. A well-known spirit guide named Silver Birch (*see page 210*), when asked about the nature of guides' individuality, explained that it was not possible to separate spiritual identity in the same way as physical individuality. This is because there can be many facets of one spiritual diamond. He explained:

This is the oversoul, the greater individuality, and the facets are aspects of it which incarnate into your world for experiences that will add lustre to the diamond when they return to it.

Also there are people who, although separate persons, are aspects of the one individuality. For instance, my medium [Maurice Barbanell], his wife and myself are parts of one individual. So you can have facets of the one guide. You can call these extensions if you like, but it comes to the same thing. Only an infinitesimal part of the whole individuality can be manifested in physical form on earth.

It is probably overstating the case, but it has been suggested that at a very deep level all humans are connected, allowing telepathy and other paranormal phenomena to occur. Some people even interpret this to mean that at a soul level 'we are one another' because we all belong to a group soul. But as far as our lives on earth are concerned, we are all very different individuals and it is that individuality which helps prove our identity when communicating from the next world.

It soon becomes obvious to those exploring mediumship that as well as lifting the veil between this world and the next they need to penetrate the deepest recesses of the human mind and explore its tremendous potential, in their quest for greater understanding of spirit communication.

1 Matthew Manning, *One Foot in the Stars*, Piatkus (2003).

Chapter 4

Searching for Psychic Clues

Murders, assassinations, terrorism, hijackings, rapes, child abuse, bank robberies – the list of crimes that dominate the media is almost endless. Governments and police departments around the world devote vast sums of money and millions of man-hours in pursuit of the culprits in order to bring them to justice. They need all the help they can get. So why, if the spirits of the dead are aware of what is happening in this world, do they not lend a hand? At the very least, you would expect that the victims of particularly vicious crimes, speaking from beyond the grave, could bring their murderers to justice quickly and easily by naming them and providing indisputable evidence. Yet such cases are exceedingly rare.

Medium or psychic?

Here I need to make a very clear distinction between psychics and mediums. Most people mistakenly regard these words as interchangeable. A psychic is an individual with the ability to 'read' your past, present or future, perhaps with the help of tarot cards or a crystal ball. This information is apparently 'picked up' by some form of extrasensory perception (ESP) that is not attributed to contact with spirits. A medium, on the other hand, is someone who is in touch with the next world and through whom spirits communicate. When it comes to paranormal crime-busting, the majority of those offering help are 'psychic detectives' using a variety of non-mediumistic techniques.

The first editor I worked for at *Psychic News*, as a freelance reporter, was Fred Archer. What Archer lacked in vocal skills – he had a serious speech impediment – he made up for in the quality of his writing. One of his paranormal books was *Crime and the Psychic World*, and as well as introducing me to some of the best stories of psychic crime-busting it also opened my mind to the untapped potential of mediumship.

Using psychic skills to locate missing people

At that time, a Dutchman named Gerard Croiset was making headlines due to his ability to locate missing people, usually children. Sadly, in most cases he was able only to indicate where a body would be found, since many youngsters drowned in the Dutch canals, but his psychic skills proved helpful to the police in several cases. From 1945 Croiset's psychic detection was studied by Professor Willem Tenhaeff, founder and director of the Parapsychology Institute at the State University of Utrecht, the Netherlands. Of 47 psychics and sensitives who co-operated in experiments with Professor Tenhaeff, Croiset was undoubtedly the star performer and was a willing subject for psychic experiments. In fact, Croiset even moved to Utrecht to be closer to the university's research department.

Although the Dutch psychic sometimes visited the scene of a crime or disappearance to pick up clues, he also claimed that he had the ability to 'see' over long distances and to predict when and where a dead body or a missing person would be found. Croiset, incidentally, refused payment for this work on the basis that his psychic powers were a divine gift.

On the trail of kidnappers
When an Australian woman named Muriel McKay was kidnapped from her home in Wimbledon, south-west London, a few days after Christmas in 1969, I wondered whether Gerard Croiset

might be called in to assist. The woman's husband Alick McKay, deputy chairman of a major newspaper group, soon received a telephoned ransom demand for £1 million from someone claiming to represent 'Mafia, M3', who also revealed that the original intention was to kidnap the wife of the group's Australian chairman Rupert Murdoch, who had just acquired the *News of the World* and the *Sun* newspapers in Britain. As Murdoch was out of the country, McKay had use of his Rolls-Royce, causing the kidnappers to misidentify him. Over the next weeks, Alick McKay received further demands, as well as pleading letters from his wife, but two attempts to leave a ransom were foiled by a mixture of bad luck and police incompetence.

Desperate to get Muriel McKay released, the McKay family decided to ask for Gerard Croiset's help and he quickly travelled to London to offer psychic assistance. He told the family she was no longer alive, adding that two men who were in an old farm dwelling were involved in the crime. The Dutch psychic began to trace the route he believed they had taken after bundling her into their car. He 'saw' the vehicle being driven from south-west London, into the heart of the capital and then out to the north, but eventually the psychic leads faded.

The police were not impressed. Eventually, they arrested brothers Arthur and Nizamodeen Hosein, who lived on a farm near the village of Stocking Pelham in Hertfordshire. Even though no trace of Mrs McKay could be found, they were found guilty of kidnapping, blackmail and murder. There has been speculation ever since that the brothers cut up their victim's body and fed it to the pigs. Though Gerard Croiset's psychic abilities did not assist the police in this case, later events and the brothers' conviction confirmed how accurate he was in his psychic attempt to reconstruct the crime and identify the killers.

I have a personal interest in the Muriel McKay case since it indirectly resulted in my deciding to leave *Psychic News*. When news of Croiset's involvement was revealed, BBC radio interviewed me about the use of psychics in solving crimes and I spoke positively, though guardedly, about the contribution they could make. Later Paul Beard, president of the College of Psychic Studies in London, invited me to lecture on the subject, and a transcript of my talk was published in *Light*, the college's magazine.

Surprisingly, my views did not meet with the approval of *Psychic News* editor Maurice Barbanell, with whom I had worked for close on eight years as assistant editor. He insisted that the newspaper's unwritten editorial policy was that mediumship was meant to be used only to provide evidence for life after death, not to solve crimes. I had no problem with that being the newspaper's policy, as long as I was free to express a different view, always making it clear that I was speaking personally and not acting as the newspaper's spokesperson. However, he insisted that as I was employed by the newspaper, I was not at liberty to express in public any view that differed from its official policy. Even after all these years, it still strikes me as strange that he did not see the irony of wanting to restrict my freedom, when Spiritualism had only won its religious freedom less than two decades earlier. Besides, I felt very strongly that if I were a murder victim and found it possible to communicate from beyond the grave, I might want to make the circumstances of my death known in order to bring the culprit to justice and perhaps prevent other murders.

A medium helping in a murder case

The medium Estelle Roberts featured very prominently in a murder case over 30 years earlier, in 1937. She displayed much the same abilities as Gerard Croiset but also, with the help of her spirit guide, Red Cloud, made contact with the victim, ten-year-old Mona Tinsley. Estelle was an excellent clairvoyant and trance medium, as well as a powerful physical medium, and I discuss other aspects of her mediumship elsewhere (*see page 203*).

She at first had misgivings when approached by a newspaper to become involved in the case of Mona Tinsley, saying that rival newspapers would regard it as a stunt, which would affect her reputation and that of Spiritualism. But she was persuaded that the girl's parents needed her help. At the parents' request, the chief constable at Newark-on-Trent forwarded a pink silk dress to the medium, who knew that the girl was dead the moment she handled it.

Many mediums use psychometry to help them tune into the next world. This functions when they handle an object and pictures of events in its history come into their minds. It is not uncommon, at a private sitting, for a medium to ask if he or she can initially hold a ring or watch to establish a rapport with the sitter. Estelle Roberts recorded what happened next in her book *Fifty Years as a Medium*[1]:

> Then, with Red Cloud's help, Mona spoke to me, saying she had been strangled. She gave me a picture of a house, with a water-filled ditch on one side, a field at its back, a churchyard close by and an inn within sight. In my vision I was taken to a graveyard, over a bridge and across some fields to a river beyond. There I stopped, unable to go further.

The police were impressed with this description, which tallied with their own investigations. They invited Estelle Roberts to travel by train to Newark-on-Trent, from where the girl had disappeared, and said she would be met by a police car at the station. On her arrival, two police officers took her to a house, which she recognised immediately as the one she had seen in her vision. It was empty and she was allowed to walk around inside. She told the police officers accompanying her that Mona Tinsley had been strangled in the back bedroom and that the murderer had put her body in a sack and carried it out of a side door, past the churchyard and across a bridge, and then dumped it in a river that was out of sight. 'The river holds the secret of the child's whereabouts. If you've dragged it already and found nothing, you must drag it again.'

Days later, the police charged Frederick Nodder, whose house Estelle Roberts had been taken to, with the abduction of Mona Tinsley. He was found guilty and sentenced to seven years' imprisonment. Many weeks later, Mona Tinsley's body was found, still in the sack in which Nodder had carried it, in the River Idle, beyond the fields at the back of his house. It had become jammed in the mouth of a drain. Frederick Nodder was brought from prison, charged with the child's murder and subsequently executed.

The Genette Tate case – still a mystery

Like so many other cases of paranormal detection, the accuracy of the clues is confirmed only after normal detective work solves a crime – sceptics call it 'retro-fitting' – which is why police forces treat psychic assistance with caution. Following up normal leads is a time-consuming business. When the police are also asked to respond to psychic leads, it adds to their burden.

A good example of this is provided by the events that transpired after the disappearance of 13-year-old schoolgirl Genette Tate while delivering newspapers in Aylesbeare, Devon, on 19 August 1978. According to one newspaper, 'over 200 mediums and people interested in psychic detection' came forward with suggestions, all of which needed to be followed up. Andrew Wilson, a TV scriptwriter, led a research group of psychics in a special week-long phone-in in December 1978, after which it was decided to organise a search of an east Devon plantation, with police co-operation.

Among those offering assistance was British clairvoyant Mrs Nella Taylor, who told the searchers to look for a piece of cloth. A strip of blue cloth was all that was found and it was sent off for forensic examination, but it yielded no clues to the girl's disappearance. Today, 25 years later, despite the efforts of professional and psychic detectives, the Genette Tate case remains as much a mystery as it did on the first day she vanished.

Psychic detection put to the test

Nella Taylor was one of the people Professor Richard Wiseman hoped to test for a TV documentary on the abilities of psychic detectives, in which Professor Donald West and I participated in the mid-1990s. Professor Wiseman, who began life as a magician, currently heads the Perrott-Warwick Research Unit at the University of Hertfordshire, England, and is a familiar, sceptical voice on most TV programmes dealing with the paranormal. Professor Donald West, a well-respected researcher, is a former president of the Society for Psychical Research.

With his reputation for scepticism it was likely that Wiseman and the TV company would have had problems finding psychic detectives willing to be tested. He hoped my involvement would reassure them that they would be fairly treated, but it didn't work. Nella Jones certainly rejected the invitation, and so did any other psychic of note. I had never heard of two of the three paranormally gifted individuals who eventually accepted the challenge, and the third – Chris Robinson – though a believer in spirit communication, derives his psychic abilities from dreams, not mediumship.

The experiment was, in essence, a test of psychometry, using objects connected with serious crimes and taken to the university by a police museum curator. Each participant was filmed handling the objects and giving their impressions of events associated with them. Then three students, literally plucked from the university's corridors, were asked to do exactly the same. The results, when Wiseman, West and I evaluated them, showed that the psychics did no better than the students.

It was an interesting experiment, though flawed for reasons too complex to explain here, and I expressed the view on camera that it would be wrong to draw conclusions from a single test, but it would be useful to carry out a series of such experiments. Professor West and I subsequently added our signatures to a report that Professor Wiseman prepared which appeared in a number of specialist publications, including the *Journal of the Society for Psychical Research*.

I am not a scientist, but I recognise the importance of not jumping to conclusions on the strength of a single experiment. If this test had been one in a series of a hundred, in which it was consistently shown there was no difference in the impressions given by psychics and non-psychics, then I would have welcomed its publication. I also realised that trying to test 'psychic detection' in the laboratory is almost certainly doomed to fail. The objects used related to crimes long forgotten and lacked the immediacy of a current crime or mystery in which there is an urgent need for a solution.

Mediums may sometimes know more than police

There was certainly a sense of urgency when Kevin and Nicola Wells consulted a local medium after their ten-year-old daughter Holly and her friend Jessica Chapman disappeared from their homes in Soham, Cambridgeshire, on Sunday, 4 August 2002. At that moment, two days into the search for the missing girls, the parents still hoped they would be found alive. Instead, the disappearance developed into one of the most disturbing British murder cases of recent times with the discovery of their partly charred bodies in a shallow grave near the perimeter fence of the US Air Force base at Lakenheath, Suffolk.

School caretaker Ian Huntley is now serving life imprisonment for the girls' murder. Once he was sentenced, in December 2003, the parents of Holly Wells gave an exclusive interview to journalist Sarah Oliver, which was syndicated to a number of newspapers, in which they revealed that they had learned more about what had happened to their daughter from a Cambridge medium, Dennis McKenzie, than they did from the police.

Though sceptical, Mr and Mrs Wells took the advice of a friend to consult a local medium, hoping he would reassure them that the girls were still alive. He began by asking the couple if they wanted the unvarnished truth, no matter how terrible, or if they wanted him to keep the worst from them. The Wellses asked for exactly what he saw. 'I'm so sorry,' he said, 'but both girls are dead.' He went on to give what proved to be 'chillingly accurate' descriptions of Huntley and his partner Maxine Carr, who though not involved in the murders was sentenced for protecting him. The medium said he could see a man with dark, cropped hair and a woman with 'mouselike' features. He also mentioned an older man who, like the other two, had a northern accent, and a small, square red car.

The Wellses are now convinced that Dennis McKenzie saw Ian Huntley and Maxine Carr and the red Ford Fiesta in which the girls' bodies were taken to the shallow graves. They also believe the older man described by the medium is Huntley's father, who had nothing to do with the murders but in whose home Huntley was arrested. They passed the seance information to the police but were told that detectives dealt only in matter-of-fact evidence and mediumistic assistance would not contribute to their inquiry.

They had a second sitting with Dennis McKenzie some days later in which he told them that the girls were the victims of anger, not sex, which suggested to the Wellses that if he had a sexual intention, Huntley was thwarted. The medium added that the girls were dead before 8 pm on the Sunday night – a fact admitted several months later in the Old Bailey witness box by Huntley – and that Maxine Carr was not in the house when they were murdered, which was information not in the public domain at the time the statement was made.

'The medium also managed to reach Holly,' the Wellses told the journalist. 'We were sceptics by nature but we truly believe it was her. He offered details he could not have known, such as the name of her favourite shop in Cambridge and the nickname which she and she alone called her brother – Olls. This kind of information made us sure the other details were genuine and again we passed them on to the police. They were treated very coolly.'

Though the spirit message from Holly Wells did not affect the outcome of the Ian Huntley and Maxine Carr trials, it certainly comforted her grieving parents and showed that, in some cases, spirit communication can provide information unknown to either the sitters or the police.

Parapsychologist's murder solved by psychics

Douglas Scott Rogo knew more about mediumship and psychic detection than most researchers. This greatly respected writer was Professor of Parapsychology at the John F. Kennedy University in Orinda, California, author of over 20 books on the paranormal and a regular columnist for *Fate* magazine, for which he was a consulting editor. Open-minded to most aspects of the paranormal, his life came to a tragically early end on 18 August 1990, when he was murdered at his San Fernando Valley home in California. Police were called when a neighbour noticed his garden sprinklers had been on for two days, and found his body on the study floor. He had suffered multiple stab wounds. The only clue was a wine glass on a table that had a smudged fingerprint that was definitely not Scott Rogo's, but was also too indistinct to match with anyone else's.

It was totally appropriate, therefore, that the Los Angeles Police Department should turn to psychics and mediums for help in solving this brutal crime. American police tend to be more willing to embrace paranormal help than their European colleagues. We can be sure that the surviving spirit of Scott Rogo would also have been a willing participant in this experiment.

Detective Tim Moss, who had responsibility for the case, sought the help of a dozen individuals whom he often consulted for their psychic impressions. They came up with similar descriptions of the killer and one was so specific that a police artist was able to sketch the man, complete with long dark hair, moustache and black leather jacket. It was also reported that the killer had a Hispanic name. But it was not enough. Police interviewed everyone in Scott Rogo's address book but failed to find anyone who matched the description or who could give them a lead.

The lucky break came when detective Moss walked into the interview room one day and saw a man with long dark hair and a moustache who perfectly matched the drawing based on a psychic impression of the killer. In his car was a black leather jacket, and his name was Hispanic: John Anthony Battista. He even admitted he knew Scott Rogo – they had become friends, he said, after the writer gave him a lift when he was hitchhiking – and had visited him in his home, but that was some time before he died. The police found nothing to incriminate Battista and he was released.

The case remained unsolved for eight more months until another psychic contacted police, insisting that the killer's fingerprint was on a glass. Police had not discussed the smudged fingerprint publicly, so detective Moss went back to the fingerprint laboratory and asked them to take a fresh look at the evidence. Forensic techniques had evolved and they were able to make a better print, which proved to be John Battista's. Interviewed again, he denied murder, saying Scott Rogo must have left the glass hanging around his study after his visit. But friends knew this was impossible. The parapsychologist was obsessive about tidiness and made sure that glasses were washed and neatly put away the moment guests left. Which meant that Battista must have been in Scott Rogo's study on the night he died – perhaps to demand money – and had killed the writer when he refused to carry out his demand. A jury agreed and Battista was sentenced to 15 years: a result that would not have been possible without the combined efforts of Californian mediums and psychics.

When victims name their murderers

The most outstanding cases of spirit intervention are those in which the victim names the murderer. That is precisely what happened when José Divino Nunes was falsely accused of murdering his best friend Maurício Henriques in Goiânia de Campinas, a small town in the state of Goiás, Brazil. The weekly news magazine *Isto É* reports that an automatic writing script had saved the life of José Divino Nunes in 1979, when the spirit of Maurício Henriques wrote through the hand of 'Chico' Xavier, the remarkable automatic writing medium featured earlier (*see page 42*). Not only did the dead man clear his friend of the crime, but also he named the real murderer. The judge accepted the dead man's account and the innocent man was released, but the killer is reported to have disappeared before being put behind bars.

At around the same time, but in America, the murder of Teresita Basa, a 48-year-old Filipino, who was stabbed to death in her Chicago apartment on 21 February 1977, looked as if it would be an unsolved crime. Police uncovered few clues at the scene and assumed robbery to be the motive. No progress was made in the case for a further five months, until Basa apparently intervened from the spirit world.

In July, Remibias Chua was sitting in her Evanstown apartment with her doctor husband Jose, also from the Philippines, when she suddenly got up and walked into the bedroom. Dr Chua followed shortly afterwards and found her lying trance-like on the bed. He asked her what was wrong and she replied in a strange voice, in Tagalog (the Philippines language): 'I am Teresita Basa.' She said she had been murdered by a fellow employee at the Edgewater Hospital, a black man named Allan Showery, who had then stolen some jewellery.

On coming out of trance, Remibias Chua could remember nothing, but the same thing happened a few days later. This time, Dr Chua told the spirit talking through his wife's entranced body that the police would need evidence on which to act. Teresita Basa replied that Showery still had some of the stolen jewellery in his possession and that his common-law wife was now wearing her pearl cocktail ring. Despite this, the Chuas were reluctant to go to the police. Teresita Basa, a former socialite in the Philippines (hence the jewellery), persisted in communicating, and after her third trance appearance the Chuas told their story to the police. Just as the spirit communication predicted, Showery had the missing jewellery and his common-law wife was wearing the cocktail ring. Faced with the incriminating evidence, he confessed to the murder of Teresita Basa.

How would sceptics argue with that experience? They would

point out that Mrs Chua worked at the same hospital as the victim and had left just before she was apparently entranced by Teresita Basa, saying she was scared of Showery. Perhaps she had already deduced that he had something to do with the fellow Filipino's murder, and that subconscious deduction manifested itself as the voice of Teresita? But that does not explain how she knew about the jewellery and the fact that Showery's partner was wearing one of the rings.

How a murder victim's testimony finally convicted her killer

A far more satisfactory outcome, this time in Britain, involved a young medium, Christine Hoolahan, who was living in Ruislip, Middlesex, on the outskirts of west London, when she was visited by the spirit of a murder victim. The victim was called Jacqueline Poole, a 25-year-old shop assistant and part-time barmaid who was murdered on 11 February 1983. Her body was discovered two days later. Detective constable Tony Batters spent five hours at the murder scene in the council flat in Ruislip, taking notes of every detail.

Christine Hoolahan

A few days later he and detective constable Andrew Smith were told to visit Christine Hoolahan, who was working part-time at RAF Northolt while training to become a professional medium, and who claimed to have information about the murder.

The police had issued appeals for those who knew Poole to contact them, but the medium was not one of them. Although she lived in the same area, Hoolahan's home in Ruislip Gardens was three miles away from the murder scene and she did not know Jacqui Poole. On the day after the body was discovered, the medium experienced strange phenomena, including the lights going on and off and a feeling as if the bedclothes were being pulled off. Having heard about the murder, she asked, 'Jacqui, is that you?' Hoolahan then had a vision of a woman who said her name was Jacqui Hunt. This was, in fact, the victim's maiden name, but was not the name by which she was known in Ruislip, nor had it been used in media reports about the murder.

The spirit told Christine Hoolahan that she wanted her help in getting justice done. The medium responded by saying that she could not go to the police unless she had some concrete evidence to give them. Otherwise, they would just assume she had read about the case in the newspapers or spoken to people who knew Jacqui. At this, the vision disappeared, but Jacqui's spirit returned next evening with much more detail about the murder, which was why detective constables Batters and Smith went to interview her.

What makes this such an outstanding case is that during their investigation, the 'dead' woman responded to questions from the police officers, even talking directly to them through the medium. The victim identified her murderer by describing him very accurately and writing his unusual nickname – Pokie – on a sheet of paper. The first account of the extraordinary case, written by Tony Batters, was published not in a tabloid newspaper or a psychic publication but in *Police*, the journal of the Police Federation (December 2001).

Guy Lyon Playfair and Montague Keen, two very well-respected Society for Psychical Research investigators, have produced a detailed paper on the case based on the police evidence and their interviews with the medium and the police officers involved. Published in the January 2004 *Journal of the Society for Psychical Research* under the title 'A Possibly Unique Case of Psychic

Detection', it contains declarations from both Batters and Smith that the paper is an accurate account of the events that they reported. Tony Batters revealed his initial feelings when asked to interview the medium:

> I was at that time completely sceptical and did not wish to pursue the interview, but as a courtesy we sat down in her lounge and she started saying things that immediately shook me. I was writing them down; at a very early stage she went into what I would describe as a trance, although I'm not familiar with a trance, but her eyelids fluttered and closed and she spoke, in a normal voice, a series of very short sentences, and I produced a verbatim transcript from the original notes of that meeting which I still hold.

At the time, these impressions – given in no particular order by the medium – were not obviously impressive, and the police officers suspected there might be a normal explanation. Perhaps people were using her as a front to convey information, true or false, to the police. Their opinion of Christine Hoolahan and her mediumship soon changed, however, as Tony Batters explained to the researchers:

> We were probing – 'Where did you get this information? Surely you have been speaking to relatives? Do you know somebody in the murder squad?' And she said, 'Well look, from the questions I think you don't believe me. I'd like to do something, and Jacqui is telling me to do this, and that is if one of you will give me something that's personal to you, I will try to demonstrate something.'

Detective constable Smith gave the medium his bunch of keys. She then made three very clear and specific statements. One was that he had recently received a letter about some essential electrical work. This was correct. A building society had informed him that a property he planned to buy needed to be rewired before it would agree to a mortgage. Christine Hoolahan also informed him that he would soon be transferred to another police station. This he regarded as highly unlikely – until he was informed of his impending transfer a few days later. The third statement – actually the first she made – was clearly accurate, though Batters told the researchers 'to my dying day I could not disclose what she said. It was quite extraordinary with detail'.

Batters admits that while the medium was making these statements it 'didn't make a great deal of sense to me until we got out of the front door, where Andy (Smith) had turned white and was literally shaking. It had an enormous impact on him.'

In all, the medium made 131 statements, only one of which was shown to be wrong – Jacqui Poole spoke of being murdered on Saturday night, whereas the murder was on Friday night. Batters reassembled the information in a logical order and the picture that emerged became much clearer.

Unquestionably impressed by the medium's abilities, they decided to question at length the man who had been identified by the spirit of Jacqui Poole as her murderer. His name was Anthony Ruark. He had already come forward as one of Jacqui's acquaintances in response to their appeal. Although he had a previous criminal record, he had no history of violence and was not a prime suspect.

The session with Hoolahan changed that. Jacqui Poole's spirit had given Ruark's nickname – Pokie – and also told them to look at his alibi. Ruark had given two alibis; one of these was disproved, the other could not be corroborated. But there was not enough evidence to charge him with murder and no court would accept statements from a murder victim made through a medium. He remained a free man for 17 years until, in 2000, an informant named someone else as Jacqui Poole's murderer. The case was reopened and in the process a pullover belonging to Ruark, which had been removed from a rubbish bin and stored as possible evidence on the orders of one of the detectives, was re-examined using the latest DNA technology. In his *Police* report, Batters revealed:

The findings were completely conclusive, identifying numerous exchanges of body fluids, skin cells and clothing fibres between the victim and her killer, Pokie Ruark. The chances of error were quoted in the court as less than one in one billion.

There were 46 such matches. Ruark was arrested and charged with murder. The jury's verdict was unanimous and he was sentenced to life, at the Old Bailey, in August 2001.

The involvement of Jacqui Poole in identifying her killer was not mentioned at the trial. However, without the victim's communications through medium Christine Hoolahan, the police would not have regarded Ruark as a prime suspect and the item of clothing that eventually proved his guilt and ensured that justice was done would not have been preserved for future forensic tests.

When Irish television (RTE) featured the case on *The Late Late Show* on 23 November 2001, both Christine Hoolahan and detective constable Batters took part. The police officer declared: 'I've accepted the fact that Jacqui communicated with Christine,' and he subsequently informed the psychical researchers that all of his police colleagues with whom he had discussed the case agreed with that interpretation. Playfair and Keen also say, 'We can find no plausible alternative explanation of how the information communicated was gathered.'

1 Estelle Roberts, *Fifty Years as a Medium*, Herbert Jenkins (1959).

Chapter 5

Conversations with the Dead

Family affairs

A Scottish stockbroker by the name of Arthur Findlay accompanied his sick wife to Glasgow and stayed close by while she had an operation and recuperated in a nursing home. One Sunday evening in 1918, during her recovery, he decided to take a stroll to get some fresh air. It was a walk that would change his life and, indirectly, affect the lives of thousands of others over the years.

As he strode through the streets he came across a Spiritualist church. Intrigued, he went inside and listened to an address in which the speaker told of amazing psychic phenomena he had witnessed and of conversations with the dead. Findlay spoke to him at the end of the service. 'Do you really expect me to believe what you said tonight?' he challenged the speaker. 'Can you prove it to me?' Arthur Findlay – who prided himself on his rationalist approach to life – had issued similar challenges to clerics in the past and the usual, inadequate response was that he needed to have faith. The Spiritualist, however, was different.

He said he did not expect anyone to believe without experiencing psychic phenomena for himself, and yes, he *could* prove what he said by introducing his inquirer to a medium. Findlay accepted his invitation to meet the man on a street corner in Glasgow at 7 pm the following night and to be taken to a seance. On the way, the Spiritualist explained that they were going to the home of medium John Sloan, who held a seance every Monday night. On arrival, he found himself in the company of ten others. No introductions were made for the simple reason that the man who had taken him to Sloan's house did not know his name; nor did Arthur Findlay know the identity of the man.

Soon, the lights were turned off, a hymn was sung and then, once John Sloan had been entranced, out of the darkness a man's loud voice was heard directly in front of a woman sitting close to Findlay. She responded, telling the group later that she had been talking to her dead husband. More voices spoke, each with a distinct sound and personality, and intimate conversations took place, until Findlay – desperately trying to analyse the experience as it unfolded and suspecting the medium was somehow impersonating dead people – began to think he was the only person who would not receive a message. Suddenly, a strong voice spoke right in front of him.

'Yes, who are you?' he responded.

'*Your father, Robert Downie Findlay.*'

Describing this first seance, Arthur Findlay writes:

The voice continued speaking, and referred to something that only my father and I, and one other man, ever knew about on earth, and that other man, like my father, was dead…. It was a private matter that neither I, nor my father, nor any other man when on earth, ever spoke about to any other person. All this was extraordinary enough, but imagine my surprise when my father concluded by saying:

'David Kidston is standing beside me and would also like to talk to you about this matter.'

Now David Kidston was the name of the other man who knew about this private affair… and here I was in a Glasgow artisan's house, a complete stranger to everyone, being told by two different voices about something known only to me and two dead men.[1]

In later editions of his book *On the Edge of the Etheric*, and also in his autobiography, Arthur Findlay elaborated on this story by explaining that the message related to the business in which his father and Kidston were partners.[2] The actual words spoken by the spirit of Robert Downie Findlay began with, 'I am very sorry I did not take you into my business. I would have liked to do so but Kidston opposed it.' And when David Kidston had the chance to speak from beyond the grave, he told Arthur Findlay, 'I was wrong opposing your coming into our office. I am sorry I did it but now you need have no regrets. I am glad to get that off my chest at last.'

At that first seance, Findlay heard 30 different voices, giving their names and sometimes their addresses to the correct people and describing intimate family affairs. At times, two or three voices spoke simultaneously. At subsequent seances with John Sloan, Findlay took the opportunity to sit next to him and, when voices spoke, he would place his ear close enough to his mouth to feel him breathing. The voices, he confirmed, did not emanate from the medium's lips.

Direct voice mediumship

Sloan, incidentally, was an *independent* direct voice medium, which means that the voices that were heard did not speak through him or through any other instrument, and only occasionally it seems was a seance room trumpet (a long, thin metal cone) needed to amplify a spirit voice.

Once he was totally satisfied that the direct voice phenomenon he had experienced was genuine, Arthur Findlay began introducing others to the regular seances, always being careful not to identify them in any way to Sloan and the other sitters before they had received spirit communications.

'If he had been willing to give his gifts to the public, he would have been known as one of this country's most famous mediums,' Findlay wrote of Sloan.

Instead of this he has preferred having his friends to his house for an evening, once a week or so, and giving them the pleasure of meeting again those of their acquaintances who have passed beyond the veil....So long as he can get work he will never take money in exchange for his gift.... No one need ask him for permission to be present at a seance and fear refusal; no one need fear that he will be made to feel that a favour is being granted.

A royal connection

Among those who asked Arthur Findlay for an introduction to John Sloan was the Hon Everard Fielding, an active member of the Society for Psychical Research, who requested that a friend be allowed to sit with the Scottish medium. Findlay met the man in Glasgow; they had dinner together, and then went on to Sloan's home. Throughout this time, the visitor made no mention of his occupation and Findlay made no enquiries.

'He was therefore a complete stranger to me, and neither I, nor the medium, nor anybody present at the seance, knew anything about him,' Findlay wrote in *On the Edge of the Etheric*, which is largely devoted to Sloan and the evidence of his direct voice communications. It was a memorable seance and in time the visitor from London was addressed by a voice. When he asked who was speaking, it said:

When on Earth I was known as King Edward VII.

There followed a very natural conversation in which names were mentioned and events discussed. Finally, the voice said: 'I must thank you for all your kindness to my wife, Queen Alexandra. I do not know how she could have gone on without you, and you have relieved her of much worry and care.'

After the seance, when Findlay enquired who he was, the anonymous visitor explained that he was controller of Queen Alexandra's

73

household. This event had an even more remarkable sequel, as Findlay records:

> Queen Alexandra, when she heard about this seance, wanted to sit with Sloan and this took place in London. I am glad to say that this gave her great satisfaction. Those also present were my friends, Sir William Barrett the eminent physicist, Sir Arthur Conan Doyle, Dr Abraham Wallace and Sir Oliver Lodge, all believers in the reality of this phenomenon after years of study and experience. Besides them were Sir Thomas Lipton and Marconi, for whose opinions I cannot vouch.

Arthur Findlay moved to England to live at Stansted Hall, Essex, where Frances, Countess of Warwick, became a friend and near neighbour. Though Findlay does not say so in his book, the Countess was King Edward VII's mistress for many years. When he told her about the King's spirit communications through John Sloan, she responded:

> King Edward has often come back to speak to me. We were friends, and when he was on earth we always spoke to each other in German. After his death he has come back to me at seances, and always spoke to me in the direct voice. Just as he always spoke German to me on Earth....

In fact, the direct voice medium through whom the King spoke to the countess was a remarkable American named Etta Wriedt, who also held seances for Queen Victoria at which Prince Albert returned. Though Findlay does not tell us when the royal seances took place, we can safely say it was between 1918 and 1925. Edward VII, who did not become King until the age of 59 in 1901, on the death of his mother, Queen Victoria, died in May 1910. Arthur Findlay's first seance with John Sloan was on 20 September 1918, and Queen Alexandra, who had married Edward in 1863 when he was Prince of Wales, died in 1925.

I have dealt with Arthur Findlay and John Sloan at some length for a number of reasons. First, I wanted to show how Sloan's remarkable direct voice mediumship, for which he refused to take payment during more than 40 years, consistently provided outstanding evidence for spirit communication to people who were total strangers. I also wanted to demonstrate that, despite the natural suspicions we have about seances held in the dark, when we assess communications of the calibre experienced by Arthur Findlay and others, we have to accept that such evidence would be extremely impressive regardless of whether the lights were on or off. This observation, I must add, is true of the direct voice phenomenon but not of most other forms of physical mediumship, as we will see in the next chapter.

Arthur Findlay College

Although my focus is on the past 50 years of Spiritualism, I also felt it was important to step outside that time frame, to the earlier part of the twentieth century, because the events I have described had such an influence on Arthur Findlay that they continue to reach out and touch people to this very day, 40 years after his passing. He dedicated the rest of his life to studying Spiritualism, spreading its message and encouraging education about the movement. He wrote several books on mediumship, Spiritualism and comparative religion, all of which remain in print. *On the Edge of the Etheric* was a runaway success, going into 30 impressions in the first year of its publication (1931). He also gave his splendid home, Stansted Hall, as a Deed of Gift to the Spiritualists' National Union (SNU) in 1964, a year after his wife's passing to the spirit world and a few months before his own transition. With it came a charter indicating how he wanted his gift used.

The result is now known as the Arthur Findlay College, a private mansion in the Essex countryside that has been converted into a residential centre for the advancement of psychic science. As perhaps the most impressive Spiritualist venue of its kind in the world, it attracts visitors from many countries. Some 8,000 visitors pass through its doors each year, most of them participating in courses run by around 90 tutors whose specialities include various forms of mediumship as well as complementary subjects such as astrology, healing and philosophy.

In many ways, Stansted Hall is a monument to both Arthur Findlay and John Sloan. It is sad to record, therefore, that the form of mediumship – direct voice – which led to Findlay's conversion to Spiritualism and the gift of his home to the SNU is not taught at Stansted, though it might occasionally be included in a broader course on physical phenomena. One reason for this is that it is not a mediumistic skill that develops overnight or can be taught in a few days.

Direct voice mediumship in the twenty-first century

It generally takes years of patience and regular weekly seances with the same group of sitters before the slightest signs of physical manifestations occur or the faintest whispers are heard. In our fast-moving twenty-first century, with its numerous distractions, there are fewer people prepared to sacrifice their time to develop such phenomena. 'There isn't physical mediumship like there used to be,' the SNU's president Duncan Gasgoyne told me early in 2004. 'I think people in the movement no longer know the difference between being overshadowed, going into trance or being in deep trance. When I was younger and went to a transfiguration seance, you actually saw the ectoplasmic mask in front of the medium's face. Now, what is called transfiguration is different. You've got to squint your eyes to see anything. At the Arthur Findlay College we try to build a scientific approach into our courses.'

I have to admit that my own experiences of direct voice have not been impressive. Among the seances I attended in my early days was one with a Worthing medium, Jim Hutchings, at which the spirits of Lord Northcliffe and Hannen Swaffer apparently returned to me. My mother came back to speak to me through a levitated trumpet at a William Olsen seance in London, which was quite clever of her considering she was alive at the time and still is, three decades later. I also attended a demonstration of direct voice by Stuart Alexander, held in the library of Stansted Hall.

None of these seances convinced me that a paranormal explanation was the only one that could be applied to what I saw and heard. In each case, the mediums could have had confederates who helped them produce the results under cover of darkness. I am not suggesting that this happened, but unless sitters can rule out such possibilities, the only other way of deciding whether a seance is what it purports to be is by the standard of evidence, and it was not impressive on those occasions. I am well aware that an accomplished conman, with the right equipment and the assistance of one or more confederates, can put on a passable display of direct voice mediumship, fooling large numbers of people for several years, and I deal with the whole subject of fraud in a later chapter (see page 165).

The nearest I have so far come to hearing an actual spirit voice is through the mediumship of Mona Van Der Watt, a Scotswoman married to a South African psychologist, who emigrated to Cape Town in 1954. During a visit to Britain in the Sixties, she demonstrated at the London Spiritual Mission and I watched with fascination as she walked around the congregation, in trance, giving messages to individuals. She was accompanied by a strange sound, seemingly coming from close to her left shoulder, which was a cross between the humming of an electric razor and a high-pitched whistle. This was said to be the voices of the dead talking to her spirit guide, who then relayed their evidential messages through the entranced medium to members of the audience.

There was no doubting the reality of this voice phenomenon, but it was impossible to distinguish any voices from the humming sound. Back in South Africa, however, members of the Spiritualist church at which she regularly demonstrated had used microphones to amplify the voices and could hear what they said. UK-based George Cranley, who ran the Noah's Ark Society, which was established in 1990 'to promote, educate and encourage the development and safe practice of physical mediumship', had an unrivalled opportunity to study Mona Van Der Watt.

Cranley's family had moved to South Africa and he began investigating different religions in 1959, at the age of 16. When he first encountered Spiritualism and Mona Van Der Watt he knew he needed to look no further. For ten years he attended the church where she demonstrated, and also took part in weekly experimental sessions. During this time, he told me, the spirit voices that spoke independently of her could be clearly heard. He also made tape recordings that showed that the voices spoke faster than the human voice normally does. 'Week after week the evidence was so breathtaking it seemed almost too good to be true, yet it was,' he added. 'No super-ESP hypothesis could explain away her mediumship. Today, I would be hard-pushed to find a medium of comparable quality.' She made a number of visits to England, demonstrating twice at International Spiritualist Federation annual conferences, where a throat microphone enabled everyone in the large halls to hear the spirit voices speaking through her mediumship.

Listening to the voices

Mona Van Der Watt explained that when she was developing her mediumship, her spirit guides gave her a choice. Either she could produce a strong direct voice in a dark room, which would limit the number of people who could receive evidence, or she could reach a wider audience but the direct voice would be much weaker. She took the latter option, but it was still eight years before faint voices were heard. It has been reported that on one occasion six doctors examined her in an attempt to locate the origin of the voices. Wherever they placed a stethoscope they could hear a voice, but could not locate its source.

This particular form of direct voice is very rare, but not unique. Often during English medium Mrs Gladys Osborne Leonard's trance sittings, held in semi-darkness, whispered voices could be heard at the same time as she was speaking in trance. Psychical researcher and clergyman the Rev Drayton Thomas was able to capture these independent voices on a gramophone record.

By far the largest collection of spirit voice recordings was produced through the mediumship of Leslie Flint, who remained conscious throughout the seance and even joined in conversations with the spirit voices. Flint, who was born in 1911 in Hackney, east London, at a Salvation Army home, showed signs of psychic ability at an early age but was not keen on becoming a full-time medium, choosing to be a ballroom dancing teacher instead. After joining a development circle, however, the direct voice phenomenon manifested. This made it difficult for him to go to the cinema because, in these darkened surroundings, spirit voices could be heard not only by Flint, but also by other cinema goers who thought he was talking and hissed at him to be quiet.

Eventually, Leslie Flint developed his mediumship and readily co-operated with researchers. 'I think I can say I am the most tested medium this country has ever produced,' he declared. 'I have been boxed up, tied up, sealed up, gagged, bound and held, and still voices have come to speak their message of life eternal.'[3] He even demonstrated before thousands of people in large halls by following similar precautionary procedures, including being gagged, then entering a makeshift darkroom – a curtain-fronted cabinet on a stage – from which spirit voices spoke to the audience through a microphone.

Sidney George Woods and Betty Greene were two regular sitters with Flint who tape-recorded many of the direct voice sessions for 17 years. Their work was inspired by the spirit of Ellen Terry, the famous British stage actress who died in 1928, and told them at one seance:

You are going to have some remarkable communications. And I suggest you keep these contacts going regularly to build up the power, and to make possible this link, which has been deliberately arranged for your tapes. The tapes you record give us the opportunity to reach many people in all parts of the world....We shall bring various souls from various spheres to give talks and lectures. We need willing helpers on your side.

That promise was kept, with Mahatma Gandhi, George Bernard Shaw, Rudolph Valentino, Oscar Wilde, Charlotte Brontë, Maurice Chevalier and Sir Winston Churchill among the many well-known communicators who returned through Flint – a man of poor education – to talk about their lives in the next world. Flint, whose life story is told in the appropriately titled *Voices in the Dark*, passed on in April 1994, but his legacy is a huge library of recordings, now the copyright of the Leslie Flint Educational Trust, which makes them available through the Internet. Not all the communicators were famous – if they were, we would be right to be suspicious – and the recordings include conversations between ordinary individuals and their loved ones.

I visited Leslie Flint with a good friend and colleague, Anne Dooley, and like thousands of others before us we sat in his darkened seance room in Westbourne Terrace, west London, waiting with high expectations for contact with the next world. There were just the three of us. No singing. No hymns. Just idle chatter as we sat and waited ... and waited ... and waited. Then, as Flint announced that nothing was going to happen that day – there was never any guarantee that the spirits would talk – a squeaky voice said, 'Hello.' Flint told us it was Mickey, his spirit helper or 'doorkeeper'. Apart from that solitary word, the door to the next world remained firmly closed on that occasion.

How does spirit voice communication work?

Many people who are not conversant with the mechanics of mediumship find it impossible to comprehend how spirits can talk at seances. It is one thing to accept that the dead, existing in an invisible, spiritual realm, might be able to communicate telepathically with a gifted medium to pass messages on, but quite another to physically communicate with the same tone of voice and recognisable mannerisms. Without bodies, how can they speak?

Ectoplasm

The explanation offered by the spirit guides who make this possible is that they extract substances from the medium's body, and also to some degree from the sitters, to form ectoplasm, which is then moulded into the shape of a human voice box and the spirits wear it like a mask in order to speak through it. Ectoplasm is the mysterious substance, the secret ingredient that makes direct voice and other forms of physical phenomena possible – particularly materialisation, which I deal with elsewhere (*see page 86*). However, since it is affected by ultraviolet light, it is not an easy substance to analyse. It also takes different forms, just as water can be solid (ice), liquid or gaseous (vapour). It has a smell like ozone and displays strange properties. In the few photographs that have been taken of it, there are times when it looks suspiciously like woven cheesecloth and others when it has the appearance of a fluffy cloud.

According to the information Arthur Findlay received from the next world, when we die we exist in an etheric body, a duplicate of our physical body, and 'in etheric life, communication takes place in the same way as in Earth life. The vocal organs vibrate their atmosphere, the tongue moves, the lungs draw in and expel the equivalent to our air ... the only difference being that it is all taking place in matter of a much finer structure and at a much more rapid rate of vibration.' The ectoplasmic voice box – which has been photographed using infrared light with a number of physical mediums – is in effect an artificial mouth, larynx and lungs, made of a substance that the spirit visitors can manipulate and speak through.

To achieve these results, a large team of spirit helpers is involved in order to create the correct chemical structure of the ectoplasm, shape it, move objects around and generally organise the many spirit communicators who want to make themselves known. My own view is that we should not concern ourselves too much with *how* it happens, but focus on *what* occurs. Because *what* has occurred at the very best direct voice seances provides us with irrefutable evidence for spirit communication.

Jack Webber

A Welsh ex-miner, Jack Webber, was responsible in the 1940s for convincing many hard-bitten sceptics of the reality of spirit communication, among them Fleet Street journalists. In addition to voices speaking through levitated trumpets, a range of physical phenomena was witnessed and photographed using infrared light. In fact, these psychic demonstrations, including removing the medium's sewn-up jacket and replacing it in seconds, levitation of heavy tables and materialising objects, all of which were caught on camera, are so remarkable that accounts of his mediumship tend to focus on them, rather than on the superb evidence provided by the spirit communicators.

In his excellent book *The Mediumship of Jack Webber*,[4] for example, Harry Edwards gives us marvellous descriptions of the precautions taken to secure the medium to a chair with rope and stitch up his jacket, and the spectacular happenings that then ensued, but little about the content of the messages. Then, at the end of a chapter called 'Voice Production' comes this throwaway 'Addendum, March 1940':

On February 10th, at Lincoln, a conversation was carried on via the trumpet in French. On January 27th, at the Sanctuary of St Andrew, Harringay, conversations were carried on in Swedish, Portuguese, and a recital of Latin was given. The sitter who carried on the Swedish conversation said there was no trace of an accent foreign to the tongue. It may be re-emphasised here that Mr Webber was an unlettered man, he rarely read a book, in fact, his only reading matter was the newspapers and children's comics.

A special feature of Jack Webber's seances was that his spirit guide, speaking through the entranced medium, would regularly call for the lights to be put on throughout the seance, allowing sitters to check that Webber was still tied tightly to his chair seconds after striking phenomena were witnessed. Sometimes this would allow the sitters to see the levitated trumpets still moving and slowly settling down on the floor, untouched by human hands.

Jack Webber passed to the spirit world suddenly and unexpectedly at the age of 33, on 9 March 1940, just a month after the Lincoln seance referred to above. In the space of ten years he had developed from someone who regarded Spiritualism as 'bunk' to one of this country's most powerful physical mediums.

The medium Mollie Perriman

Another noted Welsh medium was Mollie Perriman who, as well as being a society clairvoyant, also produced impressive direct voice, sometimes without the need for darkness. One witness to her powers, J. Curr, testified:

I heard thirty spirit voices, all of them speaking in white light. We had met in the house of a friend, eight of us, to have a social evening.

Mr Perriman was playing the piano and we were all singing, when suddenly a male voice was heard saying, 'Hello,' from the vicinity of the door. We greeted the voice, which was followed by others, until each member of the company spoke to 'dead' friends. Every spirit spoke to us in light. There were two lamps, one a 100 watt and the other 60 watt. All the voices were identified by people in the room as belonging to 'dead' relatives or friends. The voices ranged in intensity, some so loud that they could be heard above the singing, while others spoke in modulated whispers. On one occasion, while I was talking to Mrs Perriman and she was replying, I heard a spirit voice speaking at the same time as she did, but from a point that seemed to be six inches behind her neck. One communicator spoke in Polish and was recognised by a sitter as his mother.

I watched Mrs Perriman when the spirit voices spoke to us, but there was no visible contact with the medium. If they used her larynx, how was she able to speak at the same time? The impromptu seance lasted for nearly two hours and a half, with spirit voices coming and going during that time. Some of the conversations were so intimate that I cannot possibly record them. It was touching to witness the reunions between families who had lost the physical presence of their loved ones.

On another social occasion, the Perrimans held an impromptu seance with three friends in their London garden, in a shaded spot away from the direct lights of neighbours' windows or from car headlights. Voices spoke 'apparently from the air', providing remarkable evidence for survival. Mollie Perriman, who remained conscious throughout her sittings, had a conversation with her dead brother, and her husband spoke to the spirit of his mother.

In a book about his wife's mediumship,[5] A.E. Perriman relates how, in the seven years after their move from Wales to London, 'we have held some 2,500 sittings, and have listened to over 10,000 spirit entities' discourse'.

One of the most puzzling aspects of Spiritualism is the question of why different forms of mediumship come and go, like the ebb and flow of the tide, providing spectacular and prolific physical mediumship in one century and very little of note in another. This is certainly true of direct voice mediumship, which has virtually disappeared. It is to be hoped that young mediums will emerge who are prepared to spend the time necessary to produce direct voice and other physical phenomena. In return, they may well have to suffer the indignities of being treated with suspicion, accused of fraud and required to be strip searched, trussed up and even gagged, before sceptical sitters are prepared to accept the genuineness of the phenomena they produce. The rewards will be few, apart from the knowledge that they have provided yet more evidence for the existence of a spirit world which most Spiritualists believe has already been proved beyond any doubt.

1 Arthur Findlay, *On The Edge of the Etheric,* Psychic Press (1931).

2 Arthur Findlay, *Looking Back; The Autobiography of a Spiritualist*, SNU Publications (1955).

3 Leslie Flint, *Voices in the Dark: My Life as a Medium*, Macmillan, London, (1971).

4 Harry Edwards, *The Mediumship of Jack Webber*, The Healer Publishing Company (1962).

5 A.E. Perriman, *Broadcasting From Beyond*, Psychic Book Club (1952).

Chapter 6

Producing Visible Spirits

For most Spiritualists, the pinnacle of physical mediumship is the ability to produce spirits who can walk, talk and be recognised by their loved ones. This rare phenomenon is called materialisation and it takes a number of forms. At its very best, it can provide conclusive proof of survival after death to those fortunate enough to witness it. At its worst, it can look suspiciously like the medium, draped in a white sheet, masquerading as a spirit. Moreover, since physical mediums cannot guarantee that their seances will always be of the highest quality, the history of Spiritualism provides us with confusing and conflicting accounts of even the most famous exponents.

Ectoplasm in materialisations

Adding to our difficulties in assessing individuals who claim such powers is the fact that the substance used to create solid spirits is the mysterious ectoplasm already discussed in the review of direct voice mediumship (*see page 81*). To produce full-form materialisations, copious amounts of ectoplasm must be extracted from the medium to 'clothe' the spirits and produce a form that is visible to physical eyes. This is usually seen coming from the medium's mouth, nose and ears, and occasionally from the region of the solar plexus.

Since ectoplasm is sensitive to normal light, such seances are usually held in darkness or with a faint red light, making accurate observation difficult. If white light is unexpectedly used to illuminate the seance room, the ectoplasm is rapidly sucked back into the medium's body, causing burns or other injuries. Sceptics, of course, believe the insistence on low lighting makes it easier for the medium to fool the sitters. The result of these contradictory elements and claims is that it is possible to pick up one book on the subject that presents a very persuasive case for materialisation, and another that argues just as cogently that all physical mediums are fakes and the witnesses of such phenomena are gullible fools.

In fact, the evidence for materialisation is very strong, though some of the researchers who investigated the Spiritualist movement's early physical mediums were not convinced that spirits of the dead were necessarily responsible for its manipulation. They preferred 'ideoplasm' theories suggesting that the minds or imaginations of the mediums were responsible for shaping the paranormally exuded ectoplasm.

Among those who made in-depth studies of the early mediums and the white substance they produced was the German psychical researcher Baron Albert von Schrenck-Notzing. He conducted experiments with all the European mediums of repute up until his death in 1929, including the remarkable Italian Eusapia Palladino and Frenchwoman Eva Carrière (better known as Eva C and also as Marthe Béraud). His discovery of the young Austrian physical mediums Rudi and Willi Schneider and his subsequent research, involving fraudproof electrical controls, resulted in a hundred very sceptical and sometimes hostile scientists who witnessed Willi's phenomena in 1922 declaring themselves totally convinced of the reality of telekinesis (the paranormal movement of objects) and ectoplasm. Indeed, enough scientists of repute had vouched for the existence of ectoplasm and materialisation by the middle of the twentieth century that it should have been beyond doubt. But since, by its very nature, it is not something that can be put under a microscope and examined, or stored in a cupboard for later examination, the sceptics continue to outnumber those who are convinced.

Medium in the dock

The continuing clash of beliefs was to make headlines in the British press in the 1940s when a Scottish medium, Helen Victoria Duncan, found herself and three others in the dock at London's Central Criminal Court, Old Bailey, accused of offences under the Witchcraft Act of 1735.

Helen Duncan

Police had raided one of Helen Duncan's seances at Portsmouth, Hampshire, in January 1944, but had failed to retrieve any incriminating evidence. A police officer testified that the sheet used to give the appearance of a spirit had been snatched away from him, in the direction of the sitters. Spiritualists argue, however, that the ectoplasm had simply returned rapidly to the medium. Nevertheless, just a month before D-Day, together with Ernest Homer and Elizabeth Jones (known as Mrs Homer), who ran the Master Temple Psychic Centre above a drug store in Portsmouth, and the medium's travelling companion Mrs Frances Brown, Helen Duncan stood accused under the Vagrancy Act of 1824, the Larceny Act and the Witchcraft Act. It was claimed they had pretended 'to exercise or use a kind of conjuration that through the agency of Helen Duncan spirits of deceased persons should appear to be present in such place as Helen Duncan was then in, and the said spirits were communicating with living persons there present.'

The case, which began in court 4 on 23 March 1944, has been described as 'the trial of the century', and it would have made even bigger headlines had the Second World War not been going on around them at the time. Indeed, British prime minister Winston Churchill demanded to know why the court's time was being wasted on 'obsolete tomfoolery'. Churchill, incidentally, had psychic abilities and it is likely that he knew more about Spiritualism than he was saying when he sent off the angry memo demanding an explanation. Famous Fleet Street journalist Hannen Swaffer even pointed out in one newspaper that three members of the War Cabinet had attended seances and he wondered why *they* had not been charged under the Witchcraft Act, too.

Hannen Swaffer was one of many who testified for the defence – giving Spiritualism a rare opportunity to proclaim the physical wonders of the seance room in a court of law. A procession of impressive witnesses told their stories. Famous trance medium Lilian Bailey took the stand to tell of seeing the materialised form of her tall, slim mother, who removed the shroud from her head to draw attention to her golden hair, of which she was particularly proud when alive. Then the very different shape of her paternal grandmother appeared and drew attention to her outsize nose, which had been a family joke. Similarly, it was her dead father's nose that impressed psychic healer Margaret Lyons when he materialised at a Helen Duncan seance – 'it was broken and went over a bit'. And she was speechless when he addressed her as 'Marget' because he had *always* dropped the second 'r' when addressing her.

Other witnesses included a wing commander, a solicitor and a flight lieutenant, none of whom was a Spiritualist, but all willingly testified to having seen phenomena they considered paranormal. In her testimony to the judge and jury, Nurse Jane Rust, a retired municipal midwife, told of being reunited with her dead husband and feeling his rheumatic knobbly knuckles. She also told of seeing her dead mother, clearly identified by two distinct moles: one on her chin, the other above an eyebrow. And even more impressive was the spirit appearance of someone she knew as 'Aunt Mary', who spoke Spanish with a Gibraltarian accent. Journalist Sir James Harris JP even testified that he had seen the spirit of his old friend Sir Arthur Conan Doyle materialise on one of the 15 occasions he had sat with Helen Duncan.

The prosecution's case was that these spirits were really Helen Duncan in disguise. Yet the witnesses' testimony would appear to have been more than sufficient to undermine such a claim, particularly in the absence of physical proof of fraud. Would the jury be prepared to believe that the 22-stone, obese and ungainly medium could impersonate men, women and children of different shapes and sizes, as well as speak a foreign language with the correct accent?

One witness, Mary Blackwell, even spoke of seeing *two* materialisations at the same time, one of which was her father, who came out of the cabinet and patted her on the head while another spirit form was also visible. Various witnesses spoke of seeing Helen Duncan's main spirit control, Albert Steward, standing by her side. Witnesses also noted how the ectoplasm of the spirits was either bright white, blue-white or self-luminous, rather than reflecting the red light used in the seance room, and a number of them drew attention to the way in which these materialised forms often disappeared – not back into the curtained cabinet that housed the medium but straight down through the floor.

The medium's senior defence counsel, C.E. Loseby, even made a sensational offer to the jury. They could have a seance with Helen Duncan to see for themselves what her mediumship was capable of producing. The judge initially rejected the offer – even though it was the defence that was asking for it – on the grounds that it would resemble a trial by ordeal, likely to harm the defence. Later, he said the offer was open to the jury's discretion but they rejected it. Loseby complained bitterly, but to no avail.

Helen Duncan was found guilty and sentenced to nine months in Holloway Prison. Mrs Brown, who had a previous conviction, received a four-month sentence. Mr and Mrs Homer were bound over. As Dr John Beloff, former president of both the Society for Psychical Research and the Parapsychological Association, observes in his introduction to Manfred Cassirer's book on the trial: 'Clearly, their lordships preferred to disbelieve the witnesses than to risk exposure to the evidence in question.'[1]

A convincing fraud?

It is even more surprising that the jury believed they could judge Helen Duncan's physical mediumship to be trickery without witnessing it, whereas Will Goldston, founder of the Magicians' Club in 1911, had this to say after he attended a Helen Duncan seance at a house in North London in 1932:

> The medium's cabinet consisted simply of two curtains drawn across the room. She was in trance within three minutes, and in the course of the next hour and a half some eight different forms were manifested, of all ages, both sexes, and each possessed of an individual speaking voice. I personally carried on a conversation with a small female form called Violet. She told me she was eight years of age, and permitted me to feel her hand. Now, there is not, so far as I am aware – and I am a magician of lifelong experience – any system of trickery which can achieve the astounding results which I witnessed that evening with Mrs Duncan.

It has to be said that, though her physical mediumship had clearly impressed many people, there were times when Helen Duncan's seances did not satisfy her sitters. She had been charged with being a fraud once before, in Edinburgh in 1933, and fined. Before her Old Bailey trial she had also given seances at the National Laboratory of Psychical Research, after which psychic investigator Harry Price put forward the claim that Mrs Duncan was able to swallow large quantities of material before a seance, then regurgitate it in order to produce white-draped figures.

Mrs Duncan was not the first medium to be accused of swallowing the evidence, as it were. A century earlier, such suggestions were well known to Professor Charles Richet, a French professor of physiology who was a foremost investigator of materialisation mediumship and became convinced the phenomenon was genuine. On the subject of regurgitation, he declared: 'How can masses of mobile substance, organised as hands, faces and drawings, be made to emerge from the oesophagus or the stomach? No physiologist would admit such power to contract those organs at will in this manner.' Another theory was that she secreted her props 'in the pelvic region' or in other orifices. Yet whenever she was subjected to intimate searches by medical professionals, including Mrs Mollie Goldney, a prominent SPR member and also a lecturer in midwifery, she was never found to be secreting anything in her bodily cavities.

On her release from prison, Helen Duncan vowed never to give another seance, but it was not long before she was producing materialisations again. The results were not always convincing and even *Psychic News*, which had championed her for years, published a warning that she should reduce the number of seances she was giving and the number of sitters she was allowing to witness her mediumship, in order to improve the quality of her work. It is likely that this advice went unheeded.

On 28 October 1956, 11 years after her Old Bailey trial, police in Nottingham raided a Helen Duncan seance that was being held in the private home of a physiotherapist and healer named Joe Timmins. Two of his patients, posing as husband and wife, were plain clothed police officers. They attended a seance and assisted when colleagues invaded the house 20 minutes after the seance began, expecting to retrieve sheets and masks. The medium was badly shocked by the event and a doctor was called. Once more, nothing incriminating was found and no charges were brought, though a report of the incident was sent to the Director of Public Prosecutions. Helen Duncan returned to Edinburgh and was admitted to hospital for three weeks, where she was treated for diabetes, from which she had always suffered. When nothing more could be done for her she returned home. She died on 6 December 1956, less than two months after the police raid, which Spiritualists believe was the cause of her death.

The Fraudulent Mediums Act
But some good came out of the drama that surrounded Helen Duncan's colourful life. The Witchcraft Act was repealed and

replaced by the Fraudulent Mediums Act 1951, which in effect accepted that there could be genuine mediums as well as fake ones – a distinction that was not possible under the previous legislation. As noted above, however, the new legislation did not protect Helen Duncan from a further police raid, five years after the act became law. Most Spiritualists still believe that Helen Duncan was a martyr who was victimised not because her mediumship was poor or fraudulent, but because it was so good. That belief rests on the argument that she had to be stopped during the war years from giving seances at which dead soldiers, sailors and airmen returned to speak to their loved ones, revealing that they were dead before official confirmation had been released.

It may sound far-fetched, but Brigadier Roy Firebrace who, as well as being head of British Military Intelligence in Scotland, was also a Spiritualist, has revealed that in May 1941 he attended a seance with Helen Duncan at which sitters were told that a great British battleship had just sunk. Two hours after he contacted headquarters, he was informed that HMS *Hood* had gone down, but he learned that the authorities had no knowledge of the sinking at the time of the seance.

HMS *Hood* was destroyed by the Nazi battleship *Bismarck*, in the Denmark Straits, off Greenland, on 24 May 1941. The sinking was a terrible blow: all but three of its 1,421 officers and men died – the largest loss of life in a single incident during the Second World War.

Firebrace also revealed that earlier in the war the police had consulted experts for advice on how Mrs Duncan could be prevented from giving out information which, for security reasons, became an increasing embarrassment to the authorities. Percy Wilson, who later became chairman of Psychic Press, has testified that in November 1941 he was informed that a spirit had materialised the day before at a Helen Duncan seance in Portsmouth and told someone he knew that the battleship HMS *Barham*, on which he was serving, had been sunk and that he had perished.

Being a high-ranking civil servant at the Ministry of War

Transport at that time, Percy Wilson made enquiries but no one knew of the sinking. In fact, the *Barham* had been hit by three torpedoes on 25 November 1941, resulting in 861 men perishing and only 450 surviving. Relatives of the dead were not informed by the Admiralty until 31 December and they were asked to treat the information as confidential until an official announcement was made, two months after the loss. Letters confirming the request for secrecy are on display in the Imperial War Museum in London. Putting Helen Duncan behind bars for nine months effectively silenced the spirits who communicated through her mediumship.

Though Helen Duncan died almost half a century ago, modern Spiritualists still feel strongly enough about what they see as a terrible injustice against a great medium that a campaign has been launched through the Spiritualist monthly *Psychic World* and also on the Internet, seeking a pardon from the Home Secretary for what is seen as her unjust conviction.

The return of Helen Duncan's spirit

Since Helen Duncan's departure from this world, few British mediums have claimed the power to produce materialisations. I discuss one of the most remarkable, Alec Harris, in a later chapter, but two who deserve our attention now both enabled Helen Duncan to make her spirit return through their mediumship. Gladys Mallaburn, a widow who lived at Chopwell, near Newcastle-upon-Tyne, was a Spiritualists' National Union minister – which means she could perform weddings, funerals and similar ceremonies at Spiritualist services – who was also a noted healer and public clairvoyant. Her physical mediumship, however, was seldom demonstrated in public. After the traumatic experiences of Helen Duncan, mediums were understandably circumspect about the sitters they allowed to witness such phenomena.

In 1960, four years after Helen Duncan's death, Gladys Mallaburn was persuaded by Maurice Barbanell to give a physical seance for some of the delegates attending the International Spiritualist Federation's Congress, held at the Belgrave Square headquarters of the Spiritualist Association of Great Britain, in London. No materialisations appeared, but direct and independent voice communications occurred. When a voice said 'Nellie', Barbanell says he knew immediately it was Helen Duncan speaking from the next world. She gave her husband's nickname and spoke with feeling about her last seance, which police had raided.

By the 1980s Rita Goold, a Leicester medium, was producing impressive physical phenomena in a circle held in the home of Barry and Pat Jefferey, whose 16-year-old son, the victim of a motorcycle accident, was a constant communicator. Helen Duncan also began to put in regular appearances, materialising and speaking in direct voice. Eventually, one of the Scottish medium's large family – her daughter Gena – was introduced to Rita Goold and invited to visit the circle, where she spent an hour speaking about intimate family matters. She was reduced to tears by her conversation and confirmed to journalist Alan Cleaver that she had no doubts that it was her dead mother she had been speaking to.

Other visitors to the Rita Goold physical circle included Professor Archie Roy, a Glasgow University astrophysicist, who was sufficiently impressed with what he experienced in 1983 to arrange the recording of future seances on infrared film. This plan was thwarted, however, when Rita Goold claimed to have received anonymous telephone threats warning her not to proceed, and vicious lies began to circulate, intended to discredit her. Such episodes only serve to reinforce the sceptics' argument that the reason there are so few physical mediums around these days is because modern technology – such as infrared or low-light film – would make it very easy to detect deception or self-deception in a darkened seance room.

The Scole experiment

Helen Duncan also featured indirectly in a more recent attempt to provide the world with indisputable evidence of physical mediumship. A copy of the *Daily Mail* newspaper dated 1 April 1944, carrying the front-page story of her Old Bailey conviction, was apparently materialised (a phenomenon called apportation) during a seance held by the Scole Group in the early 1990s. This event was interpreted as an indication of the famous medium's involvement in the circle's rapid development.

The physical seances, held in the converted cellar of the home of Robin Foy and his wife Sandra in Scole, near Diss, Norfolk, attracted a number of seasoned investigators and other interested observers. The Foys had formed several Spiritualist circles over the years, and their fellow sitters at Scole included trance mediums Diana and Alan Bennett. The Society for Psychical Research learned of the Scole group's activities and, for a two-year period, three of their most experienced investigators attended sittings. Professor Arthur Ellison, Professor David Fontana (both of whom have been SPR presidents) and Montague Keen produced a 452-page edition of the society's *Proceedings*, which became known as the Scole Report, discussing their favourable findings. The SPR published the Report in 1999, since when the Scole phenomena have been hotly debated by believers and sceptics alike.

What was said to be special about Scole was that, instead of producing ectoplasm, the spirit communicators were using 'energies' for the first time. These were capable of producing remarkable effects, as Montague Keen later explained:

The purported discarnate contacts had facilitated the manifestation of spirit lights, moved furniture, created apports (objects appearing from no known source and by no known means), displayed shadowy figures described as angelic forms, and produced films, allegedly employing a novel form of energy not involving the traditional ectoplasmic extrusions, with their enervating and sometimes physically hazardous, and invariably contentious, associations. These films, the investigators were told, had been exposed in total darkness initially via cameras held by one or other member of the group. Next came similar pictures, but created from cameras apparently operated by spirit forces independently of human contact. Finally, similar pictures had been produced independently of any cameras or any other equipment: simply from rolls of virgin film. These images were generally somewhat fuzzy representations of familiar photographs, portraits or abstract forms, in some of which could be seen mirror images of persons or animals, and occasionally half formed human faces.

Having ruled out fraud as an explanation for what they experienced, the three investigators hoped to obtain indisputable evidence of the phenomena. They pressed the Scole group to allow even more stringent test conditions, to satisfy the most vociferous critics of the sessions, and they also asked for permission to introduce infrared video cameras into the seance room. Just as Professor Archie Roy was thwarted in his research with Rita Goold, so were the three-man SPR team frustrated in their efforts.

Suddenly, in October 1998, the Scole group announced that they had been instructed by their spirit team to stop experimentation 'because interference was occurring with beings in the future'. Sometimes, it was said, these were 'intergalactic beings'. Professor Ellison regarded the timing of the cessation of sittings as suspicious and the explanation as absurd. But it did not shake his belief that the Scole group had provided evidence of the afterlife.

The Scole seances have been the subject of a book,[2] as well as of the SPR's own Report, and the debate continues. Among those I have interviewed about their experiences at Scole seances is Professor Ivor Grattan-Guinness, Professor of the History of Mathematics and Logic at Middlesex University, who spoke at a day-long conference on the Scole Report, sponsored by the SPR in London. Professor Grattan-Guinness told me that during the seances he had attempted to do something he knew he should not do: he reached out for one of the tiny lights that moved at speed around the seance room and wrapped his hands around it. To his amazement, he felt the light bouncing off his hands, as if trying to escape. He then opened his hands and it moved away. Professor David Fontana has also testified to seeing 'a light moving around in the water I was drinking'. Now that the Scole seances have ended, the only tangible evidence of the physical phenomena are these first-hand testimonies, as well as the intriguing but not conclusive evidence of photographic images and apports.

Physical phenomena in a Minilab

Professor Ivor Grattan-Guinness is no stranger to psychic phenomena, for as well as his Scole experiences he has also received physical evidence of a different kind from another paranormal source and one that, remarkably, held out the hope of producing proof without requiring the presence of mediums or sitters. SOR-RAT – the Society for Research into Rapport and Telekinesis – was established in the United States in 1961 by John G. Neihardt to investigate why the classical physical phenomena of Spiritualism had declined so dramatically and to look for an alternative way of producing paranormal effects. The research concept was originally suggested by Dr Joseph Banks Rhine, the Duke University pioneer of extrasensory perception research, and it was a close associate, William Edward Cox, together with John Thomas Richards, a professor of English with a strong interest in parapsychology, who along with others developed what became known as the Minilab. This was a specially designed, securely locked glass-sided box in which tripwires were installed connected to lights and a film camera. Target objects were placed on the tripwires and any activity inside the locked box would trigger the camera.

Between 1979 and 1981 the team filmed remarkable phenomena in the Minilab, which had been placed in the basement of Richards' home in Rolla, Missouri. One of their on-going experiments involves letters with questions being placed in self-addressed, stamped envelopes, then put inside the Minilab, which is then secured with padlocks filled with superglue. Their film showed ink pens apparently standing up by themselves and writing answers on the letters. Professor Grattan-Guinness participated in these experiments. He has revealed in the *Journal of Scientific Exploration*[3] that he wrote questions on plain sheets of paper, then sealed them carefully in self-addressed envelopes, writing across the seams and applying adhesive tape. He then put stamps on the envelopes and posted them, in a larger envelope, to the SORRAT researchers, who placed them inside the Minilab.

Within five weeks, the envelopes came back to him in the post, with colourful postmarks, such as Carefree, AZ and Deadwood, SD. Inside, his questions had been answered and the envelopes also occasionally contained other items, and even sheets with questions from other researchers. But who were the communicators? Professor Grattan-Guinness tells us 'that they are the surviving residues (my word) of dead persons, and that they operate independently of our restrictions of space and time'. Other phenomena filmed in the Minilab included balloons inflating and deflating, rings linking and unlinking and objects moving around.

Having seen the remarkable film of these phenomena, veteran Cambridge psychical researcher Tony Cornell visited Rolla, Missouri, to find out more about the Minilab and to take letters from other parapsychologists to be used in tests. He was particularly interested in checking fingerprints on the sheets of paper after 'spirit' answers had been written, but the letters were posted back via a third party who opened them, which clouded the issue. He came to the conclusion that it was possible to fake all the phenomena reported, as well as the film, and to prove it he made his own film by exposing a single frame at a time, then moving an object. It took hours to achieve but was impressive. He gives a detailed account of this episode in his recent book about his 55 years of investigating the paranormal.[4] 'No concrete conclusions can be arrived at with regard to the Rolla affair,' he tells his readers. 'As late as 1998, the "spirit mail" effects were still occurring but the control conditions appear to be no better. Fraud has not been positively proved, only hinted at. The reader might well say that with such preposterous claims the hints are enough.' The major difference between Scole and SORRAT is that with the Norfolk seances many witnesses attended the sessions and had their own experiences. The Rolla phenomena appear to occur in the solitary confinement of a cellar and are seen and recorded only by a film camera.

Home circle materialisations

Even if it is genuine, the SORRAT approach to physical phenomena takes all the fun out of spirit communication. How much better to have seances at which the dead can walk and talk and prove their continued existence, as they did in the home circle of Minnie Harrison of Middlesbrough, which ran from 1946 until the mid-1950s. Fortunately, Minnie's son Tom made notes and tape recordings of the proceedings, as well as taking photographs. Red light was used for materialisations and total darkness for direct voice.

Two books have been written by Tom Harrison[5] about his mother's mediumship, and been featured on radio and TV programmes. One of the materialised spirits was Alfred Kitson, a Spiritualist pioneer. When the then general secretary of the Spiritualists' National Union, George Mack, was told of Kitson's spirit return at the home circle, he contacted the Harrisons to say that Kitson had promised to convey a certain message, if he found it possible to communicate. The next time Kitson materialised in the circle, they asked him if he had a message for George Mack. His reply was sent to the Spiritualist official, who confirmed it was the message they had agreed.

What was so impressive, throughout the years that the Harrison circle produced physical phenomena, writes Tom, was that 'my mother was sitting in the circle ... in full view of all of us'. Regular spirit visitors, who remained for as long as 15 minutes 'making it possible for photographs of the events to be taken', went back into a curtained cabinet area at the end of their allotted time. Spirits who had not visited before, however, appeared to have difficulty in coping with their ectoplasmic form, which they said was like wearing heavy clothing. They did not remain for long and to leave would 'gradually sink towards the floor'.

Sceptics will argue that a son's account of his mother's mediumship is going to be favourably biased and should therefore be treated with caution. But this was more than a family circle. The other sitters included Sydney and Gladys Shipman, a husband and wife who were both business people, and William Brittain Jones, a highly respected surgeon in the north east of England who was superintendent at Middlesbrough General Hospital for many years. They also received invited guests – usually strangers – in response to appeals from people they trusted. Among these was Roy Dixon-Smith, a lieutenant-colonel in the Indian army who had searched for a materialisation circle in 1948, following the death of his second wife, Betty. The Harrison family responded to the advertisement he placed in the columns of *Psychic News* and invited him to attend one of their sessions. Dixon-Smith's account of his experience of Minnie Harrison's physical mediumship, included in his book *New Light on Survival*[6], tells of various spirit forms which manifested and talked to those present.

The guide then announced the coming of Betty and asked us to sing one of her favourite songs. We sang 'I'll Walk Beside You', in the middle of which a tall slim figure emerged from the curtain and stood silently in view.

I rose from my chair and walked up to the figure, taking the extended hand in mine. I examined the hand, and it was just like Betty's and quite unlike the medium's. I stared into the face, and recognised my wife. We spoke to each other, though what we said I cannot remember, for I was deeply stirred and so was she and her voice was incoherent with emotion.

'Can he kiss you?' someone asked, and Betty murmured 'Yes'. I then kissed her on the lips which were warm, soft and natural. Thereupon she bent her head and commenced to weep, and in a moment or two she sank. I watched her form right down to the level of the floor at my feet where it dissolved, the last wisp of it being drawn within the cabinet.

Scientist photographed with spirit

It is to be hoped that it will not be long before materialised spirit forms will rise again in home circles, allowing themselves to be examined, photographed and filmed to provide the ultimate proof of spirit communication. That should not be impossible. It is, after all, just 130 years since one of Britain's most respected physicists, Sir William Crookes, conducted experiments with medium Florence Cook at which, in his own home and elsewhere, under strict test conditions, a spirit named Katie King materialised. She was even photographed arm in arm with the scientist, who answered sceptics by saying, 'To imagine ... the Katie King of the last three years to be the result of imposture does more violence to one's reason and common sense than to believe her to be what she herself affirms.'

1 Manfred Cassirer, *Medium on Trial*, PN Publishing (1996).
2 Grant and Jane Solomon, *The Scole Experiment*, Piatkus (1999).
3 'Real Communication? Report on a SORRAT Letter Writing Experiment', *Journal of Scientific Exploration* 13:231, I. Grattan-Guinness (1999).
4 Tony Cornell, *Investigating the Paranormal*, Helix Press, New York (2002).
5 Tom Harrison, *Visits by Our Friends From the Other Side*, Saturday Night Press Publications (1989).
6 Roy Dixon-Smith, *New Light on Survival*, Rider (1952).

Chapter 7

Recording Spirits

From Spiritualism's earliest days, spirits of the dead showed remarkable ingenuity in making their existence known by mechanical means. The ouija board and planchette (*see page 34*) are good examples of ways in which simple devices were developed to enhance spirit communication. Other contraptions followed, and they had mixed results.

The Ashkir-Jobson Communigraph, a small, circular table with a pendulum suspended underneath, was a success. As the pendulum swung it made contact with small metal plates, representing the alphabet, and this closed a circuit causing the letter to be illuminated upon the table. Its inventors claimed no medium was necessary: a number of people could communicate with the spirits just by sitting in a circle around the device. Despite its rather ponderous nature, Lady Zoe Caillard, wife of a prominent early twentieth-century industrialist and diplomat, Sir Vincent Caillard, received numerous messages from her dead husband, and published them as a book.[1] Another mechanical device for spirit communication was the Reflectograph, which incorporated a huge typewriter with extremely sensitive key-contacts. But it required the co-operation of a medium, Mrs L.E. Singleton. When she was entranced, a hand would reach out of the cabinet, tap the keys and spell out messages that were then flashed in luminous letters onto a six-foot indicator.

Experiments with photography

The invention that excited most interest among Spiritualists was photography. Although still in its infancy, by the time the Fox Sisters' famous experiences with rappings at their home in Hydesville, New York, had given birth to Spiritualism, there were 70 photographic studios in New York City alone. It was not long before images of spirits began appearing on the daguerreotype plates at some of the studios.

We must, of course, treat such claims with great caution. Double exposures and darkroom trickery could account for most of the results, particularly those where the face was strangely shrouded or out of focus, but there were reports of immediately recognisable images, produced under what would appear to be fraudproof conditions and sometimes showing spirits who had never had their photographs taken when alive.

Among those who sought evidence that her husband had survived his death was Mary Todd Lincoln, widow of the American president. Soon after his assassination on 14 April 1865, she arrived at the studio of psychic photographer William Mumler, dressed in mourning and with a veil over her face which she did not lift until Mumler was ready to take her photograph. When the result was developed, the photographer recognised the spirit form standing behind her, with his hands on her shoulders, as President Lincoln. Mary Todd confirmed she was his widow.

Psychic photography soon became all the rage on both sides of the Atlantic, with certain individuals specialising in the production of spirit portraits. One of the most impressive twentieth-century exponents of this form of mediumship was John Myers, who was also a healer. He began his professional life as a London dentist and discovered his unusual talent after meeting Mrs Ada Deane, a psychic photographer of note. Soon he was producing remarkable results, in which sitters were allowed to bring their own marked photographic plates.

In one test for the *Sunday Dispatch* newspaper – which was

witnessed by magician Will Goldston, journalist Hannen Swaffer and the newspaper's art editor – the Marquess of Donegall loaded Myers' camera six times with his own plates, took six pictures in bright light and developed them himself. John Myers simply stood by and watched. The pictures contained 'extras' (images that should not have been there) which the sceptics present could not explain. A week later, following a further sitting, Lord Donegall accused Myers of gross trickery, saying he had substituted plates. The accusation astonished the hundreds who had received convincing evidence of his mediumship, one of whom was a wealthy New York businessman, Laurence Parish, who was so impressed with Myers' mediumship that he invited him to move to the United States and join his company. Myers eventually became its vice-president.

Putting John Myers to the test

By the time I began investigating Spiritualism, psychic photography was as rare as direct voice and materialisation mediumship. So, when *Psychic News* editor Maurice Barbanell learned that his old friend John Myers was making a rare visit to London, he asked him to demonstrate his mediumistic powers for me. A likeable man in his seventies, Myers still had a passion for photography and had just bought the latest compact camera which, because of its size, needed special film. Since this was to be a test of his powers, it was important that I bought the film that would be used.

I visited numerous camera shops before I found one that stocked this type of film, and eventually it was put into the camera under my watchful eye. Myers made a number of exposures in the hotel room where he was staying. He then removed the film and put it aside, explaining that it was a special film that required processing in the United States, and he would send us the prints. I protested to Barbanell that this made the test void, but decided to reserve judgement. After all, if faces of people I knew, who would have been totally unknown to Myers, appeared on the prints, then the way the film was developed was not so significant.

When the pictures arrived by post from America, I excitedly opened the package and found myself looking at two people whose faces I knew very well. One was journalist Hannen Swaffer. The other was Marilyn Monroe. I had never met either of them in life and thought Swaffer's interest in John Myers and me could be explained by the fact that he was one of the founders of *Psychic News*. Marilyn Monroe's spirit visit was a mystery. The more I looked at the images, superimposed on the hotel room, the more I became suspicious. Then it dawned on me. The picture of Hannen Swaffer was identical to one hanging in Maurice Barbanell's office, except that it was flipped, left to right. And the artist who painted that picture? None other than ... John Myers, who was also a gifted artist. Later, I discovered that he had also painted a portrait of Marilyn Monroe which, when I compared it to the 'psychic extra', was also an identical but flipped copy. Needless to say, I no longer shared Barbanell's enthusiasm for his friend's mediumship and nothing I have learned since has changed my mind. I discuss the whole subject of fraud in a later chapter.

The spirit radio

Having a snapshot of a dear departed loved one who has returned from the spirit world to pose before a camera may bring comfort to many people, but it does not compare to having a two-world conversation with them. As we have already seen, direct voice and materialisation mediums can make this possible. But with the development of 'the wireless', or radio, many people hoped that in time it would be possible to tune into the next world as easily as moving from one radio station to another. And it was the pioneers of radio who believed this most strongly. None lived to see this dream become reality, but there are researchers all over the world today who insist they have achieved it.

Soon after his passing in 1930, Sir Arthur Conan Doyle is said to have entranced the medium Eileen Garrett (*see page 24*) and indicated that spirit scientists were experimenting with new communication methods to enable them to speak to the living. Six years later Sir Oliver Lodge, the noted scientist and prominent Spiritualist, predicted that a form of spirit radio would one day be produced. It was Sir Oliver's work on wireless transmission that formed the basis of Guglielmo Marconi's involvement in the development of radio, although Nikola Tesla is regarded by many as its inventor.

Both men were working on radio transmission at the end of the nineteenth century, and both reported receiving strange signals that they believed must be coming from another world, since no one else was broadcasting at that time. In Tesla's case, he assumed they came from space and decided Mars and Venus were the most likely sources. Marconi, on the other hand, being a believer in life after death, decided that the spirit world must be transmitting the unexplained Morse code messages he received – though there is no record of their content. As a young man, Marconi tried to build a system that could put him in touch with the dead and it is believed he worked on perfecting this until his death in 1937.

The young Alexander Graham Bell, inventor of the 'electrical speech machine' that we now call the telephone, also attempted to build a machine that would enable the dead to speak. He made a pact with his brother, who died at a young age, that whoever died first should 'contact the survivor through a medium demonstrably superior to the more traditional channel of Spiritualism'. There are no records of how successful he was in that endeavour.

The spirit finder

Meanwhile at around the same time, another great inventor, Thomas A. Edison, creator of the electric light bulb and the phonograph, on which he made the first voice recording in 1877, was also exploring the possibility of making contact with unseen forces. He spent the last seven years of his life, until his death in

1931, developing a 'Spirit Finder' device which he hoped would locate a frequency between long and short waves to be used as a telepathic channel between the living and the dead. Edison observed:

If our personality survives, then it is strictly logical or scientific to assume that it retains memory, intellect, other faculties, and knowledge that we acquire on this Earth.Therefore ... if we can evolve an instrument so delicate as to be affected by our personality as it survives in the next life, such an instrument, when made available, ought to record something.

He confirmed his interest in an interview with *Scientific American*, but never succeeded in making contact. His assistant Dr Miller Hutchinson shared his interest, explaining, 'Edison and I are convinced that in the fields of psychic research will yet be discovered facts that will prove of greater significance to the thinking of the human race than all the inventions we have ever made in the field of electricity.'

After his death, a number of people made contact with Edison through mediums. They included John Logie Baird, the television pioneer and inventor of the infrared camera, who declared: 'I have witnessed some very startling phenomena under circumstances which make trickery out of the question.' But despite attempts to locate plans for Edison's 'Spirit Finder' and some suggested modifications which Edison is said to have given to J. Gilbert Wright, the inventor of putty, and others, from beyond the grave, the device has never been located.

Someone who claimed to have succeeded in communicating with spirits through a mechanical device was Jesse Shepard (also known as Francis Grierson), a remarkable medium who in 1921 published a book of messages received on a Psycho-Phone. Mystery surrounds its origins but it has been suggested that it could be the machine Edison was working on. It is known that Edison visited San Diego, where Shepard lived, in 1915, just six years before the book was published. But there appear to be no first-hand accounts of the Psycho-Phone being used.

Spontaneous voice messages

By this time, however, it was becoming apparent that it was not necessary to have specially designed and built apparatus to make contact with the dead. Spirits seemed to be able to communicate, often quite spontaneously, through existing electrically powered equipment. For example, a London-based SPR researcher, Zoe Richmond, and her husband were listening to a record of a favourite male singer in 1930 when suddenly, to their great astonishment, 'the most beautiful soprano voice' joined in and sang to the end. Kenneth Richmond corresponded with Sir Oliver Lodge and the record company about this remarkable happening but neither could shed any light on it.[2]

The secretary of famous crime writer Edgar Wallace reported a similar experience in 1932. In his work Edgar Wallace used an old 78-rpm record cutter and shortly after his death his secretary used it to cut a record. When she replayed it, she was astonished to hear her former employer speaking a few words. Such experiences were rare and were simply filed by parapsychologists under 'unexplained'.

All this was to change in the 1960s when it was revealed that a number of people had succeeded in recording voices on tape that appeared to have an other-world origin. For a time, this was known as 'the mediumship of the tape recorder', but the phenomenon has since broadened out to almost every conceivable form of communication. There are well-attested reports of the dead speaking over normal telephones, through radios and even on computers, fax machines and televisions.

Perhaps the spirits of Lodge, Marconi, Tesla, Edison, Graham Bell and others have been continuing their efforts in the next world, resulting in a transformation in the way spirit communication will take place in future. Although few Spiritualists share this view because the messages so far received seem to be brief and cryptic in comparison with mediumship, we should not forget that the quality of the earliest radio and telephone communications were very poor compared to the standard now achieved in our digital world.

Tape-recorded messages

The breakthrough came in 1959 when Friedrich Jurgenson, a Russian-born writer, painter and film producer, switched on his tape recorder expecting to hear bird song he had recorded in a Swedish forest. In addition to the birds, he heard the distinct and unmistakable voice of his dead mother saying, 'Friedel, my little Friedel, can you hear me?' It was to be the first of many such voices that mysteriously appeared on his tapes. They could not be called spirit messages – they were usually no more than a couple of words – and they seemed to be speaking in various languages. Listening to recordings of these snatches of speech, people heard different words, causing some sceptics to argue that they were just extraneous, meaningless sounds, perhaps stray radio broadcasts, which were being 'translated' according to individual expectations. Subsequent developments, however, indicate that such a theory fails to explain many of the later communications, particularly where meaningful conversations occur.

Jurgenson admitted 14 years later that the recording of his mother's voice was not as spontaneous as he first suggested. He had tried to obtain 'something' on tape for several months before he heard the short message.

Somehow, and completely without any known reason, there grew in me an overwhelming desire to establish electronic contact with somebody unknown. It was a strange feeling, almost as if I had to open a channel for something which was still hidden and wanted to get into the open. At the same time I remember feeling sceptical, amused and curious.

Dr Konstantin Raudive

Once Jurgenson's recordings became known, others began experimenting with tape recorders, of whom Dr Konstantin Raudive, a Latvian-born psychologist also living in Sweden, achieved the most remarkable early results. He experimented with various types of equipment, from a simple microphone and tape recorder to specially designed apparatus – the goniometer – made for him by an electronics engineer.

Raudive had no technical knowledge and is said to have relied on the voices to assist in the development and improvement of the equipment. By 1968 he had recorded more than 70,000 voice effects, which he wrote about in his book *Unhorbares wird Horbar* (The inaudible becomes audible), the English translation of which was published in England and the United States as *Breakthrough*.[3] This received so much publicity that the phenomenon came to be known by the popular name 'Raudive voices' and encouraged many others to conduct their own experiments.

What everyone wanted to know was whether the experimenter required mediumistic powers in order to get results, or whether anyone could record the voices. Raudive's response was:

In one 10-minute recording I got 200 voices. With patience there is no reason at all why anyone cannot tape the voice phenomenon. But the experimenter must develop his hearing by constant listening to tapes. What at first seems like atmospheric buzzing is often many voices. They have to be analysed and amplified, of course.

He added:

There is no doubt that we have established communication with another world.

But doubt there was, and understandably so. Raudive recorded one message which he wrote down phonetically as

'Te Mac-Cloo, mej dream, my dear, yes.' It made sense to him as a combination of Latvian, Swedish and English and he claimed it came from Sir Winston Churchill. But why would the former British prime minister speak in three languages (two of which he did not speak when in this world) when one would do?

Two British researchers listened to the tape and offered alternative all-English versions. One thought he heard 'Hear, Mark you, make believe, my dear, yes,' while the other said it was 'Mark you, make thee mightier yet.' Both of which suggest a deterioration in Churchill's oratorical skills since death. Among the other famous communicators Raudive claimed to have recorded were Hitler, Stalin, John F. Kennedy, Tolstoy and Nietzsche.

Are the recordings just stray radio broadcasts?

Among those who were not convinced was David Ellis, who received a grant from Cambridge University to study the Raudive voices, which are now more commonly called Electronic Voice Phenomenon (EVP). He decided that, since the air is full of radio transmissions, no wavelength in the normal range can be guaranteed to be clear. He even traced one message back to a Radio Luxembourg programme hosted by disc jockey Kid Jenson. However, he also thought that Raudive might have produced some of the voices telekinetically (using mind over matter) after having received them from spirits telepathically and 'clothed in words from his own subconscious mind'.

In the United States, Attila von Szalay, a commercial photographer and natural psychic who over the years had been aware of a tiny voice speaking close to his body, agreed to participate in a series of experiments with researcher Raymond Bayless. The aim was to amplify such voices and record them on tape, and the sessions, which started in December 1956, produced impressive results. Their research findings were first published as a letter in the

American Society for Psychical Research's *Journal* in 1959,[4] the same year that Jurgenson recorded his mother's voice on tape.

'Scientific proof of afterlife'

A decade later, also in the United States, scientist and inventor George W. Meek decided to retire and live off the proceeds of a variety of patents, in order to devote his life to researching life after death. For the next quarter of a century, having established the Metascience Foundation in Franklin, North Carolina, he travelled the world encouraging specialists in a variety of fields to become involved in his research.

Together with his colleague Bill O'Neil, Meek developed a form of electronic spirit communication known as Spiricom. This large, radio-like device incorporated a set of 13 tone generators spanning the range of the adult male voice, which gave off a droning sound that filled the room in which they conducted research.

O'Neil, whose natural psychic abilities are said to have played a key role in the work, tested the apparatus for many months. Eventually, another voice was heard, which responded to his questions. It has been identified as that of Dr George Jeffries Mueller, a NASA scientist. The two men – one living, one dead – collaborated on developing Spiricom further between 1979 and 1982, during which they had over 20 hours of dialogue. It was now time to unveil it to the world. Meek, as Metascience Foundation's president and director of research, chose Easter week 1982 to make 'two rather startling announcements':

1. For the first time in the history of Western man we have electronic proof that the mind, memory banks, personality and soul
   survive death of the physical body. What is our proof? During the
   past four years we have had many hours of conversation with
   some among the 'so-called dead'. Most useful have been the
   extensive conversations we had during the year 1981 with an

> *American scientist, Dr George Jeffries Mueller, who suffered a heart attack and died thirteen years before.*
>
> 2. *An elementary start has been made toward the eventual perfection of an electromagnetic-etheric communications system that will someday permit those living on earth to have telephone-like conversations with persons very much alive in higher levels of consciousness.*

Metascience Foundation research colleagues in London, Paris, Rome, Zurich, Frankfurt, Tokyo and Manila made the same announcement on the same day.

It seemed that a group of spirit entities were making a concerted effort to establish the first electronic system for prolonged, two-way communication. What a story. But it was not quite as simple as Meek's statement and press release suggested. He conceded that the researchers faced a number of problems, one of them major: 'We frankly admit that our present crude devices do not work every day. In fact, there may be many weeks or even months between successful communication.' As scientists, however, they took such problems in their stride.

Media representatives were issued with an hour-long tape recording, containing 14 excerpts of conversations, and invited to obtain the foundation's 100-page technical manual describing the equipment used and future research possibilities. George Meek then went on a world tour, sharing all this information with interested parties, in the expectation that there would be further breakthroughs and improvements in the quality of the phenomena reported. And that certainly appears to have happened.

Among those who decided to conduct their own experiments was Maggy Harsch-Fischbach of Luxembourg. She started in 1985, using a tape recorder and following the methods outlined by Konstantin Raudive. Maggy and her husband Jules soon met other researchers, hosted weekly recording sessions, and published their own newsletter. They had a strong hunch that Raudive, who died in 1977, would try to make contact with them. In August 1985 they were listening to their small clock-radio when the music stopped and was replaced with a rushing sound, followed by a deep voice that boomed over the speakers: 'This is Konstantin Raudive. Soon it will work everywhere!'

A year later, by which time they were recording regular communications, a new high-pitched, computer-like voice was heard that seemed almost too perfect and synthesized to be of human origin. During a group session in which a question about God was asked, this voice responded with the words: 'Please address this question to me.' Maggy asked, 'Who are you?' and received the reply:

We are what we are. It is difficult to explain to you but I am not an energy being, not a light being. I was never human, never an animal, and was never incarnated. Neither am I God! You know the picture of two children walking across a bridge? Behind them is a being that protects them. This is what I am to you but without wings. If you insist on giving me a name, call me Technician.

Letter from beyond via computer

The improvements in the voice communications apparently enabled George Meek to receive remarkable personal evidence of survival of death from his wife Jeanette, who died in the spring of 1990 after a long illness. She chose Maggy and Jules Harsch-Fischbach's computer as the means of proving her continuing existence.

Just a few months after Jeanette Meek's death, Meek visited the Luxembourg researchers and was in their laboratory when, after the computer had finished its routine summary of weekend activities, it paused, and a short message appeared on the display screen: 'Hello Sweetheart, Jeanette.' Sceptics at this point may suspect the couple of typing that surreptitiously into the computer to give Meek some words of comfort. Jeanette Meek, it seems, was well aware of such scepticism, so she later produced a signed letter and somehow inserted it into the Harsch-Fischbaches' computer. When they discovered it, they printed it out and posted it to Meek in Boulder, North Carolina. It discussed three personal items known only to the Meeks or their assistant Molly. The letter read:

Dear G.W.

Well, it seems there are still people who do not believe in the contacts your friends here in Luxembourg are having. Hence I will give you some personal details known only to you and Molly.

First story. In 1987, end of April, our tenant Debbie called to say her refrigerator was off. It must have been on a Thursday morning. . . .

Second story. On April 29, 1987, Ann Valentin wrote a letter from California saying she had not received the 'Magic of Living Forever' booklets she had ordered, but instead had received a box of Harlequin novels.

Third story. John Lathrop shut off the electricity at our rental house to put in the new yard light. He wasn't down there very long but charged $20 service in addition to $40 for the bulbs, plus tax. The charge seemed high.

Don't try to explain this, Honey. My never-ending love to you. I miss you so much, but I know we will be together . . ..

Love forever, Jeannette Duncan Meek

The second story meant nothing to George Meek, but when he checked with Ann Valentin in California he found that a box of novels *had* arrived mysteriously in 1987, and to this day she has no idea who sent them. The other two items he was able to confirm from his own memories.

The Harsch-Fischbaches' experiences were not unique. Researchers in several countries began receiving unsolicited computer printouts from spirit communicators. Among them was Kenneth Webster in England, who reported receiving 250 communications via several different computers claiming to be from a person who had lived in his sixteenth-century home, written in speech consistent with that historical period.[5] Others reported recording fleeting images of the dead on computer screens. At the prestigious Monroe Institute, emails purporting to come from its dead founder, Robert Monroe, began arriving – sometimes when the computer was not even connected to the Internet. With this apparent growth of communication methods, a new name – instrumental transcommunication, or ITC – was coined.

Mark Macy, who became a close collaborator of George Meek and established the International Network for Instrumental Transcommunication (INIT), coined the phrase 'Enhanced ITC' to describe this phase of the communications. He pointed out that between 1995 and 1997 researchers received messages by telephone – the dead Konstantin Raudive phoned people regularly – tape recorders, radio, TV, computers and even fax machines.

It was mind boggling, not only for non-believers but also for many of those involved in the research. Those whose results were not of the highest quality began questioning the genuineness of others, claiming conversations were too long and too clear, or images were too perfect, to be real. As a result, disharmony and mistrust caused splits and schisms that have affected ITC results. Since 2000, claims Mark Macy, there has been a distinct drop in the type of communication received. He is optimistic that in time the phenomena will be recorded just as strongly as before and urges everyone involved to work in harmony in order to achieve that goal. But there are warnings for those who decide to experiment in this field, which focus on who the voices are. Mark Macy believes that they can emanate from three sources:

1. Ethereal realms, whose inhabitants are mostly entities who have never lived in a physical world.
2. Astral realms, which are Earth-like and of great beauty, populated by people with astral bodies, much like our own.
3. Quantum realms, which are 'dark, dismal pockets of fear and confusion'.

Macy believes that all three sources can make contact through ITC methods, and has himself received a telephone call from 'a demonic sounding voice' falsely claiming to be Konstantin Raudive.

Research project to authenticate voices

Time will tell whether these efforts will add to our understanding of the next world or just cause more confusion. The Institute of Noetic Sciences, established by astronaut Edgar Mitchell to 'explore the frontiers of consciousness', has announced a collaborative research effort between itself and the Global Association of Instrumental Transcommunication (GAIT) to examine ITC claims scientifically. GAIT is a loose association of experimenters, technicians, theorists and others, mostly in South America, interested in authenticating electronic spirit communications. A joint statement says that it is expected that laboratories will be designed and built to test, replicate and authenticate the phenomenon.

Among those involved in ITC research in the UK is Professor David Fontana, former president of the Society for Psychical Research. As current chairman of its Survival Research Committee he reported, in the SPR's Annual Report for 2003, that he has been present in the French and Spanish studios of Portuguese ITC researcher Dr Anabela Cardoso and studied her research protocols and results. During these experiments he has also 'obtained and recorded communications' that responded to two specific questions he had put to the entities concerned.

Addressing SPR members in London during May 2004, Dr Cardoso, who is a career diplomat, revealed that there were an estimated 70,000 individuals around the world who were conducting ITC experiments, with varying degrees of success. The main spirit communicating with Dr Cardoso is Carlos de Almeida and he does so from a transmitting centre in the spirit world known as Timestream Station, from which many groups work. The latest communication methods, she told her audience, involve 'being able to modulate radio waves with thought' and the direct radio voices (DRVs) produced, manifesting through the radio's loudspeakers, are much louder and the conversations much longer than the early EVP recordings.

This is clearly a breakthrough. At the outset, in the 1960s, researchers heard nothing during their experiments. It was only when they played back their tape recordings that they discovered voices. Now the research has entered this new ITC phase, in which researchers can hear and record audible answers to their questions, it has become a very promising area for exploring the possibility of spirit communication. Dr Cardoso reported that among her many recordings are some that last over one hour. Even so, they are not always easy to comprehend. Their interpretation can be difficult mainly because of the background noise of the radios on which the words are modulated. The semantics of the sentences can be complex and difficult: the usual structure of the phrases might be altered, the grammar distorted and the language is sometimes symbolic. Several languages might also be used in the same communication, though normally ones that the receiver can understand.

'In my case,' says Dr Cardoso, 'I receive messages in my mother tongue, Portuguese, but sometimes with a Brazilian or even an African accent. I have had words or sentences in Spanish, English, seldom in French and Italian. When Carlos de Almeida speaks, the white noise of the radios is suddenly silenced and his voice sounds loud and clear. This does not happen with all the transcommunicators of Timestream Station.'

Most of the people involved in ITC research are not Spiritualists, but have come to much the same conclusions as Spiritualists have about the afterlife and spirit communication through their independent research. Their hope to achieve regular spirit contact without the use of a medium, however, appears to be premature and optimistic, for it seems that those researchers who get the best results are often individuals with psychic powers. It's a fascinating area of study – even if many of the claims made are difficult to accept without independent corroboration – but there certainly seems to be no prospect of mediums being made redundant by spirit radios for the foreseeable future.

1 Lady Zoe Caillard, *A new Conception of Love,* Rider (1934).
2 D. Scott Rogo and Raymond Bayless, *Phone Calls From the Dead*, Prentice Hall (1979).
3 Konstantin Raudive, *Breakthrough*, Colin Smythe (1971).
4 'Correspondence', *Journal of the American Society for Psychical Research*, No. 53, Raymond Bayless (1959).
5 Kenneth Webster, *Vertical Plane*, Grafton Books (1989).

Chapter 8

Spiritualism and Healing

Spiritualism's greatest impact in the United Kingdom in the mid-twentieth century came not from seances but from spiritual healing, and it laid the foundations for what today is perhaps the most enlightened attitude to healing in the modern world.

A remarkable healer

For Harry Edwards, the remarkable Spiritualist whose efforts were largely responsible for this change, it was an uphill struggle but one he was prepared to shoulder. He had to take on the might of the British Medical Association (BMA) and the Church of England, but he did so with the knowledge that spiritual healing, given a chance, could make a vital contribution to the health of millions. Now, in the twenty-first century, spiritual healers often work closely with the medical profession, and their involvement is welcomed as part of an integrated approach to healthcare.

It all began for Harry Edwards, a printer, at the age of 44, when he visited a small Spiritualist Church in Clousdale Road, Balham, South London. A medium singled him out and told him he was 'born to heal'. Intrigued, he decided to join a development circle to see what would happen and soon found himself going into trance. He also made tentative attempts at 'absent healing' or 'distant healing', which – as the name implies – involves directing healing thoughts to people who are not present. He achieved many notable successes and soon his home was crowded with people seeking his help.

After the Second World War Edwards' healing career really took off. By 1947 he had given up his printing business and opened a healing sanctuary in Shere, near Guildford, Surrey, which became a focal point for sick people needing help – usually after doctors had said they could do no more for them. As well as the many people he saw by appointment, arriving by car, train or coach at his Burrows Lea sanctuary, he also dealt with a mountain of letters each week requesting absent healing. Added to this, he helped John Britnell found the National Federation of Spiritual Healers in 1955, and served as its president for many years as well as allowing Burrows Lea to be its headquarters.

In addition to his healing powers, incidentally, Harry Edwards also took a keen interest in other forms of mediumship, particularly physical phenomena, and published books about his intensive studies of two outstanding mediums, Jack Webber and Arnold Clare.[1, 2] He was convinced through his own experiences that his mission to heal the sick was orchestrated by a discarnate spirit team whose members included French scientist Louis Pasteur and the founder of antiseptic surgery Lord (Joseph) Lister. He received confirmation of this from a number of mediums and made no secret of it.

Patients who sought Edwards' help were largely unaware of these spirit influences. All they saw was a cherubic, genial man with a compassionate smile, direct manner and caring eyes that held their gaze as they talked about their ailments. Placing his hands on their bodies, he would close his eyes and 'tune in' to the power that flowed through him. After a few minutes of treatment he would intuitively know that an improvement had occurred. Edwards would then ask the patient to demonstrate this change by doing something they had not been able to do before, such as touch their toes or stretch their arms above their heads.

Whether the healing took place in Edwards' sanctuary or on a public platform in front of thousands, the method was always the same. There were no histrionics or casting out of demons, no evangelical singing or dramatic sermons, just the laying-on of hands by a man who claimed to be no more than a channel for healing power. Nonetheless, the miraculous results he often achieved set Harry Edwards apart as one of the most remarkable of twentieth-century healers.

Edwards' cures made national headlines, his public demonstrations filled Britain's largest halls and his fame spread around the world. He often pointed out that although healing was an important aspect of Jesus' life, Christianity had virtually abandoned healing. Instead, Edwards was doing the work the Church ought to be doing. In the early 1950s the Church of England responded by setting up a commission to investigate the subject. This would not have been necessary had Edwards' healing ministry not had such a tremendous impact on the British public and led to thousands seeking healing help across the country.

The Archbishop of Canterbury, Dr Geoffrey Fisher, established the Commission on Divine Healing in 1953, the same year he conducted the coronation of Queen Elizabeth II. It consisted of a medical panel appointed by the British Medical Association as well as ecclesiastical representatives, one of whom was the Rev Maurice Elliott who, as well as being a clergyman, was a staunch believer in Spiritualism. His inclusion is said to have angered the archbishop. 'And what are you doing here? Who sent you?' Dr Fisher asked Elliott. The clergyman simply pointed to heaven and turned away.

Harry Edwards' evidence

Edwards willingly presented evidence to the commission at Lambeth Palace in July 1954. He and other healers had been asked to provide details of six cases for investigation by the medical panel. Edwards did not need to dig very deep for such evidence. In fact, he forwarded details of 70 successful cases, all of which had occurred in the previous three months, where doctors had declared the patients to be incurable. Despite this, he faced a barrage of hostile questions.

One commission member said all the healings could have been spontaneous or natural healings and that too many doctors were diagnosing people as incurable when they were not. Another member, Dr David Stafford-Clark, who was famous as 'the TV psychiatrist', dismissed Edwards' account of healing a 'blue baby' (a child born with cyanotic heart disease) as 'impossible', and when Edwards continued to discuss the case he turned his back on him. The biggest absurdity, however, was that the healers were asked to provide medical verification of their cases, which was something they could not do because patient-doctor confidentiality prevented it, and rightly so. The commission members, on the other hand, *could* have applied for that information, but chose not to do so.

An alternative, which Edwards preferred, was for the commission to select its own patients for healing, and to compare their medical conditions before and after spiritual healing. The offer was rejected. However, on 25 September 1954, an audience of 6,000 people at the Royal Albert Hall attending a public demonstration of healing by Harry Edwards were joined by 17 members of the Archbishop's Commission, as well as representatives of the Church's Council of Healing and the BMA. During that event, a girl of eight who had suffered from cerebral palsy from birth raised her arms above her head for the first time and two people who were crippled with disease walked away from the platform unaided.

Yet the BMA panel's findings were exactly what had been predicted by Edwards long before they were published in 1956. 'As I anticipated, and as I have told you several times, the BMA findings are purposefully evasive, misleading and a distortion of the truth...,' he said in a letter to the Rev Eric Jay, the secretary to the commission.

It is obvious the doctors are hostile. To ask them for an impartial judgment is asking them to agree that spiritual healing can succeed when they have failed, and this they do not want to do, whatever the evidence ... If the commission is willing to accept the BMA report at its face value, that is its responsibility, but if, on the other hand, it cares to question this report, I shall be prepared to co-operate.

Edwards never received a reply, so he issued a statement to the press pointing out the BMA panel's errors, as well as giving full details of eight cases with which they had been presented. He challenged the doctors to have these cases independently assessed, but they never responded. It was not altogether surprising that when the Church finally published its 'Commission's Report on Healing' two years later, it decided not to include any of the extensive evidence provided by Harry Edwards, which the medical panel had rejected but which the healer had so vigorously defended. Instead, it talked about encouraging a patient to 'confess' in order that he would have 'a real sorrow for his sins' before receiving healing, and advised clergy to discover whether patients were Christians, baptised, confirmed or communicants before treatment was given.

The most absurd of the recommendations was the suggestion that to induce healing, a priest should bless a bottle of olive oil, soak a piece of wool in this, draw a cross on the patient's forehead and, after reciting a prayer, burn the wool. As Harry Edwards pointed out: 'If Spiritualist healers did this, they would be rightly laughed at.'

Not surprisingly, one national newspaper said the report was a 'jungle of theological jargon' that reached back to 'the dark superstitious beginnings of man himself', adding that it was also a 'tremendous attack' on other denominations, including Spiritualism. The leading article in a London evening newspaper asked, 'Why, for instance, didn't the commission probe and test the evidence of a man like Harry Edwards...? Because, they say, it was outside their terms of reference.' The newspaper was blissfully ignorant – because the report did not reveal the fact – that Edwards *had* provided an abundance of evidence, which was ignored.

In a nutshell, the purpose of the commission was to reinforce the Christian view that healing should be performed only by clergy and in the name of Jesus, and the BMA used it to reassert what it regarded as the supremacy of medical science over all other forms of treatment. As it happens, Harry Edwards and spiritual healing were the eventual winners in this battle.

Public proof of healing

Within a month of the report being published, Edwards was back in front of a capacity audience at the Albert Hall in London, this time demonstrating his gift against a backdrop of 300 white-coated healers. Sharing the platform with him was George Rogers, a Labour Member of Parliament and Spiritualist whose wife Mary was also a very powerful healing medium. Also on the platform were some of the 'incurables' whose cases Edwards had presented to the commission. The evidence of their healings had been omitted from the report but they publicly confirmed the efficacy of the healing they had received.

The BMA had made a bad miscalculation by not realising, when it published its medical panel's dismissive findings, that many doctors had a tremendous respect for Harry Edwards and sought his co-operation in giving spiritual healing to their patients. To underline this, Edwards held up 200 letters from doctors seeking such assistance at a public meeting in Bloomsbury in 1959. They had all been received in the short time since the medical report was released. Moreover in that same year, despite the BMA's antagonism towards spiritual healing, Britain's National Health Service (NHS) announced that it was giving permission to spiritual healers to treat the sick in hospital, if requested to do so by patients or relatives.

The medical establishment finally accepts healing

Sadly, Harry Edwards did not live to see an even greater medical breakthrough. In 1977, a year after his passing, the General

Medical Council, which has the legal powers to protect, promote and maintain the health and safety of the British public, gave permission to doctors to refer patients to healers. Had they done so before this change was announced, they would have been disciplined or struck off. Today, many doctors take advantage of that enlightened view, and there are even medical doctors who are also spiritual healers.

Healing through my hand

During the 1960s I attended many of Harry Edwards' public healing demonstrations, interviewing patients and following up cases. He deliberately selected people from the audience whose conditions would show demonstrable improvement. With him on the platform were his healing assistants, husband-and-wife team George and Olive Burton, who also worked with him at his Burrows Lea sanctuary. Olive's healing abilities were particularly good with eye problems. In fact, one of the peculiarities of spiritual healing is that healers are very different in their approach and methodology, often getting better results with one type of disease or disability than another.

One of my most memorable experiences from that period was being given the opportunity to sit alongside Harry Edwards in his Surrey sanctuary and watch at close quarters how the healing took place. I have read newspaper reports that describe Edwards *manipulating* the patient. In all the years I saw him at work, this never happened. He simply placed his hand over the afflicted area – an arthritic knee, a painful back, a large goitre on the neck – and sat quietly for a minute or so, no more. He never claimed that a single healing session would produce a cure, suggesting instead that the patient received absent or direct healing for a period until the condition was totally gone. But when he lifted his hand there was almost always a noticeable improvement.

As I sat watching Edwards' simple technique, a woman came

forward and explained that she had a painful back problem that made it very difficult for her to bend. Edwards turned to me and told me to put my hand on the small of her back. I did so. He then placed his right hand over mine and his left hand somewhere on the front of the woman, either her chest or maybe her forehead. We sat together for a short period, united in healing. 'What can you feel?' he asked the patient. 'Intense heat in my back,' she replied. Then, turning to me, he asked, 'And what do you feel?' 'Nothing,' I responded, feeling that my spiritual sensitivity had somehow failed a crucial test, but puzzled that I could not feel the heat. 'Precisely!' he said with a broad smile. 'You are not receiving the healing, this lady is, so it passes through your hand and into her body, which registers the healing power as heat.' And to prove that she had benefited far more than by getting a warm feeling from the famous healer's hands, via mine, the patient stood up, bent down and touched her toes without a flicker of pain.

Theories about how the healing works

Harry Edwards had no doubt that spirit entities were responsible for the healing,[3] although he would not have argued with the suggestion that they, in turn, were conduits of healing from an even greater source. Indeed, he used a cross in a circle as his sanctuary's symbol. It mattered not what religion his patients followed, or whether they were atheists or sceptics: their need for healing was as great as anyone else's. Nor did he pontificate on the rights or wrongs of healing methods, though his advice to all would-be healers was to keep it as simple as possible. Attunement with the source of healing, whoever or whatever that may be, was the most important aspect of successful healing. He argued convincingly that for most healings to take place, there had to be an 'intelligence' at work. To produce the complicated chemical and physiological changes capable of instantly freeing locked joints or improving eyesight required a sophisticated intervention from the spirit world that went far beyond what one could expect from the patient's own self-healing mechanisms.

Having already satisfied myself that mediums could receive communications from the spirit world, I had no difficulty in accepting the view of Edwards and most other spiritual healers – the majority of whom were Spiritualists – that they were channelling healing power from the next world. One thing, however, did puzzle me, and still does to some extent.

If discarnate beings are responsible for most healings, then why is it that our relatives and loved ones who have gone on to the spirit world before us and who, it seems, continue to monitor our activities closely, do not seek healing for us? If I go to a healer asking for help, I will receive it from his or her spirit team of medical specialists. So why couldn't a dead relative of mine, aware of my needs, also ask the spirit team for healing to be directed to me? I put that question to Harry Edwards at one of our meetings. He thought for a while, and then suggested that there seems to be a spiritual law that requires a request for healing to come from someone in the physical world. I won't pretend to accept this explanation fully, but I guess it's the only one that makes any sense. Clearly, we still have a lot to learn.

My personal experience of healing

What I do know for sure is that spiritual healing works. I knew it anyway from watching public healing demonstrations. But personal experience is the best teacher and it arrived unexpectedly one morning when I reached out to turn off my bedside alarm. I must have slept awkwardly because suddenly there was an audible 'click' in my neck and I knew something unpleasant had happened. It wasn't until I tried to turn my head that I experienced an excruciating pain. I could move my head to the left, but not to the right. Crossing the road on my way to the office was a problem: I had to turn the whole of my body to the right in order to check that no cars were coming.

I had obviously slipped a disc in my neck, I decided, and would have to visit a doctor, probably have some form of traction and maybe even wear a neck brace. When my editor, Maurice Barbanell, learned of my problem he immediately advised me to go to a healer, suggesting Leonard Morris, who lived in St John's Wood, north-west London, as the most convenient and accessible.

I'd met Leonard a few times socially and written about his healing powers, so I made an appointment for that afternoon, after his return from a funeral. He and his wife lived in a very pleasant apartment block and as I sat in his lounge, on the chair he used for healing, I admired a painting above the fireplace. It was one he had painted. He placed one hand on my neck, the other on my head, and continued chatting about the painting and his interest in art. I was expecting to feel an intense heat, just as the woman patient had described at Harry Edwards' sanctuary, but I felt only the pleasant warmth of the healer's hands. I decided that the healing clearly wasn't working, and began planning a visit to my doctor's surgery that evening.

After a couple of minutes, Leonard lifted his hands from my head and said, 'That's it. You're OK now.' He stepped in front of me, placed an index finger on each of my cheeks and moved my head effortlessly from left to right. The agonising pain had gone; mobility had returned. All I was left with was a soreness that he said would be gone in a couple of days, advising me to apply a hot salt poultice to the neck to speed up the process. He had *not* manipulated my neck. I had *not* felt anything pop back in or realign. As far as I was concerned, nothing had happened. Yet he knew it had and that was because Morris' healing powers, like Edwards', were controlled by spirits who communicated with him and inspired his actions.

A healer guided by a voice

Another prominent healer of that period was Ted Fricker, who worked first from his home in Tottenham, north London, and then opened a consulting room in the Harley Street area of London, which is where many medical specialists have their practices. From an early age he had heard a spirit voice and it was this that guided him when giving healing.

I spent a day at Fricker's north London home, watching and marvelling as a procession of people filed through in rapid succession. There was no appointment system so they would start waiting outside his front door early in the morning. By the time I arrived, the queue snaked out of his front gate and down the street. The neighbours didn't seem to mind – many of them had probably benefited from his powers. His method was much the same as that of Edwards and Morris, except that he liked to play loud music (sometimes pop, sometimes classical) and his hands would vibrate intensely as the healing took place. Then, acting on instructions from the spirit voice, he would instruct the patient to do something that had previously been difficult or impossible for them to do.

I remember very well a woman, accompanied by her son, who had a slipped disc – a condition Fricker specialised in – and who was in such pain that others in the queue allowed her to move ahead so that she could take a seat in the crowded waiting room. When she joined us in the healing room, Fricker motioned for her to sit on the upholstered stool in the centre of the room. He turned up the music and placed his hands on her back and her stomach. Eyes closed, his body seemed to shake from head to toe, but it was his hands that vibrated the most. Healing over, he stretched out his hands and helped her to her feet. 'You're better,' he declared.

The woman looked pleased but perplexed, as if not daring to believe that in just a couple of minutes she had been cured. 'Any pain?' he asked. She shook her head and smiled. Then he motioned to an armchair in the corner of the room. 'Sit down.' She backed towards it but shook her head. 'I can't,' she said, as she recalled the agony she would have felt just minutes earlier. 'Yes you can.' She began, then stopped herself. 'I haven't been able to sit in a chair like that for ages,' she explained. Perhaps she feared that the action of sitting might undo the healing and bring the pain back. Fricker then took matters into his own hands, which he placed on her shoulders and then gave her a sharp push. She fell back into the chair with a cry of astonishment. I caught a glimpse of her son's expression – it was one of horror, but he was too slow to reach out and grab her. But to her surprise, there was no pain. She stood up. Then sat down again. The healing really *had* worked.

I followed the woman outside and watched as she stopped to talk to people in the queue – the same people who had allowed her to go inside because she was suffering so much – and told them with tears in her eyes how wonderful Ted Fricker was. Later, back in his treatment room, after I had witnessed many more healings, he said it was time for us to have a break. He lifted the upholstered lid of the healing stool and inside were bottles of whisky, gin and other drinks. We had a small drink together, then he closed the lid, opened the door to his still crowded reception room, and called, 'Next'. It gave spirit healing a whole new meaning.

Spiritual healing in Britain today

Most people who give any thought to spiritual healing believe it is something that happens on a small scale and affects very few people. In fact, there are now over 8,000 healers in the United Kingdom, the majority of whom are members of the National Federation of Spiritual Healers. Most share the views of Harry Edwards, Leonard Morris and Ted Fricker that spirit teams work with them in treating the sick.

Healing services are a feature of virtually every Spiritualist church's activities, and all the major Spiritualist organisations encourage spiritual healing, making it freely available to those who need help. Some healers may prefer to give credit to guardian angels, to Jesus or to God himself as the source of their powers. It matters not. As long as they are attuned to a source of healing that they can channel through their bodies, bringing about an improve-

Doris Stokes became such a popular clairvoyant she was able to book the London Palladium for demonstrations. © Psychic News

Ena Twigg, clairvoyant and trance medium consulted by bishops and clergy. © Bryce Bond (courtesy of Psychic News)

Four famous mediums (pictured 1971, left to right): Helen Hughes, Estelle Roberts, Lilian Bailey and Nan McKenzie. © Studio Raphael (courtesy of Psychic News)

Hester Dowden used a planchette to receive automatic writing communications from spirits.
© unknown (courtesy of Psychic News)

Brazilian automatic writing medium Francisco Candido 'Chico' Xavier signing a copy of one of his numerous spirit-dictated books.
© unknown (courtesy of Psychic News)

Geraldine Cummins, in a light trance, produces automatic writing at astonishing speed, watched by Miss E. B. Gibbes. © Psychic News

Musical medium Rosemary Brown with scores dictated by dead composers.
© presumed property the Hulton Archive

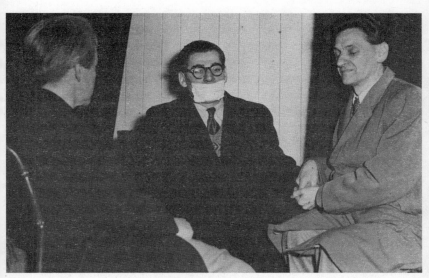

Even though British medium Leslie Flint had his mouth taped, independent spirit voices were heard during seances under test conditions. © Psychic News

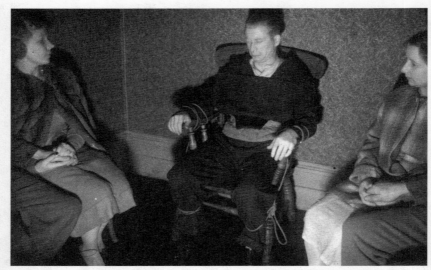

Although securely tied to his chair, the jacket of Welsh spirit medium Jack Webber was routinely removed by the spirits. This photograph, taken with infra-red light, catches the event in progress and is physically impossible since it shows the back of his jacket in front of his body, with his arms still in the sleeves. © Psychic News

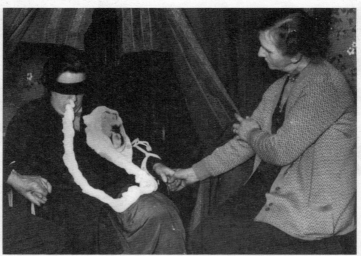

A face appears to be forming in the ectoplasm produced by Scottish materialisation medium Helen Duncan. She was searched before her seances and is tied to the chair as well as having her hands held by sitters. © Psychic News

Eileen Garrett, Irish-born medium who moved to the US and founded the Parapsychology Foundation. © Psychic News

Konstantin Raudive's experiments pioneered a breakthrough in 'spirit radio' communications. © Mary Evans Picture Library

Most of the English football squad had healing from Spiritualist medium Eileen Drewery. © Rex Features

Medium and healer Doris Collins with two of her famous clients: Frankie Howerd (left) and Michael Bentine. © Psychic News

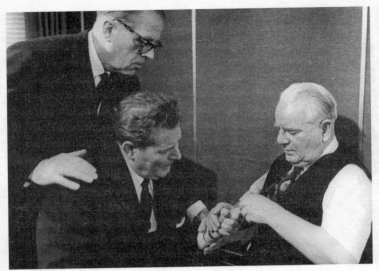

Harry Edwards gives healing to a patient's hand, helped by assistant George Burton.
© Psychic News

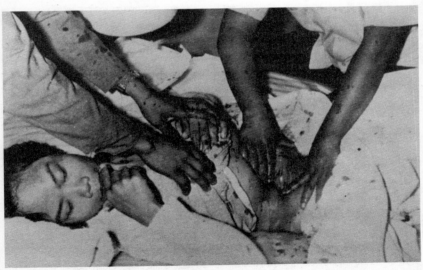

Psychic surgery is said to involve actual operations carried out without anaesthetics or instruments. The healer in this picture in Filipino Tony Agpaoa. © Psychic News

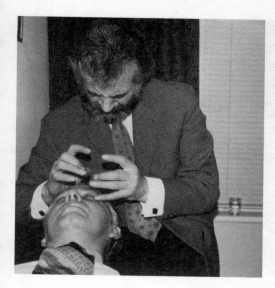

George Chapman, entranced by the spirit of surgeon William Lang, carries out a spirit operation on a patient.
© Michael Chapman

This portrait of spirit guide Silver Birch, whose philosophy inspires many Spiritualists around the world, was painted by clairvoyant artist Marcel Poncin. © Psychic News

Jenny Cockell's memories of living as Mary Sutton (pictured left) in Ireland resulted in the reunion of her past-life children. © Jenny Cockell

East London medium Tony Stockwell's public demonstrations of mediumship challenge the sceptics. © Tony Stockwell

Psychic barber Gordon Smith impresses with his very specific spirit messages. © Gordon Smith

ment in their patients' health, it makes no sense to worry about labels and beliefs.

I remember a very powerful London-based healer, Gordon Turner, refusing even to use the prefix 'spiritual', explaining: 'I'm just a healer.' But how do we know which healers are accredited and which are not? And does it matter? Just because a healer belongs to a recognised association does not make him or her a good healer, and many who work independently get very good results. However, healers in the United Kingdom are now beginning to work closely together – regardless of their beliefs – as part of the government's and the European Union's requirements for self-regulation of complementary and alternative therapies.

UK Healers, formed in 2000, has formulated common basic standards of good practice, with the result that most of the healing organisations have joined this umbrella organisation and share its objectives. It is also supported by the Prince of Wales Foundation for Integrated Health. The long-term view is that this greater acceptance of complementary medicine at all levels of society will ultimately result in spiritual healing being available in the United Kingdom on the National Health Service. A motion to that effect was narrowly defeated in the House of Lords in 1990 (by only four votes) and it is just a matter of time before it is finally included as a beneficial option in healthcare programmes. This is all a far cry from the days when Harry Edwards took on both the Church and the BMA in his determination to prove the value of spiritual healing.

The use of healing in football and other sports

Astonishingly, changing attitudes to spiritual healing in recent times owe as much to football as to the Church or medicine. At the end of 1997, in the run-up to the World Cup, newspapers began to speculate on the relationship between England's player-turned-coach Glenn Hoddle, and a 56-year-old grandmother named Eileen Drewery.

Eileen Drewery

Glenn Hoddle's marriage had just ended after 18 years and he had moved in with Eileen Drewery and her husband, resulting in wild speculation. It transpired that their daughter had been Hoddle's girlfriend when they were teenagers, and that during that period he had been cured of a hamstring injury by Drewery, whose healing powers had been discovered after she visited a Spiritualist church. Since then Hoddle had benefited from her healing for many football injuries, as well as receiving spiritual guidance.

Most football fans and the media regarded this as just a quirk of the England manager. However, there were more revelations to come. In April 1998, just two months before England's first game in France, against Tunisia, Hoddle revealed that Eileen Drewery's services as a spiritual healer had been used by three-quarters of the 32-strong England football squad during the previous 18 months. They had sought her help of their own volition, having seen the benefits that Hoddle and other colleagues had received from her healing hands.

'I've seen plenty of people go to see Drewery cynically and it changed their lives,' Hoddle told the media. 'From my Swindon days, she's saved players' careers.' Among those willing to back their boss and testify to the healing received was Arsenal captain and England striker Ian Wright. 'I've been going to Eileen for eight or nine months now,' he admitted. 'She's helped me to be positive. She means a lot to me. I feel very close to her. She's blessed.'

It must be remembered that football is big business, and clubs and national teams depend heavily on the fitness of their top players.

Injuries are common in such a physical sport, so a range of medical and physiotherapy treatments are available to get players back on their feet as quickly as possible. It says much for spiritual healing that it was the treatment of choice for so many of the England squad and their manager.

Eileen Drewery's explanation for her powers was simple: she was merely a channel, and these remarkable results were accomplished not by her but by her spirit guide, an Egyptian named Zyphos.[4] Nor was she the only healer helping football teams. While writing a book about Manchester United, Jim White came to the conclusion that the widespread use of healers was 'the hidden secret of football'. He discovered that former United and England captain Bryan Robson had referred injured players to a healer.

Hoddle, meanwhile, had enemies in the media who made fun of his beliefs and after England was knocked out of the World Cup, an interview with a reporter from *The Times* in which he discussed his views on reincarnation led to his dismissal. That was not the end of the story. It soon transpired that his replacement as care-taker coach, Kevin Keegan, had also received healing from Eileen Drewery during his playing career, and that his wife was even training to be a healer.

Spiritual healing has also had an impact in other sports. Let me give just one example, taken from an earlier book of mine, on heal-ers and healing.[5] The sensational New Zealand runner John Walker has admitted that he was in so much pain from a knee injury in 1974 that he even had trouble getting out of bed. It had been troubling him for two years and was getting worse, although he had mentioned it to very few people.

One morning Walker tuned in to a local radio talk show and heard an interview with English clairvoyant and healer Doris Collins, who was touring Australasia demonstrating her medi-umship. The 23-year-old immediately made his way to the radio station – where he had often been interviewed about his achieve-ments – and as soon as she saw him, Doris Collins referred to the knee problem. 'Mrs Collins put her hands on my spine and on my knees,' he told a journalist later. 'I felt vibrations coming through her fingertips! It was uncanny. Incredible. Then, after about five minutes, she asked me to stand up and there was no more pain! The next Saturday I ran 400 metres 15 times. If my knee was going to hurt, it would have hurt then. The next day I ran a 17-miler. No trouble!'

As a result, when Walker flew to Gothenburg, Sweden, in August 1975 to compete in a major athletics event, he did so with the knowledge that he was running better than ever before, thanks to spiritual healing. In fact, he ran straight into the record books, shaving 1.6 seconds off the old world record for the mile by running it in an incredible three minutes 49.4 seconds.

I suspect there are thousands of similar stories of successful spiritual healings that go unreported.

1 Harry Edwards, *The Mediumship of Jack Webber*, Rider & Co. (1940).
2 Harry Edwards, *The Mediumship of Arnold Clare*, Rider & Co. (1941).
3 Harry Edwards, *Thirty Years a Spiritual Healer*, Herbert Jenkins (1968).
4 Eileen Drewery, *Why Me?*, Hodder Headline (1997).
5 Roy Stemman, *Healers and Healing*, Piatkus Books (1999).

Chapter 9

Trance Healing

In this form of healing the trance medium's body is taken over by a spirit, and patients consult the spirit about their problems. Before I describe this process in more detail, it is important to recognise that trance healing, in various forms, has been an important aspect of spirit communication and of the Spiritualist movement since its earliest days. In fact, Leah Fox – one of the sisters through whose mediumship modern Spiritualism was born – is reported to have received a visitor, E.W. Capron, who mentioned that his wife was affected by a severe and troublesome cough.

The entranced medium declared: 'I am going to cure Rebecca of the cough.' After giving an accurate description of Mrs Capron, the spirit speaking through Leah Fox declared her to be cured. Returning home, the husband is said to have found his wife 'extremely well' and the trouble never recurred. This anecdotal account is unconvincing. I quote it simply to indicate that trance healing is not new.

In the twentieth century, its UK exponents included Nan Mackenzie, a remarkable woman whose Native American spirit guide, 'Running Water', continued to give healing until the medium was a hundred years old. Another well-known trance healer, Fred Jones, was also controlled by a Native American spirit guide named, aptly, 'Medicine Man'. They produced many remarkable healings, but their spirit guides' identities were secondary to the healing. William Lang, on the other hand, was a surgeon whose identity *could* be verified by people who knew him, which is precisely what happened when he communicated through George

Chapman. The Chapman-Lang partnership therefore provides us not only with evidence for spiritual healing, effected from beyond, but also for individual survival of death. As such, it is a story worth telling in some detail.

There is a major difference in the way the Chapman-Lang partnership works, compared with the healers I have already discussed. Chapman is a trance medium whose body is taken over by the spirit of Lang for several hours at a time, during which patients consult the dead surgeon about their problems. They lie down on an examining couch – one that actually belonged to Lang during his earthly life – and after an examination he treats their condition not by laying-on hands but by performing 'spirit operations'.

The surgeon and the medium

I first spoke to William Lang some 40 years ago. It was an exciting and curious encounter. Although I have spoken to him many times since, and regard him as a friend, I still find it hard to shake off the rather incredulous feeling that engulfs me whenever we meet. William Lang, after all, died 67 years ago. In his day, he was a well-known surgeon and ophthalmic specialist, with a thriving private practice in London and busy hospital commitments. George Bernard Shaw was one of his patients and William Morris was a good friend.

Lang, a small, bearded, bespectacled man, had a long and happy association with the famous Middlesex Hospital in London, and when his days of operating on and caring for patients came to an end he continued to lecture and demonstrate there for several years. Eventually, he gave up all medical work and spent many years in retirement before dying in 1937 at the age of 84.

There the story of William Lang should have ended – if a final curtain had descended – but it did not and the compassionate surgeon, having survived the change we call death, decided he wanted to continue treating the sick from the next world. To do that, he needed a healer through whom he could work. We do not know what process was involved in making that choice, but the person he selected was a Liverpudlian named George Chapman, who was brought up by his grandparents in a poor part of the city.

George Chapman

George Chapman was only 17 years old when Lang died. Their paths had never crossed and they were blissfully unaware of each other's existence, but a powerful spiritual partnership was about to develop between them, resulting in a two-world healing mission that has benefited many thousands of people around the world.

After leaving school, George Chapman had a number of jobs. He was a butcher, garage hand and a professional boxer before joining the Irish Guards and then the Royal Air Force. He was stationed at RAF Halton, married a local girl, Margaret, and after leaving the RAF, joined the Fire Brigade and settled down in Aylesbury. Their first child, a daughter named Vivian, unfortunately died within a month. This sudden bereavement led to Chapman searching for answers about life and death and investigating Spiritualism. It was not long before he discovered his mediumistic potential. He was entranced by a variety of spirits, one of whom identified himself as William Lang and said he had returned to heal the sick. It was only after Lang and Chapman had established a good working relationship that the dead surgeon revealed more about himself, enabling verification to be made. Yet most people who sought his help were not interested in checking whether he was who he said he was. They just wanted to get better.

It would be easy for me to cite many cases of successful healing, such as that of Barrie Miron, the wife of dental surgeon Joe Miron, who was treated successfully by Lang after the extraction of a tooth caused damage to the roof of her mouth that failed to respond to dental treatment.

I could give a detailed report on the case of a Parisian shop assistant, Joseph Tanguy, who was referred to William Lang by his own doctor after surgeons had been unable to remove no more than a small part of a malignant brain tumour. His wife was told he had six months to live, but following a spirit operation by Lang the tumour began to shrink and eventually disappeared completely.

A Swiss artist, M. Salvaen, has reason to be thankful for William Lang's intervention. He was taken to see the dead surgeon by Dr Guinvarch after cataracts on both eyes made it impossible for him to paint any more. After being operated on by the dead ophthalmic surgeon, the artist was able to pick up his brushes and paint, and his eyesight stabilised.

There is no shortage of such testimonies. When a survey was conducted of 121 patients treated in France over a two-day period, it was found that only one reported no improvement. There are many outstanding cases of healing to be found in the books about Chapman and Lang. What I intend to do, however, is to concentrate on the evidence for life after death provided by this remarkable mediumistic partnership.

How William Lang operated on me

My first meeting with George Chapman and William Lang was in the early 1960s, and although I had no medical problems I asked the dead surgeon to examine me. I did so in order to see how he worked. Like hundreds of patients before me, I lay down on the examination table in the dimly lit consulting room and watched as Chapman, his eyes tightly closed, waved his hands over me and the spirit of William Lang spoke through him.

Chapman, then in his early forties, spoke in a markedly different way when in trance. Lang's speech mannerisms and use of language were what I would have expected from a cultured, well-educated professional man who had lived and worked at the turn of the century. He had the charm of a doctor who had developed the perfect bedside manner from years of treating the sick.

William Lang completed his examination and announced that all was well, apart from an indication that at some time in the future I might experience trouble with my tear ducts. He would, therefore, correct them. I watched as his fingers began to 'operate' just an inch or so above my face. He seemed to be handling surgical instruments, which were passed to him by invisible hands whenever he snapped his fingers, yet his hands were empty. I felt nothing and when the 'operation' was completed there was no visible sign that I had been operated on. According to William Lang, however, my etheric body (which serves as a go-between for the physical and spirit bodies) had been treated in order to rid me of a problem that would creep up on me in later years.

Was it a charade? Was Chapman a clever actor who had learned enough medical terminology to bluff his way through these healing sessions? Or had I really been operated on by a dead surgeon? I admit that the last possibility seemed so preposterous that fraud was the easier explanation for my mind to cope with. One thing intrigued me, however. As far as I knew there was nothing wrong with my tear ducts – but my mother *had* had such trouble, to the extent of needing surgery to replace the ducts with artificial ones. Her elder sister had also had the same operation. So it was clearly a rare genetic weakness and one to which I may well have been susceptible in later life. I'm pleased to report that I still have my own tear ducts!

Encounters with the dead surgeon's daughter

Over the years my friendship with both Chapman and Lang developed and I collaborated with the medium on a couple of books.[1] I was also shown the Lang Museum, a collection of items that had once belonged to the ophthalmic surgeon, and learned of some of the high-profile patients who had consulted the dead surgeon – although I am not at liberty to identify them.

There was another secret that Chapman kept from most people

until 1977. In May of that year he phoned me to say that his Auntie Lyndon had died in a north London nursing home. He had visited the 94-year-old lady regularly during her brief illness following a fall, and had sat at her bedside discussing the times they had spent together over the previous 30 years. But she was not his aunt. In fact, they were not related at all, although she looked on him as a son and he regarded her with the affection one normally feels for a mother. The remarkable truth is that she was Marie Lyndon Lang, daughter of the surgeon who speaks through him, and when he was in trance she would address him as 'Father'.

Chapman and I revealed the full story in our book *Surgeon From Another World*, which explained how their remarkable relationship came about. George Chapman's healing abilities started to be reported in the press, with the result that he received an invitation from a Mrs Connie Newey in 1946 inviting him to travel from Aylesbury to Edgbaston, a south-west Birmingham suburb, to give healing to 12 patients. What Connie Newey did not reveal was that she had known William Lang during his earthly life. She and her sister Mrs Nora Hanson had taken their mother, who was a patient of William Lang, to see him on a number of occasions. There was another link with the family, for Nora Hanson's husband had met and become friendly with Lyndon Lang when they both served in France during the First World War.

George Chapman knew none of this history when he arrived at Hagley Road for the healing session. As soon as he was in trance, the group plied Dr Lang – as his earthly patients always called the surgeon – with questions about his identity. His answers left them in no doubt that he *was* the person he claimed to be, except that he was now living in another world. Some time later, Mrs Nora Hanson wrote this testimony to Chapman:

When Mr Lang was in practice on earth I went with mother to consult him about her eyes. There in his consulting room I watched him examining mother's eyes; helping her and advising her what to do. His daughter was a great friend of mine. I often visited her in their home. The son,

Basil, who is now in spirit and assists Dr Lang in the healing, was also a friend of mine. I have stayed with Basil Lang and his wife at their London flat. When I meet Dr Lang in spirit it is to me a really wonderful experience. He is helpful, friendly and kind. We have discussed the professional visit mother and I made to him and many other personal reminiscences. The talks I now have with Dr Lang make me realise it must be the Mr Lang I knew in the past to whom I am talking.

It wasn't long before Lyndon Lang heard about her father's spirit return and the fact that those present, who knew him well enough to judge the authenticity of the communication, were unanimous in their verdict. She decided to find out for herself by arranging a private meeting with Chapman at Aylesbury. She didn't use deception: she told the medium who she was when she wrote to him. She reasoned that if her father really was communicating through the medium, he would be able to tell her things that Chapman could not research from any other sources.

Thus it was that in 1947, ten years after William Lang's death, his 64-year-old daughter found herself talking to him again. Her memory of him and of shared events in their lives was still very lucid, so she asked penetrating and personal questions, all of which he answered fully and without hesitation. It would have made a sensational story, but Lyndon Lang knew that publicity would also disturb her happy life. She had no wish to be in the spotlight or to have to deal with constant questions from believers and sceptics alike. Chapman respected her wishes. Their friendship lasted for 30 years, during which time she spoke to William Lang through Chapman's mediumship on many occasions. By the time she reached her nineties, and had deteriorating health and poor eyesight, it was clear that it would not be long before she joined her father in the spirit world.

Chapman and I had just started collaborating on a book for the French market, because William Lang's healing services were in great demand in that country, where a number of medical professionals supported his work. He discussed this plan with Lyndon

Lang and to his surprise she said she would like to write something for the book. She was aware that she would no longer be on Earth by the time the book was in print. This is her testimony, dictated to Chapman but signed by Marie Lyndon Lang:

I came to know of George and my father's return in 1946. George was invited to my home to meet old colleagues of father's. We asked many questions of father about things which only he could know. He knew all the answers and, better still, he asked questions in return. Some of the questions we could not answer. In 1947 George accepted a contract with myself and of a group of aged doctors. I am the only one left....To all readers of this book I can truthfully say the William Lang who operates via the body of George Chapman is, without a doubt, my father.

Her statement enabled us to write a much broader book than we originally planned, and it also took the lid off another story, which she touched on in a private visitors' book that Chapman keeps for doctors or well-known patients willing to write brief testimonies. Lyndon Lang had asked to make the first entry. It reads:

I would like to be the first to write in this little book and to put on record that George Chapman first visited my flat in 1947 to give sittings to myself and to friends and medical contemporaries of my brother. We all questioned and tested George and my father William Lang, and we could only come to the conclusion that the person who speaks through George Chapman and claimed to be William Lang is, without a doubt, my father. George came under a contract to a group of medical men whose names are in a sealed envelope, which was given to George in 1956 and must not be opened until my passing. Since then, George has kept the gentleman's agreement of visiting London every two weeks for the few of us who are left to talk with father and receive healings. It is a fact that William Lang, my father, is as much alive today, continuing his work from the spirit world, and helping mankind back to health as best he can.

After 1956, George Chapman left the Fire Brigade to devote himself full-time to trance mediumship and healing, and his commitment to 'Auntie Lyndon' and the medical group – most of whom were colleagues of Basil Lang, who had died of pneumonia in 1928 – became a weekly one and continued for 20 more years. As well as providing the written statements, Lyndon Lang – a very private person – allowed herself to be filmed briefly, talking to her dead father through Chapman's mediumship, and the films are now in the healer's extensive archives.

Confirmation from other relatives

Other members of William Lang's family have added their confirmation that it is the dead surgeon who has returned through the mediumship of George Chapman. One was Susan Fairtlough, William Lang's granddaughter, who decided to tell her story to a journalist writing for the mass-circulation French magazine *Paris Match* in 1974. He came to England to research a feature on the Chapman-Lang partnership and visited the Fairtloughs in their Surrey home. As a child, Susan had been taken to have tea with her grandparents in their London home on many occasions and she had a very precise memory of William Lang. She told Robert Barrat:

This is why, six years ago [1968], when I heard that a healer was pretending to be my grandfather, I found it grotesque. I rang this journalist Hutton [Joe Hutton had written a book about the healing partnership[2]] and told him: 'I am going to put this quack to confusion.' I obtained an appointment from this Chapman fellow. I had bought a tape recorder for the purpose and there I was at St Bride's, Aylesbury. To my great horror, or rather stupefaction, the man who was in this room was indisputably my grandfather. It was not him physically, but it was his voice.... His behaviour. It was unquestionable. He spoke to me and recalled precise events of my childhood. And I was so impressed that all I could say was, 'Yes, grandpapa. No, grandpapa.' I was so strongly affected, in fact, that I never went back to Aylesbury. However, when George Chapman came to visit us in this house, a phenomenon occurred which confirms his quality as a medium. I have here three objects that used to belong to my grandfather. Chapman walked through the house and recognised them immediately.

Susan Fairtlough died five months after this interview was published but I was able to confirm its accuracy – and much more besides – in subsequent interviews with her husband Andrew and daughter Amanda.

The other family member who has added his testimony is Gavin Dunlop, William Lang's great-grandson. Living in South Africa, he had taken an interest in the Chapman-Lang partnership from a distance and corresponded regularly with the medium. Then, in 1978, he visited Chapman in England, writing on his return that it was 'tremendous fun seeing again so many familiar pieces of furniture, pictures, books, etc, and remembering them from so long ago – and more recently in the case of those which Lyndon Lang had in day-to-day use'.

Dunlop was disappointed, however, that the many portraits of William Lang that people have given the medium over the years – mostly based on black-and-white photographs – do not do him justice. So Duncan, a talented artist, produced a much better likeness that now has pride of place in Chapman's home. It is exactly as his great-grandson remembers him from the 1920s. And he added the personal note that it is 'very comforting to know that we can always turn to you, if in need, for a consultation with Dr Lang, or for distant healing'.

There is one final piece of this remarkable two-world jigsaw that reinforces Marie Lyndon Lang's acceptance of her dead father's spirit return and explains why Gavin Dunlop recognised so many items of furniture on his visit to Chapman's home. It is to be found in her will, which she made and signed on 22 September 1964, at the age of 81. She left all her personal effects – many of which had belonged to Lang – to Chapman, and after making bequests to the likes of the Royal Society of Medicine, and instructing her Trustees to make various other payments and investments, she bequeathed the rest of her estate to the trance healer 'in the confident expectation that he will make good use of this bequest'. It enabled him to continue her father's work not only in the United Kingdom, but also in many other countries.

By the time he reached his eighties, George Chapman was living in semi-retirement in Wales, but a privileged few still occasionally have an opportunity to talk with Lang through his amazing mediumship and to receive healing from the dead surgeon, who has been helping the sick, from the spirit world, for the best part of 60 years. But most patients requesting healing are passed to his son, Michael, who lives nearby with his wife and family in Machynlleth. Though not a trance medium, Michael Chapman – like his father – has the support of a large team of spirit helpers, led by Lang's son Basil.

George Chapman's healing mission came to an end with his passing, on 9th August 2006, leaving Michael to continue his healing work.

There are other trance healers who work in a similar way to Chapman and Lang, with a spirit guide operating on the etheric bodies of patients. They often produce impressive results, and are making their own, unique contribution to the growth of spiritual healing. But I make no apologies for devoting this chapter entirely to George Chapman and William Lang, for I know of no other two-world relationship that provides such strong evidence not only for healing but also for our continuing existence beyond the grave. And that, says William Lang, is one of the main objectives of his spirit return. It is a case of unparalleled significance and no review of spirit communication in the twentieth or twenty-first century is complete without it.

1 George Chapman and Roy Stemman, *Surgeon From Another World: Extraordinary Encounters*, W. H. Allen (1978).
2 Joe Bernard Hutton, *Healing Hands*, W.H. Allen (1966).

Chapter 10

Psychic Surgeons

India has a reputation for fakirs and holy men capable of many wonders, but the subcontinent has nothing to compare with the Rev Alex Orbito – which was why the Filipino psychic surgeon caused such a sensation when he toured India in April 2002 to demonstrate his extraordinary powers.

Whereas mediums like George Chapman, described in the previous chapter, enable a spirit surgeon to operate on the patient's etheric body, psychic surgeons like Alex Orbito appear to carry out real operations. They plunge their hands into a patient's body, blood flows, and a tumour or diseased matter is pulled out; then the wound miraculously closes and the area is swabbed with cotton wool, leaving no scar. If real, this is an astonishing demonstration of physical phenomena, performed in bright light, which shows the extent to which spirits can interact with our world. If faked, it is brilliant sleight of hand that has fooled numerous competent observers. But perhaps, some suggest, it is somehow a combination of the two.

A psychic healer in India

Alex Orbito's story and his experiences in India encapsulate the dilemma we face in trying to make sense of a phenomenon whose origins could be regarded as momentous or scurrilous depending on your point of view. Born on 25 November 1940, near Manila, the fourteenth child of a farming couple whose mother is one of the founders of the Philippine's Spiritualist movement, Alex Orbito became aware of his destiny at an early age through a spirit voice that has guided him ever since.

Orbito is now one of the Philippines' leading psychic surgeons but spends up to 300 days of each year travelling the world. Since 1990 he has visited 70 countries to demonstrate his mediumistic abilities, including the United States, where he performed psychic surgery on Oscar-winning actress Shirley MacLaine and some of her Hollywood friends in her California home. She described the experience in one of her many books on the paranormal.[1] Members of the Saudi royal family and one of India's most admired singers, Jagit Singh – 'the ghazal king' – are among the one million people he claims to have treated during more than three decades as a psychic surgeon.

Among those welcoming the Filipino medium to India was Devarayapuram Ramasam Karthikeyan, a man who should be able to detect a fake in a single glance. A former police officer who became the state of Karnataka's head of intelligence, then Inspector-General of the Central Reserve Police Force's southern sector at Hyderabad and Joint Director of the Central Bureau of Investigations (CBI), D.R. Karthikeyan was put in charge of the Special Investigation Team (SIT) that probed the assassination of former Indian prime minister Rajiv Gandhi in May 1991. Under his leadership, the SIT identified 26 culprits who were involved in the crime, all of whom were found guilty.

After retiring as CBI chief in 1998, Karthikeyan was appointed director-general (investigations) at the National Human Rights Commission, based in Delhi. Since leaving that post, he has been actively involved in promoting spirituality in India and abroad. It was during a visit to Grosseto, Italy, that he had a chance meeting with Alex Orbito, and saw his bare-hand surgery at close quarters. The psychic surgeon impressed him as 'very simple, humble and pious'.

Orbito responded to Karthikeyan's 'exceptionally positive aura and spiritual energy', extending an invitation to him to attend a healing festival in Manila. Karthikeyan refused, on the grounds that he knew nothing about spiritual healing, but eventually accepted after receiving several emails telling him he would be a special guest of honour. If he had any lingering doubts about the psychic surgeon, they would certainly have been dispelled by one of the delegates he was introduced to on his arrival at the festival.

Fidel Valdez Ramos, the military hero of the 1986 People Power Revolution that toppled Ferdinand Marcos' dictatorship and who went on to be the president of the Philippines from 1992 to 1998, is one of Alex Orbito's staunchest supporters. He had served under Marcos as head of the Philippine Constabulary, the country's national police force, so he would have had much in common with D.R. Karthikeyan when the two men met in Manila. An invitation for the psychic surgeon to demonstrate his powers in four Indian cities soon followed.

Controversy accompanies Alex Orbito wherever he goes, and his four-city visit to India in 2002 was no exception. He spent two days in Mumbai where, according to journalist Sudeshna Chatterjee, those who received treatment reported they 'just feel a prick, a light floating feeling and a gush of energy emanating from the doctor who performs the surgery'. Then Orbito moved on to Bangalore where, according to another reporter, N. Bhanutej, he addressed 'a massive gathering of Bangalore's elite where he was introduced in terms reserved for gods'. D.R. Karthikeyan told the gathering that, as an investigator, he had initially been sceptical but after going to the Philippines and undergoing surgery himself he was convinced. One of the organisers of the event, incidentally, was a surgeon at Bangalore's Victoria Hospital, Dr Ramesh Mahadev Tambat. The report, in the *Week* (8 September 2002) continued:

Orbito was invited to perform his psychic surgery at the Vidhana Soudha, the seat of government, where several ministers and legislators lay down on his surgery table. The rush of politicians and the photographs of them being 'operated' upon by Orbito's bare hands completed the publicity campaign. The next two days, Orbito went on to perform his surgery on about 150 patients ... at the healing camp that was organised at Le Meridian Hotel .... Orbito apparently removes 'negativities' from the body by plunging his hands inside the abdomen. The negativities materialise as bloody clots, which he disposes into a trashcan. The operation lasts less than two minutes. The 'blood' is wiped off with tissue paper. Several retired judges, serving bureaucrats, doctors and lawyers were convinced that they were seeing a miracle.

But the journalist did not agree, as was indicated by the headline on his report: 'Filipino Psychic Takes Indians for a Ride'. That verdict was based in part on the experiences of Amita Sharma, 38, the mother of three daughters who was dying of cancer. She had surgery for breast cancer in 1998. Three years later, cancer had spread to the liver and then the hip bones. Her husband, Satish Chandra Sharma, a cardiovascular and thoracic surgeon, knew that Orbito was her last chance of a miracle. So many wanted to be treated by the Filipino psychic surgeon, however, that the Sharmas were originally declined. The intervention of an industrialist friend, Chandrashekara Raju, who is blind, saved the day. He gave free accommodation to Orbito's assistants in his four-star The Chancery Hotel in return for being put on the waiting list with Amita. There were chaotic scenes as people waited for treatment while politicians were ushered in to be operated on immediately.

Meanwhile, a lawyer had filed a public interest litigation before the High Court, pleading that Orbito be restrained from performing psychic surgeries. The court decided that the state health department should study the surgery and report back, and its principal secretary, A.K.M. Nayak, arrived with a team of officials to investigate. They were hardly made welcome, and their opportunities to ask penetrating questions or get up close to the action virtually evaporated when medical education minister A.B. Maalakaraddy came for treatment, as did former home minister P.G.R. Sindhia, who is the Janata Dal (United) floor leader in the legislative Assembly. The bureaucrats had to bow to the wishes of the politicians.

Also present was Bangalore's police commissioner H.T. Sangliana, who was challenged to stop the event by Dr P. Janardhana Rao, chairman of the anti-quackery committee of the Indian Medical Association's Karnataka branch. He replied: 'Everyone seems to be happy except you. It is a matter of faith and divine power.' Then, according to the newspaper report, Sangliana also had a session with Orbito and announced that the pain in his waist had gone. Dr Hanume Gowda, registrar of the Karnataka Ayurveda Board and the only officer appointed by the government to identify and prosecute quacks, was also at the Bangalore event and he rushed to the Director-General of Police, V.V. Bhaskar, and asked him to arrest the Filipino psychic surgeon. That, he was told, was the police commissioner's responsibility. But Sangliana would not hear of it. 'Orbito has never claimed to be a medical man,' he responded. 'He has the prefix 'Reverend' and not 'Doctor' attached to his name. Therefore, he cannot be arrested for quackery.' (His title, incidentally, comes from being a Philippines Christian Spiritualist Movement minister.)

It seems there were many people present who were very pleased to be treated and who, presumably, benefited. Amita Sharma and blind industrialist Chandrashekara Raju were not among them, even though they were both operated on by Orbito. When Amita returned to the hospital for an MRI (magnetic resonance imaging) scan it revealed that she still had a tumour and its size had not changed. And Raju is still blind. India's health minister Kagodu Thimmappa was soon declaring the Filipino psychic surgeon a fake and, having received the report it commissioned from the health department, the High Court ordered Orbito's arrest.

By then, however, Orbito had left India and returned to his Pyramid of Asia healing centre in Pangasinan, an extraordinary recently built, scaled down version of the Great Pyramid of Giza, which Fidel Ramos, the former Philippines president, inaugurated in 1999. To make the grand opening a momentous event, said a press release at the time, the pyramid would host a five-day international healing festival and seminar. Members of the Philippine Healers' Circle, of which Alex Orbito is president, would complement a foreign contingent of specialists, conducting bare-handed surgery, magnetic healing, tooth extraction, boiling oil therapy, spiritual readings, crystal healing, pranic applications, bone setting and psychic consultations.

Confused? Join the club

If, after reading the story of Alex Orbito, you are totally confused, you are not alone. I know individuals who have stood within inches of patients having psychic operations and they still do not know whether to believe the evidence of their own eyes – and rightly so. Magicians earn good livings by apparently performing miracles, and most of us cannot see how they do their tricks. We're not supposed to. Perhaps psychic surgery is no more than a trick. Before I deal with that question, let me tell you a little more about this fascinating subject.

Healers of the Philippines

I first heard about psychic surgery when an illustrated manuscript called 'Wonder' Healers of the Philippines by Harold Sherman arrived at Psychic News in the 1970s. Maurice Barbanell decided to publish a UK edition and I was asked to edit it. It was a fascinating eyewitness account of operations conducted by a number of psychic surgeons, but principally by Antonio (Tony) Agpaoa. Sherman was careful to make his readers aware of the suspicion of fraud that had been raised by some observers, but he also offered compelling evidence that many people were cured by psychic operations.

Such books, as well as TV documentaries, had turned psychic

surgery into an international tourist opportunity, and Tony Agpaoa was not alone in making a lot of money from his abilities. As well as treating the sick, he ran his own travel agency, Diplomat Tours, which organised groups from Europe, North America, Japan, Australia and New Zealand. Agpaoa also decided to demonstrate his powers in the United States in 1967, only to be indicted for fraud in connection with psychic surgery. He forfeited a $25,000 bond when he jumped bail and headed back to the safety of his home country.

The Philippines Medical Association and the government denounced Agpaoa as a fraud and a charlatan, but that did not prevent thousands of Filipinos and overseas visitors continuing to flock to his home in Baguio City, 250 kilometres northwest of Manila, which is where most of the psychic surgeons are based. But when Agpaoa was sick he consulted doctors in Baguio, rather than fellow healers. He even had his appendix removed in a San Francisco hospital and took his son to the United States for treatment, but the boy died. Tony Agpaoa himself died from a stroke in 1982.

Probably the most famous Filipino psychic surgeon today – of the 400 who are believed to be practising – is Ramon (more commonly known as Jun) Labo, a colourful character with a large ego who, according to one report, was briefly incarcerated in Russia in 1998 after one of his patients there lodged a complaint against him. It is possible that Andy Kaufman, the comic actor who played Latka Gravas in the television sitcom *Taxi*, might have sought his incarceration, too – had he lived.

Kaufman went to the Philippines in June 1984 after being diagnosed with terminal lung cancer. His journey led to the door of Jun Labo, who duly performed psychic surgery. I have seen pictures of the operation, which show what appear to be copious amounts of blood as well as tissue being removed from the actor's chest. He returned to Los Angeles expecting to be told that the cancer had been eradicated, but hospital X-rays showed no surgery had been performed and Kaufman died two months later.

Such reports have not, apparently, harmed Jun Labo's reputation. As well as being a much sought-after psychic surgeon, he has twice been elected mayor of Baguio City. The first two-year term came to an end when his Filipino citizenship was questioned and he was accused of adopting and retaining his second wife's Australian citizenship after marrying her. He was eventually reinstated as a Filipino citizen by the Supreme Court and was elected again as Baguio City mayor. Right now (April 2004) he is standing as vice mayor of Baguio in the city's forthcoming elections.

Australian tennis star and Wimbledon champion Tony Roche is another celebrity who turned to psychic surgery for help. It was for nothing more than a sore tendon – though for a professional tennis player that's pretty serious – but Placido Palitayan, another Baguio City healer who has been practising for 40 years, managed to cure the problem. During a visit to the United States in 1989, however, Placido Palitayan was arrested in Oregon and exposed as a fake. He was using cow organs to simulate the removal of human parts from his patients.

The extent of the problem with psychic surgery was well known 30 years ago when, in 1974, Donald F. Wright and Carol Wright were among 48 witnesses who testified before a US Federal Trade Commission (FTC) hearing in Seattle investigating travel agents promoting tours to visit Filipino healers. The Wrights, from Iowa, were into magnetic healing, and travelled to the Philippines a year earlier to study psychic surgery. They became convinced that what they saw was not surgery but trickery, and were eventually taught by their surgeon how to shop for animal parts, how to hide them and how to transfer them onto the patient. The FTC's four-year review concluded that it 'could find no evidence that psychic surgery was effective'.

At the time when the Wrights were visiting the Philippines, a Minnesota surgeon, Dr William A. Nolen, was also there, seeking personal experience of psychic surgery because he believed the American Medical Association was wrong not to investigate the subject. In the book he wrote about his exploits[2] he says he made a 'very sincere effort not to prejudge the merits of psychic surgeons' he saw during his investigation. He even underwent surgery at the hands of Jose Mercado and Placido Palitayan.

Among the tricks he observed were an 'appendix' removed by Josephine Sison that turned out to be a wad of cotton; a 'hysterectomy' conducted by Jose Mercado in which the uterus consisted of chicken intestines; and the removal of an eye of Joaquin Cunanan, a retired businessman who promoted psychic surgery, by Juan Flores, which was accomplished by means of a dog's eye which the healer produced at the right moment. A 'tumour' Mercado apparently removed from the American surgeon proved to be 'clumps of fat soaked in a reddish liquid that was said to be blood'. Dr Nolen observes:

> *I've done about 6,000 operations. I've taken out lungs, gallbladders, appendices, uteruses and various other organs. I've operated on the head, the neck, the chest, the abdomen and the extremities. I've had my hand inside all the cavities of the body. I know quite a lot about surgery, and when I watch someone operate, I'm able to evaluate what he is doing. This is the background that most others lack who have observed and been treated by psychic surgeons. And as I learned over and over again during my two weeks in the Philippines, it's almost essential to have experience as a surgeon to appraise the psychic surgeons with accuracy. If you haven't done or watched many operations – if you haven't seen a lot of blood – you can easily be fooled.*

Psychic surgery in Britain

Psychic surgery was something that seemed to happen only in other countries and I was not expecting to have an opportunity to witness it for myself in Britain. But in 1966 it arrived, in London, in the tall, wiry form of Lourival de Freitas, who called into the *Psychic News* offices unannounced with a translator. Editor

Maurice Barbanell asked my colleague Anne Dooley to interview them.

The Brazilian psychic surgeon agreed to give a demonstration of his powers at the Spiritualist Association of Great Britain's headquarters in London's Belgravia, and I was given the task of reporting it. I also made an 8mm film of the event, which was one of the most bizarre I have ever encountered. The cream of Britain's healers was there to witness psychic surgery for the first time, including Harry Edwards, George Chapman and Gordon Turner. Maurice Barbanell also managed to find a couple of 'volunteers' to be operated on. One was a man who was dying of stomach cancer but was not aware that his illness was terminal. Another was the wife of Marcel Poncin, a famous psychic artist.

As it transpired, they were the only two to have 'surgery' because Lourival de Freitas' theatrical performance took up most of the time allocated. He was soon entranced by Nero, the emperor of ill-repute – his chief spirit guide – puffing on cigarettes, playing a guitar and singing, and (though apparently a teetotaller in his normal state) downing neat whisky straight from a bottle, which appeared to have no effect on him, except to deepen the trance state.

The operation on the man with stomach cancer involved shoving cotton wool on the end of scissors into his mouth, making him retch and producing a lump of gristly matter that he spat into a bowl. Meanwhile Mrs Poncin had a sharp wooden-handled knife, which I had bought from Woolworth's along with other accessories, pushed under her eyelid. When the entranced medium removed it, a small object on the end was dropped into a glass of water. It was said to be a cataract.

The bizarre, stomach-turning but strangely entertaining proceedings were finally brought to an end when, annoyed by something, the entranced de Freitas threw the knife across the room and it buried itself in the wood panelling above the heads of the distinguished but horrified observers. Sadly, the man with cancer passed away a few weeks later, and when Mrs Poncin had her eyes checked the ophthalmologist confirmed what she already knew: there was no change in her vision.

As for most of those present, this confirmed my worst fears about Lourival de Freitas' 'psychic surgery'. But Anne Dooley had meanwhile interviewed others who were sure they had witnessed him performing genuine surgery and she decided to journey to Brazil to find out more, and maybe have an operation to alleviate the inoperable bronchiectasis from which she had suffered for years. In her fascinating book,[3] which contains graphic photographs of her operation and a gruesome account that should be enough to put off most people from following in her footsteps, Anne told not only of the benefit she received but describes other operations she witnessed which indicate that something paranormal certainly occurred.

Strange events in Brazil

José Arigo

The story of the most famous Brazilian psychic surgeon of them all, José Arigo, suggests that there really are spirit-controlled mediums capable of carrying out complex operations. Arigo (real name José Pedro de Freitas, but no relation to Lourival) became known as the 'surgeon of the rusty knife' because he used unsterilised implements while controlled in trance by the spirit of a German doctor Dr Adolphus Fritz, who had died in 1918.[4]

Arigo was twice imprisoned for illegally practising medicine, in 1958 and 1964. His first sentence, of two and a half years, was cut short by a pardon from the Brazilian president, Juscelino Kubitschek. The reason was that Arigo had saved the life of Kubitschek's daughter after medical experts had said there was nothing more they could do for her.

José Arigo became a national hero, as well known as that

other great Brazilian, the footballer Pelé. There was usually a queue of 200 people waiting to see him when he opened his surgery in Congonhas do Campo at 7 am each morning. Treatment was swift and sometimes even brutal, although few people felt pain and there was little blood. Not everyone had psychic surgery; Dr Fritz wrote rapid prescriptions for many of them, sometimes without even asking about their symptoms. 'I simply listen to a voice in my right ear and report whatever it says,' he explained. 'It is always right.'

Both the medium and the spirit control willingly co-operated with investigation teams. One of the most impressive testimonies I have heard came from Dr Andrija Puharich, whom I interviewed in London in the 1970s. He told me he was so impressed with what he witnessed on a personal visit to José Arigo that he returned with a team of doctors between 1963 and 1968, when he was a senior medical researcher at New York University, to investigate and film the phenomenon. Writing about the experience later, he said:

These people step up – they're all sick. One had a big goitre. Arigo just picked up a paring knife, cut it open, popped the goitre out, slapped it in her hand, wiped the opening with a piece of dirty cotton, and off she went. It hardly bled.

Psychic surgery captured on film

Thousands of operations were performed in an environment that he likened to a train station in the rush hour. Recalling what happened next, Puharich rolled up the sleeve of his right arm and pointed to an area near his elbow. For seven years, he told me, there had been a lipoma there – a lipoma is a small, fatty tumour that rolls around freely under the skin when it is examined. He had it checked regularly and his doctor advised him not to have it removed because it was directly over the ulnar nerve, which controls the movement of the hand, and also close to the brachial artery. There was a small risk that either of these might be damaged in the otherwise simple, 20-minute operation that would be required to remove it, and if this happened it might affect his finger control.

Puharich decided to ask the Brazilian psychic surgeon to remove the lipoma. José Arigo asked someone for a pocket knife, told Puharich to look away and in front of 90 witnesses and under the watchful gaze of the film camera, made two incisions with the knife. The skin split wide open, revealing the tumour, which the psychic surgeon squeezed out as one would deal with a boil. The whole procedure took five seconds. Puharich was able to take it back for analysis, together with a film record of the operation, and he confirmed that his finger control was unaffected.

I have watched a film of José Arigo operating on patients and can confidently say that sleight of hand trickery did not form any part of the surgery I witnessed. Whereas the bare-hand surgeons use no instruments, giving rise to suggestions that they or their assistants hide pouches of animal blood and body parts, Arigo quite clearly used any sharp instrument available to lance abscesses, make incisions to remove tumours and generally prod around inside and outside the patients' bodies. It is said that when Arigo saw a film of himself doing these operations he fainted.

Although José Arigo died in a car crash in 1971, Dr Fritz apparently lives on, working through Rio de Janeiro medium Rubens Faria. There are some excellent accounts of his healing work, but the British *Guardian* newspaper reported (2 February 1999) that he is 'under investigation for murder, tax evasion, charlatanism and money laundering', though I have not read anything since to support that claim.

Another Brazilian psychic surgeon said to have incredible powers is Joao Teixeria de Faria, known to his followers as John of God. It is claimed that he performs more operations in 24 hours than a small hospital achieves in a month. The president of Peru is said to have awarded him a medal of honour in gratitude for healing his son.

Against these impressive reports we must also balance stories of people travelling thousands of miles to see such psychic surgeons, only to be bitterly disappointed not only by the experience and treatment, but also by the lack of any benefit to their health. In some cases sick patients may even refuse conventional medical treatment in the belief that psychic surgery will cure them – and then when they discover it has failed, it is too late.

Sleight of hand?

So how do we equate the varying reports on psychic surgery? It's not easy, and any attempt to do so is likely to sound like wild rationalisation. But to do justice to the subject there are a couple of observations I must make. The first relates to patients' needs. In the West, it seems, we can accept the concept of the laying on of hands to allow healing to flow into our bodies. In other cultures, such as Brazil and the Philippines, patients need to witness something far more tangible, preferably with blood. Unless they see the cause of their illness being physically plucked from their bodies, they will not believe they have been cured. Since belief, as we will see shortly, does have an influence on the result, psychic surgery reinforces it. Seeing, as they say, is believing.

Tony Agpaoa is reported to have explained: 'I merely plant the seed with my surgery. The patient's mind does the rest.' So what is removed from the patient may not be a diseased organ at all. It is even suggested that psychic surgeons may have the ability to materialise blood and flesh to stage these performances, so that what we see is truly paranormal but not what it purports to be. In which case, why have so many of them been caught using animal parts?

The answer is that those particular 'psychic surgeons' do not have the ability to materialise, but they do have healing powers, so they use props – animal blood, etc – in order to bolster their patients' belief in the healing and make it more effective. But different cultures have different beliefs. Many Filipinos are convinced their illnesses are caused by evil spirits putting foreign objects into them. So the psychic surgeons often 'remove' objects such as pieces of tin foil, coins, a chicken's foot or other unlikely objects. That would not impress Westerners, so for them the psychic surgeons imitate more orthodox, medical-type operations.

Mind over matter

We must not overlook the well-documented placebo (mind over matter) effect, either. Harvey J. Martin III, author of several books on Philippines Spiritualism, deals with this in some depth in an essay titled, 'Unravelling the Enigma of Psychic Surgery'. In the 1950s, he tells us, several American doctors conducted an experiment to determine the merits of surgical procedure for angina pectoris.

In the experiment, three of five patients received the operation. The other two were merely placed under anaesthesia and given a surface incision, which was then sutured. Once awakened, the five patients were monitored during their recovery from the operation. To the amazement of the physicians, a significant percentage of the patients who had received placebo operations were cured.

In 1961, he adds, Dr Henry Beecher reviewed two double-blind studies of the placebo operations which convincingly demonstrated that the actual operation produced no greater benefit than the placebo operation. In a separate study, conducted by Dr Leonard Cobb and his associates, placebo surgery proved to be *more* effective than the real thing. They found 43 per cent of the patients who received placebo surgery reported both subjective and objective improvement. In the patients who had received the real operation, only 32 per cent reported satisfactory results.

'What this research established,' Martin adds, 'is that the mere form (metaphor) of surgical procedures can produce the same results as the actual surgical procedures.'

This, perhaps, is what psychic healers of the Philippines, or their spirit guides, realised long before Western medicine began exploring the possibility: it's a combination of sleight of hand and sleight of mind.

The question of belief

Another important factor that needs our consideration is the whole question of belief. Some observers in the Philippines and Brazil have come to the conclusion that if an individual expects to see fraud, that is what he will experience. If, on the other hand, he believes in the reality of the phenomenon, he will witness genuine psychic surgery. I have problems with that theory, since it implies that the psychic surgeons have to be prepared, consciously or unconsciously, to satisfy the needs of both believers and non-believers. Logic tells me that it would be far better if all the psychic surgeons were genuine and all the sceptics were converted into believers. I examine the question of belief in greater depth in the next chapter.

So, what do I really think about psychic surgery? I am convinced that a few individuals – José Arigo in particular – have demonstrated the ability to carry out psychic operations on their patients' physical bodies, under spirit control. I am just as convinced that clever sleight of hand and the collaboration of assistants can explain the majority of such surgeries, but that trickery may not have any bearing on the healing results. My most important conclusion, however, is that there really is no need to travel halfway round the world to be poked and prodded into getting better, when there is ample evidence that the laying on of hands or other healing techniques, all readily and usually freely available in Britain, other parts of Europe, and the United States, are just as effective as psychic surgery.

1 Shirley MacLaine, *Going Within*, Bantam Press (1989).
2 Dr William Nolen, *Healing: A Doctor in Search of a Miracle*, Random House (1974).
3 Anne Dooley, *Every Wall a Door*, Abelard-Schuman (1973).
4 John Fuller, *Arigo: Surgeon of the Rusty Knife*, Thomas Y. Cromwell Company (1974).

Chapter 11

Believers and Sceptics

Beliefs play an important part in our lives, whether we realise it or not. Our cultures and upbringing shape our thinking in surprising ways. Religious and political views are often determined by what we are taught from childhood and can stay with us throughout our lives. But breaking free and thinking differently can be important stepping stones in an individual's spiritual development. Those who examine Spiritualism will notice that there are two aspects that make it very different from other belief systems.

A living religion

First, Spiritualism is not founded on a 'holy book' of scriptures written more than a thousand years ago. It is a 'living' religion which accepts that spiritual guidance continues to be given to us now, and every day, through mediumship. This is done through many teaching guides, who discuss spiritual and philosophical subjects rather than giving evidence of survival. Spiritualists can choose which ones they listen to because they are not told who or what to believe.

Freedom of interpretation

Freedom of interpretation has always been an essential part of Spiritualism and the spirit guides themselves advise people to follow only those teachings that are acceptable and reject those that are not. After all, individuals evolve and what may make no sense to someone right now may have greater significance at a later stage on their spiritual path. I deal in greater detail with religion and spirit guides in the next two chapters.

Additionally, Spiritualism is not primarily about belief. When asked 'Do you believe in Spiritualism?' many people respond with the words, 'I don't *believe*, I *know!*' By this they mean that the cornerstone of Spiritualism – communication with the next world – has been proved to them beyond a shadow of doubt.

Attitudes towards Spiritualism

There are, however, many people who, because they turn to Spiritualism in their grief at losing a loved one, allow their critical faculties to take a back seat as they grasp any morsel of evidence that life after death is a fact. Sadly, in that state of mind, they make easy victims for individuals who claim to be in touch with the next world but have no real mediumistic powers or are outright charlatans. On the other hand, there are individuals who refuse even to accept the *possibility* that life continues beyond the grave and who therefore dismiss everything associated with Spiritualism as lies, fraud or self-deception. There are also religious fanatics who insist spirit communication is wrong. Every medium is therefore a sitting target for sceptics and religious extremists.

Occasionally, when someone I meet learns that I have an interest in Spiritualism and mediumship, they respond by saying, 'Oh, I don't believe in all that.' It's a sweeping statement that has to be challenged. I therefore ask them to define what they mean by 'all that'. Usually they mention astrology, fortune-telling and tarot readings. So I tell them that none of those has anything to do with Spiritualism; that some Spiritualists may be interested in them but many others do not believe in any of them.

'Spiritualism,' I go on to explain, 'is about spirit communication – talking with the dead.'

'Oh, I don't believe in that, either,' they usually respond.

'So you have investigated it?'

'Er, no.'

'Then how can you not believe in something you have not investigated? I've taken the trouble to investigate it, and on the basis of what I have seen and experienced I believe spirit communication *does* take place.'

'I just don't believe it.'

At which point, I usually change the subject, having at least made the point that Spiritualism is about much more than belief – that it's something that can be examined and researched. Of course, if I get a different response, such as 'That's interesting, what convinced you?' I offer one or two examples of spirit communication from personal experience.

It never ceases to amaze me that so many people are dismissive of subjects about which they know nothing. They seem to assume that because they have not considered a subject worthy of their attention, there can be nothing about it worth studying. Even worse are those individuals who decide that there is no truth in certain claims, and choose to conduct a personal crusade against the subject and the people connected with it, rather than question the origins of their own beliefs. It seems that the only thing sceptics are not sceptical about is their own scepticism. What particularly annoys me about many such people is that they claim what they are doing is scientific, whereas science requires, at the very least, that they do not prejudge a phenomenon until they have studied it thoroughly.

There are a number of fallacies about Spiritualism, fraud and scepticism that I would like to dispose of at this juncture.

Fallacy 1: magicians can duplicate everything mediums do

I'm a great fan of magic and have been known to perform a few conjuring tricks to entertain family and friends. But magic has its limitations. It is true that magicians appear to be able to perform miracles, making themselves or their assistants disappear and re-appear; transforming objects, reading minds and levitating people. But when we see these things happen we know we are being deceived. So how do we know we are not being deceived by mediums? There is one major problem with that theory.

Magicians are in control: they use props, assistants, confederates and a variety of techniques to create the illusion of achieving the impossible. In Spiritualism, the sitter is usually the one in control – being able to book a sitting with a mental medium under an assumed name, for example. And in the case of physical seances, mediums usually submit to a range of controls decided by the investigators. They undergo intimate searches; allow themselves to be tied up; sometimes wear luminous bands on their hands and feet so that every movement can be seen; are wired to electrical contacts that would signal the slightest movement; take liquid into their mouths and have their lips taped; and yet still phenomena occur.

Imagine what response you would get if just before master magician David Copperfield starts to 'fly' through the air you asked if you could search him for hidden harnesses or wires. In my experience, most mediums are happy to have their medi-umship tested and to take part in experiments without any previ-ous knowledge of what will be involved. Few magicians would accept such a challenge. And don't forget that a number of famous conjurors and illusionists, having attended physical seances, have declared that what they witnessed could not have been achieved by trickery.

Fallacy 2: clairvoyance is just 'cold' or 'hot' reading

The favourite explanation sceptics put forward to 'explain' mental mediumship is that mediums use 'cold' reading methods, which means making general statements with which most people can identify, then elaborating on these once they pick up clues from the sitter's body language or verbal responses.

This theory is far more likely to be true of general psychic readings in which emotional, physical and career aspirations are discussed, than with a medium, where the sitter is looking for evidence that identifiable individuals have survived death.

An alternative theory, known as 'hot' or 'warm' reading, suggests that mediums acquire or are fed information on their sitters, available from normal sources, which then forms the basis of the reading. For over a century, parapsychologists have been well aware of such possibilities and have therefore devised tests and experiments to eliminate these possibilities, even to the extent of having one medium followed by a private detective to see if she was conniving with others to gain information – a subterfuge that exonerated her completely.

Fallacy 3: all Spiritualists are gullible

In fact, most Spiritualists, and even mediums, start out as sceptics. Our upbringing does not generally encourage us to believe that spirit communication is possible, and most of us are likely to go along with the belief that science has found no evidence for an afterlife – until we know better. So when first encountering mediumship and receiving a spirit message, the majority of people treat it with caution or disbelief – I know I did. Has the medium read my mind? Was it a lucky guess? Could the medium have known my identity? These and other doubts buzz around inside the heads of all but the most gullible of sitters. It often takes years of study, reading extensively on the subject as well as watching mediums at work and having personal experiences, for many Spiritualists to be totally convinced that they have been in touch with the spirit world.

Fallacy 4: Spiritualism is riddled with fraud

Spiritualism does attract a few heartless and unscrupulous individuals keen to make a living at the expense of grieving individuals when they are at their most vulnerable. I know, because I have encountered some of them. But the Church, medicine, police force, law and social services are similarly afflicted by people whose motives in being involved in these professions or activities are less than pure. I don't believe that fraud is more prevalent in Spiritualism than in any other walk of life, but by its very nature it does provide a 'cover' for crooks and conmen making wild claims or pretending to have special powers.

It's always best to get a personal recommendation from someone who has had good results with a medium, or to check that they belong to one of the major Spiritualist organisations and comply with its code of conduct before you part with your money.

Fallacy 5: it's always outsiders who expose frauds

Sceptics never give credit to Spiritualists for exposing most of the frauds that have been reported in the movement's history. In the eight years I worked at *Psychic News* we uncovered several frauds and were also critical of the standards of a number of other mediums. Spiritualists believe in spirit communication but that does not mean they do not continue to apply their critical faculties whenever they encounter mediumship. They are also keen for frauds to be exposed as soon as they are detected, for the good of the movement.

Just a few years before I became involved in Spiritualism, *Psychic News* and its editor, Maurice Barbanell, had exposed one of the biggest rogues in twentieth-century Spiritualism – a crook posing as a direct-voice medium who worked under the name of William Roy. He used a variety of equipment, including extension rods and earphones, which he wore under cover of darkness in the seance room, enabling accomplices to feed him with information they had gleaned from sitters who gathered in an anteroom before the seance. He denied the allegations at first, but eventually sold his story to a national newspaper, revealing the sophisticated methods he used. Later, he began operating under another name, and I believe that among those who attended those later seances were some, if not all, of the Beatles.

Let me underline the Spiritualist movement's commitment to exposing fraud by recounting another case in which I was involved. It concerns a Preston, Lancashire, 'materialisation medium' named James Gardner. I had heard some good reports of his mediumship but a few complaints as well. So when I was told he would be giving a few private seances in London I managed to make a reservation under an assumed name.

The seance was held in a private house, in a large room lit only by a small red light, and the 'medium' sat in a curtained-off cabinet in which, after a while, various 'spirits' appeared. There had been no examination of the 'medium' or the room beforehand, and the 'spirits' never ventured from the cabinet. Sitters were invited to walk up to the cabinet to talk to the 'materialised' forms, and when my turn came I was confronted by Gardner's 'spirit guide', who appeared to be the 'medium' wearing a stocking over his face and holding a large ring under his nose by curling his lip beneath it. I believe he was hoping he looked like a Zulu.

The 'guide' then said he would partially dematerialise, from the floor up. The long, flowing 'ectoplasm' that touched the floor began to rise and I could see very clearly his hands gathering it up in a ball, to give the appearance in the dimly lit room that he had only half a body, floating in the air.

At the end of the session I confronted James Gardner, told him who I was and said that when I wrote my report on the seance I would be telling readers that he had not offered any evidence of genuine mediumship. He was unhappy with my verdict and turned to his local newspaper – which carried an advertisement for his church each week – and invited a reporter and photographer to attend a materialisation seance.

He must have thought it would be easier to fool journalists who knew nothing about Spiritualism than one with a reasonable grasp of the subject. If so, his plan misfired badly. Next week, the local newspaper published a picture of a spirit who had 'dematerialised' his bottom half, just as I had seen. The headline above the picture was: 'The Spirit Who Wore Trousers'. Unfortunately for Gardner, he had not taken into account that the white flashlight would be able to see a lot more than the human eye can detect in red light.

Fallacy 6: Spiritualists always protect their own

Spiritualists feel so strongly about the need to prevent fraud that no one in the movement is above suspicion or too important to be accused of deception if there is evidence to support such charges. Gordon Higginson, who did a superb job as president of the Spiritualists' National Union (SNU) for many years, was accused on a number of occasions of looking at church records in order to acquire information that would be useful in his always impressive demonstrations of clairvoyance. He was also 'exposed' by a Sunday newspaper, which claimed he had hidden props under a chair seat at Stansted Hall, which is run by the SNU, to be used during a materialisation seance.

Higginson vigorously denied all these allegations, was cleared of most of them after thorough investigation and continued to serve Spiritualism for many years afterwards. Interestingly, he was one of those who arranged for another newspaper to expose Paul McElhoney, a young medium noted for producing 'apports' such as flowers in the seance room. A search uncovered flowers hidden in the battery compartment of a tape recorder. Even though the media has been involved in some of these exposures, it is usually Spiritualists who suspect fraud and orchestrate the unmasking or publicising of their suspicions.

Fallacy 7: sceptics' criticisms are useful

Scepticism has become the new religion. The numbers of sceptics are growing and spirit communication is just one of a wide range of targets, such as alternative therapies, religion and evolutionary theories, which they have in their sights. Are they useful? Not at all. They have become the self-appointed 'protectors' of what we should and should not believe; seeing themselves as mind police determined to stop people thinking beyond the boundaries of what they tell us is acceptable. In fact, they are not sceptics, they are opponents.

Perhaps the best-known opponent of Spiritualism at the current time is magician James Randi, who visited Britain in 2003 to participate in a pre-recorded television programme called *The Ultimate Psychic Challenge*. He was introduced to the studio audience as a psychic and proceeded to give a cold reading that was so dreadful, according to psychical researcher Montague Keen, one of the other participants, that the embarrassed studio manager stopped the recording, blaming a 'technical fault'. That part of the show was not screened.

Randi then did a 'hot' reading, using information acquired in advance by a researcher – the studio audience's names and addresses were known in advance, of course, and they were there by invitation. But neither hot nor cold reading methods could explain the single most impressive piece of evidence shared with the studio audience, but also edited out, of an anonymous and untraceable booking made by a grieving father for a private reading with medium Keith Charles, a former London policeman. He described to the sitter the detailed contents and design of a sealed letter that had been placed, unbeknown to the father, in the coffin of his daughter by her sister.

Randi's name is closely associated with the Committee for the Scientific Investigation of Claims of the Paranormal (CSICOP), a group that in my view is as narrow-minded as born-again Christians. Real scepticism is essential in examining mediumship and psychic phenomena. But CSICOP members are *not* real sceptics. They are people who have prejudged the subjects they claim to investigate, which they dismiss as 'pseudoscience'. Randi's premise is that spirit communication is not possible and therefore not only can it not be proved scientifically, but anyone claiming to be in touch with spirits must be deluded or a fraud. It is hardly surprising that few mediums are willing to co-operate with someone who is so negative about what they do.

Fallacy 8: sceptics know best

The only people who believe sceptics are right about Spiritualism and mediumship are the sceptics. It seems to be the only subject about which they are *not* sceptical. While most parapsychological organisations are having a hard time financially, CSICOP has recently opened a new headquarters in New York – a shrine to belief in nothing. I am delighted, therefore, that believers are now beginning to bite back and sceptics are increasingly coming under fire from individuals who are tired of their attempts to stifle interest in the paranormal and the spiritual.

Among the voices being raised against the sceptics is *New York Times* best-selling author Michael Prescott, whose first novel was *Comes the Dark* and whose latest is *In Dark Places*.

Michael Prescott

Prescott confesses that he was once 'a full-fledged sceptic, atheist and rationalist' who read and enjoyed James Randi's 1980 book *Flim-Flam*,[1] 'which reinforced my belief system at the time'. But, 20 years later, he read the book again – 'having changed my mind about many things' – and responded very differently.

He was particularly struck by the book's 'tedious nastiness' and its 'hectoring, sarcastic tone', in which psychical

---

researchers are depicted as medieval fools. Michael Prescott therefore decided to check on a few of Randi's claims in detail. His findings are too long to include here but can be found on his website (http://michaelprescott.freeservers.com/), together with Randi's responses. But let me give you a simple example which demonstrates Randi's criticism. In Chapter 8 of his book, he deals with the psychic experiments of two well-known parapsychologists, Russell Targ and Harold Puthoff, describing them as 'the Laurel and Hardy of psi' and arguing that their experiments were a tissue of ineptitude, gullibility and dishonesty. This is how Michael Prescott responds to that:

> The first thing I noticed was that Randi never gives any indication that Targ and Puthoff have any scientific credentials or accomplishments. The casual reader could be forgiven for assuming that they are not 'real' scientists at all. For the record, Targ is a physicist credited with inventing the FM laser, the high-power gas-transport laser, and the tunable plasma oscillator. Puthoff, also a physicist, invented the tunable infrared laser and is widely known for his theoretical work on quantum vacuum states and the zero point field... If these two are 'Laurel and Hardy', at least they come with good résumés. Randi, by contrast, has no scientific training.

How did Randi respond to that point? 'No, I did not specify the scientific credentials of Targ and Puthoff,' he replied. 'They were laser scientists, which does not serve as any validation of their scientific – or other – ability to witness these matters.' Why wasn't Randi prepared to let his readers decide the relevance of that information when he wrote his book? In my view it was because it would have diminished the case he was trying to make against the two scientists. He would, however, have been quick to pounce on such an omission if a Spiritualist or medium had been so selective in presenting data.

To those who believe that sceptics are making a vital contribution by trying to eradicate belief in the paranormal, I would quote the words of Francis Bacon: 'Let the mind be enlarged ... to the grandeur of the mysteries, and not the mysteries contracted to the narrowness of the mind.'

Fallacy 9: Spiritualism is in decline

Sceptics have been predicting the demise of Spiritualism for decades. Its growth after the First and Second World Wars was naturally attributed to the huge number of deaths in combat. During a relatively peaceful period of history, however, Spiritualism continues to thrive. Televised mediumship is making more people aware of spiritual realities and, although organised religion is on the decline, belief in the paranormal, according to opinion polls, is increasing. I particularly like the observation made by Dean Radin in his book *The Conscious Universe: The Scientific Truth of Psychic Phenomena*,[2] which sheds light on the way beliefs change:

In science, the acceptance of new ideas follows a predictable, four-stage sequence. In Stage 1, sceptics confidently proclaim that the idea is impossible because it violates the Laws of Science. This stage can last for years or for centuries, depending on how much the idea challenges conventional wisdom. In Stage 2, sceptics reluctantly concede that the idea is possible but that it is not very interesting and the claimed effects are extremely weak. Stage 3 begins when the mainstream realises not only that the idea is important but that its effects are much stronger and more pervasive than previously imagined. Stage 4 is achieved when the same critics who previously disavowed any interest in the idea begin to proclaim that they thought of it first. Eventually, no one remembers that the idea was once considered a dangerous heresy.

A quantum leap

Spiritualism is a comparatively new religion, being just over 150 years old, and its image and organisation will almost certainly change in the years ahead. But the spiritual realities it embodies will continue long after the words of the most vociferous sceptics are forgotten.

We should also not lose sight of the fact that while sceptics are encouraging us to regard the paranormal as 'pseudoscience' not worthy of study, science itself is taking us into areas that make the claims of Spiritualism look positively tame. Winston Wu, a Taiwanese researcher, has written an excellent paper called 'Debunking the Sceptics' in which he observes:

> In fact, new discoveries in quantum physics each year are shattering the materialistic reductionist view we had of the universe, making psychic phenomena and other dimensions more plausible. These include the non-locality (meaning distance and space do not exist) of twin particles (discovered by Alan Aspect in 1982), string theories that postulate several other dimensions beside our own, the discovery that particles behave differently when observed (making psychokinesis more probable), etc. Each new discovery seems to prove the sceptics wrong and moves us further from their views and closer to metaphysical paradigms.

The experimenter effect

In fact, what we believe may have a far greater impact on things around us than we previously imagined. For many years, parapsychologists studying extrasensory perception (ESP) and other psychic phenomena in the laboratory have been getting conflicting results. Like all scientists, what they are looking for is replicability. When an experimenter devises a test that gives positive results, he or she hopes that other researchers will confirm the findings by producing similar results. But that was not happening. Some individuals were getting above-chance results consistently over long series of tests, while others, apparently conducting the same experiments under the same conditions, were not producing results of any significance.

This seemed to point to what became known as 'the experimenter effect', dividing the field of parapsychology into believers and sceptics, for it became clear that the researchers who were getting significant results believed psychic phenomena were possible, whereas those with negative or chance results were sceptical of such phenomena. Some believers even suggested that the experimenter effect in itself was evidence of a psychic phenomenon. Sceptics, on the other hand, though not suggesting fraud, argued that perhaps the researchers who believed were more lax in their controls than the sceptics.

The experimenter effect has now become a hot topic following a series of experiments conducted in the UK by arch sceptic Professor Richard Wiseman at the University of Hertfordshire and in the US by a believer in psi, Dr Marilyn Schlitz of the Institute of Noetic Sciences in Petaluma, California. The experiments involved checking subjects for physiological evidence that they were being stared at via a closed circuit television link.

Predictably, Wiseman's tests were not significant, but Schlitz's were consistently 'on the knife edge' of significance. Could differences in the two laboratories or the human subjects they used account for this? To eliminate those possibilities, the two parapsychologists and others are now trying to modify their experimental protocols in an attempt to isolate the reason for this remarkable finding.

If it can be shown scientifically that belief in something can make it happen, and that scepticism can help repress it, then scientists everywhere may need to re-evaluate their studies on a whole range of subjects, not just the paranormal. Individuals who attend seances will also be encouraged to set aside their scepticism and believe that spirit communication is possible if they want to increase their chances of getting messages from their loved ones in the next world.

1 James Randi, *Flim-Flam*, Prometheus Books (1982).
2 Dean Radin, *The Conscious Universe: The Scientific Truth of Psychic Phenomena*, HarperSanFrancisco (1997).

Chapter 12

Spiritualism as a Religion

Guided by Spirits

Ask anyone what religion they associate with spirit communication and the answer you are most likely to get is Spiritualism. And yet, as we will see, spirit communication has inspired other world religions. Let us begin, however, with Spiritualism – one of the newest world religions – whose humble origins just over 150 years ago I discussed earlier. It has no 'holy' book on which its teachings are based, nor does it have a single spiritual leader. But it does have Seven Principles to which most Spiritualists subscribe, whether they are 'ordinary' Spiritualists or those who are associated with other variations, such as Christian Spiritualism and Spiritism. Spiritualism's Seven Principles are:

- The Fatherhood of God
- The Brotherhood of Man
- The Communion of Spirits and the Ministry of Angels
- The continuous existence of the human soul
- Personal responsibility
- Compensation and retribution hereafter for all the good and evil deeds done on earth
- Eternal progress open to every human soul

These simple guidelines for everyday living were received, appropriately enough, through a medium – the remarkable Emma

Hardinge Britten (1823–99), a British psychic, inspirational speaker and writer who also founded the Spiritualist publication *Two Worlds*. Spiritualists tend to view God not as a person but as a universal force or energy, and so terms such as 'Supreme Being' or 'Great Spirit' are more likely to be heard in a Spiritualist church than the word 'God'. The other important element of its beliefs is that we do not become spirits when we die, but are spirits already, clothed in a physical body.

Spirit communication plays an important part in almost every Spiritualist service. It is also accepted that we each have a guardian angel – or spirit guide – who watches over us and attempts to help us, if we choose to listen. Although many Spiritualists do not like or use the term 'karma', they accept that we each have personal responsibility for our actions, and that we will suffer or be rewarded for these in either this world or the next.

The numbers of Spiritualists

Calculating how many Spiritualists there are in the world is difficult since many do not become members of the churches they occasionally attend. They may decide, once they have encountered Spiritualism and received evidence for survival of death, that there is no longer any need to visit a Spiritualist church. Many millions who have watched televised demonstrations of mediumship may also have become convinced of spirit communication without feeling the need to attend a church. Spiritualism itself does not make worship at one of its churches a religious necessity. We *all* survive death, whatever religion we follow, and attending church services should make no difference to the conditions we find ourselves in when we get to the next world. What matters is how we live our lives now and how we treat our fellow human beings.

Having said that, I can report that there are an estimated 120,000 Spiritualists in the United States and 50,000 in the United Kingdom, both of which follow a similar form of Spiritualism.

Those figures are, however, based on people who actually belong to church congregations and attend regularly. In reality, the real numbers are probably twice as high. Robert Egby, who produces the monthly *Parapsychic Journal*, tells me that when she was touring the United States in around 1870, Emma Hardinge Britten reported there were an estimated ten million Spiritualists in that country. 'If anyone were to do a survey today,' he adds, 'I think there are many more millions who believe the Spiritualist way.' Of the various organisations in both countries, the National Spiritualist Association of Churches has 133 churches in the United States and the Spiritualists' National Union in the United Kingdom has 368 affiliated churches. But there are also Christian Spiritualist and other organisations in both countries that follow Spiritualist teachings but with a special focus. In the US, there are around 16 different Spiritualist organisations and in the UK the number is probably seven, though there are numerous independent societies satisfying local needs. The International Spiritualist Federation (ISF) is a UK-based organisation with 600 members in 26 countries, as well as 20 affiliated spiritual groups. The largest numbers of its members are in the UK, the US and Finland.

As well as Spiritualist churches, there are also Spiritualist camps – a uniquely American phenomenon – the most famous of which is Lily Dale, where 30,000 people consult mediums each year. Situated 60 miles south of Buffalo in New York State, this unique development on Lake Cassadaga stands within the town of Pomfret and is now the permanent home of many Spiritualists. In fact, only Spiritualists are allowed to buy a home in the 167-acre gated membership community. Founded as a summer camp in 1879 at the suggestion of a spirit communication – which makes it 'the world's oldest and largest community of Spiritualists' – it quickly evolved as a focal point of American Spiritualism and today is also home to the headquarters of the National Spiritualist Association of Churches, which was established 14 years after Lily Dale came into being. Over the decades it has experienced its fair share of scandals, being duped by unscrupulous frauds. Famous escapologist and illusionist Harry Houdini even turned up to expose one of them. Today, Lily Dale's management is more circumspect about the types of mediumship that can be demonstrated with the result that only 36 mediums are currently registered to work there and physical seances are banned. But despite this it still attracts the big names. Recent years have seen Deepak Chopra, John Edward and James Van Praagh taking centre stage.

A fascinating book about Lily Dale, past and present, has been written by journalist Christine Wicker, who was a reporter with the *Dallas Morning News* for 17 years before going freelance. In the pages of *Lily Dale: the true story of the town that talks to the dead*[1], we meet not only the mediums who keep Lily Dale alive but also some of the visitors who testify to the benefits they derive from their sessions. It's a very human and often hilarious chronicle of a major landmark for thousands of enquirers seeking proof of life after death.

The growth of Spiritism

Another form of Spiritualism – known as Spiritism – has grown rapidly in South America and in Europe and is now beginning to make an impact in the United States. According to the excellent Internet website Adherents.com, Spiritism stands at number 14 in the 'top 20' world religions, with 14 million followers. It says that whereas the 1997 *Encyclopedia Britannica Book of the Year* gave the world total of Spiritist adherents as 10,292,500, a recent poll from Brazil alone indicates '15 million professed Spiritists', as well as a fringe following of up to 50 million, which it describes as 'not officially professed but possibly quite avid'. They combine Spiritualist practices with beliefs drawn from other sources, including Roman Catholicism.

Adherents.com believes a fair estimate of worldwide Spiritists is 20 million, which makes it a larger religion than Judaism, with

14 million adherents, but much smaller than Buddhism (360 million), Hinduism (900 million), Islam (1.3 billion) and Christianity (two billion).

Spiritism in Europe, but also in South America, is largely influenced by the work of H. Leon Denizard Rivail, better known by the *nom de plume* Allan Kardec. Born in Lyon, France, in 1804, he was an impressive intellectual who taught many subjects and ran free courses for the underprivileged. At the age of 50 – just six years after the birth of Spiritualism – he learned of the growing interest in the paranormal that was sweeping the United States and Europe and, though sceptical, was persuaded by friends to investigate.

Kardec satisfied himself of the genuineness of the phenomena he witnessed, then set about submitting questions to different mediums in various countries. He compared, analysed and organised the responses of these spirits, whose replies showed a remarkable consistency, and published them in book form. The best known of the books is *The Spirits' Book*,[2] first published in 1857, which contains answers to 1,000 questions on God, creation, the universe, the spirit world and much more besides. Where its teachings differ from mainstream Spiritualism is in advocating reincarnation. Let me give you a flavour of his work by quoting just one question and answer from it:

Has matter existed from all eternity, like God, or has it been created at some definite period of time?

God only knows. There is, nevertheless, one point which your reason should suffice to show you, namely, that God, the prototype of love and beneficence, can never have been inactive. However far off in the past you may imagine the beginning of His action, can you suppose Him to have been for a single moment inactive?

Other books compiled by Kardec include *The Book of Mediums*, *The Gospel – Explained by the Spiritist Doctrine*, *Christian Spiritism*, *Heaven and Hell* and *Genesis*.

Spiritism in the US

Indicative of the impact that Spiritism is having in the US is the fact that there are some 22 Spiritist centres in the state of Florida alone, the majority being on the east coast. Yvonne Limoges of The Spiritist Society of Florida, who has an extensive knowledge of the Spiritist movement worldwide, tells me that her organisation is a member of the Florida Spiritist Federation, and that although meetings are held in English, they also speak Portuguese and Spanish. Florida clearly has the lion's share in terms of centres, since Limoges puts the total of officially listed centres in the US at 66, though she points out that there are also many independents. There are also two international bodies within the Spiritist movement: the International Spiritist Council (ISC), which was founded in 1992, and the Brazilian Spiritist Federation (FEB), which has been in existence for 120 years. Angola, Poland, Italy, Japan and Sweden are among the 28 countries with centres that belong to the ISC. In addition, the Pan-American Spiritist Confederation (CEPA) has a membership that extends to 12 countries, including the US, South America, Cuba, France and Spain.

Differences between Spiritualism and Spiritism

Most Spiritualists believe that the only difference between their beliefs and those of Spiritism is that reincarnation is a cornerstone of the latter's teachings. But Lionel Owen, a former International Spiritualist Federation president, has discovered that there are many other differences. During his long association with the ISF, Owen became very familiar with Spiritualism in Europe and other parts of the world. Then, two years ago, he moved from the UK to Orlando, Florida, and within six months decided to relocate to Rio de Janeiro with his new Brazilian wife. He was amazed at the size of the congregation attending a Spiritist meeting in Rio. Several hundred turned up to hear what was, in essence, a lecture on astrology. In the even larger centres in Rio and São Paulo, they number their congregations in the thousands.

Writing about the differences between Spiritualism and Spiritism (*Psychic News*, 1 May 2004) he reports:

> Spiritualism is virtually unheard of in Brazil. There are one or two small centres, but the overwhelming number of centres and churches are Spiritist. Spiritism has many similarities to Spiritualism, but there are marked differences also....
>
> [About three years ago] Spiritists codified [Kardec's] works, which I think means they are no longer allowed to accept teachings about the spirit world and mediumship other than those of Kardec, plus any received through their own trance mediums. The focus on trance mediumship is not hard to understand because Kardec received all the information for his books through trance mediums....
>
> You will find no public demonstrations of mediumship in Spiritist churches or centres. These are reserved for members only at private seances which, I believe, consist mostly of trance mediumship.

Owen added that many Spiritists 'believe clairvoyants are in contact only with the dark side of the spirit world or else with "mischievous spirits".' As someone brought up on a diet of British Spiritualism, with its emphasis on evidence and proof, Owen finds this attitude towards public demonstration and private sittings 'very difficult to accept'. But he pays tribute to the tremendous work Spiritism does in Brazil to help people living in poverty and to give healing to the socially disadvantaged.

Spirit-inspired Christianity

Religious teachings are open to interpretation, or misinterpretation, which has been a cause not only of schisms in all the major religions but also to wars and untold bloodshed. It is possible to find in the Bible or the Koran a solitary sentence to support almost any argument, and there are many who have done that to justify their beliefs and their violent or cruel actions.

Most Spiritualists take the view that the Great Spirit sends His messengers to enlighten humanity and teach spiritual and moral concepts that are essential in a physical world. Christian Spiritualists follow the leadership of Jesus Christ, but other Spiritualists see Jesus, Buddha, Mohammed and other prophets of long ago as of equal status, each playing an important role in the spiritual development of the human race. What made them different to other men, as far as Spiritualists are concerned, is that they were all mediums, or channels, for divine guidance. This is a view shared by some Christian clergymen and is sometimes expressed through the publications and at the conferences of the Churches' Fellowship for Psychical and Spiritual Studies, which was founded over 50 years ago and whose *Study Notes* include 'Paranormal Experiences', 'Psychical Studies and the Bible', 'Communication and Mediumship' and 'Healing'.

Incidentally, I was delighted to learn that Canon Michael Perry was one of five recipients of the Lambeth Degree, an annual academic award that was decided by and presented to him by the Archbishop of Canterbury, Dr Rowan Williams, on 6 October 2003. The award recognises Canon Perry's 'contribution to the study of the ministry of deliverance and his leadership in the Churches' Fellowship for Psychical and Spiritual Studies'. Canon Perry has edited the Fellowship's theological quarterly *The Christian Parapsychologist* for 25 years and is its current president. He was Archdeacon of Durham from 1970 to 1993, and then served as the Bishop's senior chaplain until 1998, when he retired. The Fellowship numbers among its patrons lay and ordained members from the main Christian Churches, including the Archbishop of York, the Bishop of London and Professor Frances Young.

As well as taking a keen interest in psychics and mediums, many of the Fellowship's members argue that a full understanding of the

Bible can be achieved only if it is read in the light of modern para-psychological experiences. Certainly, many of the Old and New Testament stories are puzzling without such knowledge. An early Church of England supporter of Spiritualism, the Rev Maurice Elliott, had this to say in his book, *The Psychic Life of Jesus*[3]:

> Without the possession of psychic gifts and the exercise of them Jesus could not have done what he was called to do. Indeed, we should not have heard much about him, and there would have been no Christian Church and no New Testament.

Elliott, whose other books included *When Prophets Spoke: Spiritualism in the Old Testament* and *The Bible as Psychic History*, was secretary of the Churches' Fellowship for Psychical and Spiritual Studies from 1954 and served on the Archbishop of Canterbury's Commission on Divine Healing from the same year.

Horace Leaf, one of Britain's top mediums in the mid-1950s, shared similar views to those of Elliott, which he published in a small book called *The World's Greatest Mediums*.[4] In his foreword, he points out that 'Mediumship, which gave rise to modern Spiritualism and psychical research, also helped to lay the foundation of at least four of the great living religions, as well as the science of ethics'.

Leaf regards Moses as a great medium through whom the spirit of Yahweh (the Old Testament God) communicated, enabling him to liberate his people from slavery in Egypt. Yahweh, Leaf observes, 'was in the habit of selecting different modes of manifestation; sometimes appearing as a fire; sometimes speaking out of a cloud; occasionally being a voice, and at least on one occasion appearing in solid form'. The Bible also tells us that Yahweh (or Jehovah) sometimes appeared to others at the same time. 'Moses, Aaron and Abihu, and seventy elders went up and beheld Jehovah from afar' (Exodus, 24). It was Yahweh who gave Moses the Ten Commandments, first orally and then written on tablets of stone.

There are those who argue that none of this has anything to do with spirit communication; it is God communicating directly with Moses. What, then, is their response to the extraordinary event that happened on the Mount of Transfiguration? The Bible tells us that Moses and Elijah (both of whom, of course, had died many years before) appeared to Jesus, with three of his disciples as witnesses. For Jesus, suggests Horace Leaf, their appearance would have been a clear indication that he was in touch with the spirit world and that the two great prophets were helping him with his spiritual mission.

Jesus' materialisation

Leaf also sees Jesus' resurrection and appearance to the disciples in terms of a well-known mediumistic phenomenon – materialisation. One would have expected Jesus to be 'whole' again, after dying on the Cross, but he showed his Crucifixion wounds to the startled disciples as evidence of his identity, just as materialised spirit forms have done in the seance room.

The author and medium also points out that many Bible scholars have problems explaining another aspect of Jesus' postmortem appearances. Why was it that people who had known him well did not recognise the resurrected Jesus immediately he appeared to them? The Bible tells us he walked with two disciples for some time without being recognised and, because of the lateness of the hour, they even invited him to stay the night with them. On refusing the invitation 'their eyes were opened and they knew him, and he vanished out of their sight'. When he appeared in Jerusalem he was not recognised by one of his female followers, and even his disciples 'knew not that it was Jesus'. Horace Leaf believes this reinforces the Spiritualist interpretation that Jesus materialised, and we know from accounts of modern materialisation seances that identification is not always immediate, depending on the conditions.

Saul experiences direct voice mediumship

Lastly, we have the conversion of Saul (who became Paul) while on his way to Damascus to eradicate followers of Jesus. Suddenly, we are told, there was a light from heaven and, falling to the ground, Saul heard a voice saying, 'Saul, Saul, why do you persecute me?' When Saul asked whose voice it was, the reply came, 'I am Jesus, whom you are persecuting.' He was told to enter the city, where he would be told what to do.

Was this a subjective experience? Imagination? Not at all. The Bible tells us that the men who were travelling with him stood speechless, 'hearing the voice but seeing no one'. The light had blinded Saul and he had to be led into Damascus where he neither ate nor drank for three days. Then a disciple in the city named Ananias had a vision in which Jesus told him to go to a specific house where he would find Saul, and that he should lay his hands on him.

Ananias knew of Saul's reputation and protested. But Jesus told him, 'Go, for he is a chosen instrument of mine to carry my name before the Gentiles and kings and the sons of Israel, for I will show him how much he must suffer for the sake of my name.' The disciple obeyed and when he gave healing something like scales fell from Saul's eyes. Within days, Saul, the former enemy of Jesus, was proclaiming in the synagogues, 'He is the Son of God.'

It is also reported that Saul told King Agrippa that during his vision, Jesus spoke to him in the Hebrew tongue, commissioned him to his mission and said he would appear to him in future when necessary to give him instruction. The interpretation of Horace Leaf and many other Spiritualists is that Saul (Paul) was unwittingly a powerful medium and that Jesus talked to him through direct voice mediumship, enabling others who were present to hear the voice as well. Having been converted by the experience, Saul went on to become the medium ('a chosen instrument of mine') through whom Jesus regularly communicated.

I know that many Christians will take issue with the Spiritualist interpretation, maintaining that Jesus was the Son of God and that what is reported in the Bible is proof that he was divine. But Spiritualists in the twentieth and twenty-first centuries have seen many similar wonders, including levitation (Jesus walked on water) and the production of apports out of thin air (the same ability that enabled Jesus to produce enough loaves and fishes to feed a multitude). Nor were such abilities restricted to Jesus. Paul became a powerful healer, among other things. Writing his Epistles to the Corinthians he made a point of recommending the use of paranormal abilities (1 Corinthians 12):

> Now concerning spiritual gifts, brethren, I would not have you igno-
> rant.... There are diversities of gifts, but the same Spirit ... to one is
> given by the Spirit the word of wisdom; to another the word of
> knowledge by the same Spirit; to another faith by the same Spirit; to
> another the working of miracles; to another prophecy; to another the
> discerning of spirits; to another divers kinds of tongues; to another
> the interpretation of tongues; but all these worketh that one and the
> self-same Spirit, dividing to every man severally as he will.

Clergy who embrace mediumship

Those Christians who take an interest in the phenomena of Spiritualism will know that spirit communication did not cease after the Bible was written. If anything, it is more prevalent today and many churchmen are broadening their spiritual horizons by embracing it. When the Unitarian Society for Psychical Studies held its annual conference at Manchester College, Oxford, in 1977, I was invited to speak to the delegates about Spiritualism.

I knew that Unitarianism had its roots in Jewish and Christian traditions and is open to insights from world faiths and science. I was agreeably surprised, however, to hear the Society's chairperson, the Rev Florence Whitby (wife of its president), tell the conference that Spiritualism had been of immense help to her at a time of need. I also met the Rev Basil Viney, who told me that he had received many spirit communications from his wife. As well as being a Unitarian minister he declared himself to have been a Spiritualist for many years.

I have already written about the mediumistic experiences of Dr Mervyn Stockwood, Bishop of Southwark (*see page 8*). Let me add to that with a personal experience involving another bishop – the controversial American Episcopalian James Pike, former Bishop of California.

James Pike

James Pike agreed to be interviewed by me during a visit to Britain in 1968, and spoke openly about the spirit communications he had received from his son Jim two years earlier, through London medium Ena Twigg. Their two-world conversation took place just a month after Jim took a gun and committed suicide in a New York hotel room. A detailed account of the sitting can be found in Bishop Pike's book *The Other Side*.[5] Incidentally, in addition to his son Jim's spirit communication during Bishop Pike's first sitting with Ena Twigg, another spirit kept interrupting the boy's messages. The medium described this man as having a foreign accent, which she thought was German, and said he was giving his name as Paul. She added that he had a powerful intellect and wrote philosophical treatises. As well as telling Bishop Pike not to worry about his dead son – 'he's in safe keeping; he is surrounded by our love' – he also discussed the bishop's difficulties within the Episcopal Church. Then he added, 'Thank you for dedicating your new book to me.'

Bishop Pike was astonished. He recognised the communicator immediately. It was his good friend theologian Paul Tillich, Jim's godfather, who had died a year earlier. The bishop's new book, *What Is This Treasure?*, which was not then available to the public in the United Kingdom or the United States, carried this dedication:

To
PAUL TILLICH
Principal Mentor and
Dear Friend much missed

Canon John Pearce-Higgins, who had accompanied Bishop Pike to Ena Twigg's home for the sitting and was taking copious notes, told me later:

When Paul Tillich came through my eyes nearly jumped out of my head. And I only wish this could really be put across, because if these wretched American theologians who don't believe in anything realised that their great hero, Paul Tillich, was still alive and kicking it might produce some sort of impact. He said to us: 'My faith in God was justified but I did not know that this was possible.'

A year after my meeting with him, Bishop Pike and his wife Diane were in Jerusalem. They set off from the Intercontinental Hotel on 1 September 1969, in a hired Ford, in the direction of Qumran, where the Dead Sea Scrolls were discovered. Taking a wrong turn, they ended up in the wilderness and eventually the car got stuck in the sand. After walking for two hours Bishop Pike collapsed. Diane decided to go for help and her husband advised her to call out 'Help me! Help me!' as she walked. She was eventually found by a group of Bedouin workers.

Meanwhile, Ena Twigg, her husband Harry and Canon John Pearce-Higgins, Vice-Provost of Southwark, had gathered in the medium's home to pray and send healing thoughts to the couple, whose disappearance had now been reported in the world's press.

Suddenly, the spirit of Bishop Pike controlled Ena Twigg. 'Help me! Help me!' he cried, echoing the words he had told Diane to call out. Then, in a more subdued tone, he said, 'Where am I? I'm lost. I'm nowhere and I don't belong anywhere. Help me.

> Help me.' When Canon Pearce-Higgins asked who he was, he replied, 'You *know* who I am.'
>
> It was clear that this was a spirit communication and that Bishop Pike was dead. Ena Twigg called me with the news and within a couple of hours I was listening to the tape recording. We agreed that it should be published, even though many people – including Diane Pike – were still hoping that the bishop had found shelter from the heat, was alive and would be rescued.
>
> But could we be *sure* he had died? I put it to Ena Twigg that maybe he was unconscious or his spirit was out of its body and able to communicate with her, but that he had not died.
>
> 'But he *is* dead! He's here. I can see him,' she exclaimed. She seemed as surprised as I was by this sudden vision. 'I think he must have climbed up something and fallen down.'
>
> Sadly, these psychic impressions were confirmed a day later when a trail of discarded clothing led rescuers to Bishop Pike's body.

At a later press conference, Diane Pike revealed, 'He climbed down into a boxed canyon, then fell seventy feet. Doctors said he must have died instantly.'

Among more recent commentators on Christianity and the paranormal is Hugh Montefiore, who at one time was a suffragan bishop to Mervyn Stockwood, Bishop of Southwark, whose interest in mediumship has already been discussed. Montefiore served as Bishop of Kingston and of Birmingham. His own introduction to the paranormal came through two encounters with psychometry, which he defines as 'the alleged ability to tell the future or the past of individuals by simply handling some object that belongs to them'. Stockwood, incidentally, had told him that medium Ena Twigg had been able to give him 'a rundown on his life' simply by holding his episcopal ring.

In his book *The Paranormal: a Bishop Investigates*[6] he writes: 'The upshot of this enquiry has been that the paranormal seems to me a subject of real importance, and I find it deplorable that scientists deride it and religion ignores it.' He deals very thoroughly with a range of phenomena, including spirit communication, concluding that there is 'genuine communication with the dead' in some cases.

Catholicism permits 'dialogue with dead'

The Roman Catholic Church has in the past been a vociferous opponent of Spiritualism and spirit communication, but times are changing. Father Gino Concetti, the moral theologian who writes regularly for the Vatican newspaper *L'Osservatore Romano*, had this to say during a recent interview:

> According to the modern catechism, God allows our dear departed persons who live in an ultra-terrestrial dimension to send messages to guide us in certain difficult moments of our lives. The Church has decided not to forbid any more the dialogue with the deceased with the condition that these contacts are carried out with a serious religious and scientific purpose.

I believe this decision confirms that the Roman Catholic Church has a far greater awareness and understanding of psychic phenomena and spirit communication than it admits. This is perhaps not surprising, given the phenomena and miracles that have been attributed to many of its saints and mystics over the centuries.

Catholicism and the electronic voice phenomenon

Catholic support seems to be particularly strong for the electronic voice phenomenon (EVP) (*see page 112*). Two Catholic priests, Father Ernetti and Father Gemelli, who were collaborators in music research, were among the earliest researchers in this field. Ernetti was an internationally respected scientist, physicist, philosopher and music lover. Gemelli was president of the Papal Academy. They stumbled on the voice phenomenon by chance in 1952 while recording a Gregorian chant. A wire on their magnetophone kept breaking and in exasperation Gemelli looked up and asked his dead father for help. To their amazement, his father's voice was recorded on the magnetophone, responding: 'Of course I shall help you. I'm always with you.' They repeated the experiment and this time a very clear voice declared: 'But Zucchini, it is clear, don't you know it is I?' Gemelli stared at the tape in disbelief. No one knew the nickname his father had teased him with as a boy. Though understandably delighted to have had this spirit communication, the priest was also deeply troubled about its possible conflict with Catholicism's teachings. Eventually, the two men visited Pope Pius XII in Rome and recounted their experience. To their surprise, the Pope said: 'Dear Father Gemelli, you really need not worry about this. The existence of this voice is strictly a scientific fact and has nothing whatsoever to do with Spiritism. The recorder is totally objective: it receives and records only sound waves from wherever they come. This experiment may perhaps become the cornerstone for a building for scientific studies which will strengthen people's faith in a hereafter.' Although reassured by these words, Gemelli did not publicly reveal this remarkable experience until the last years of his life.

Pope Pius' cousin, the Rev Professor Dr Gebhard Frei, co-founder of the Jung Institute, was also president of the International Society for Catholic Parapsychologists and worked closely with Konstantin Raudive, an EVP pioneer. Friedrich Jurgenson, the Swedish EVP researcher whose work inspired many others to attempt radio communication with the next world, was a friend of Pope Paul VI from whom he received a Knight Commander of the Order of St Gregory in 1969 for the film he made about him. The Pope was well aware of Jurgenson's ten years of EVP research. 'I have found a sympathetic ear for the voice phenomenon in the Vatican,' Jurgenson wrote to a publisher. 'I have won many wonderful friends among the leading figures in the Holy City.'

The Vatican has even authorised its priests to carry out their own EVP research. Father Andreas Resch not only made recordings but also ran courses on parapsychology at the Vatican's school for priests in Rome. All the indications are that this support from the Roman Catholic Church of research into spirit communication continues, though Catholics are generally unaware of it.

Catholicism and automatic writing

British psychic and healer Matthew Manning tells of being introduced to two Vatican emissaries – Archbishop Hyginus Cardinale and Monsignor Bruno Heim – friends of his publisher, Peter Bander, who had close ties with the Roman Catholic Church. Manning had developed a talent for automatic writing in which medical diagnoses were given for individuals whose birthdates were supplied to him. The Vatican emissaries provided Manning with some dates and received psychic diagnoses for each one. Eventually, a Sunday newspaper splashed the story that the Vatican had consulted Manning about Pope Paul VI's health. Monsignor Heim confirmed that he and Archbishop Cardinale had met Manning but denied they had discussed the Pope's health with him.

What actually happened was revealed by Manning in his book *One Foot in the Stars*[7]:

On this occasion I was asked to tune into a birth date to get a diagnosis of the person in question through automatic writing. It did not take too long for several sheets of paper to be filled with details of the anonymous person's health problems. The two men read them with interest and went into a lengthy discussion about the contents before explaining to me that the birth date in question was that of Pope Paul VI, who was unwell at the time with some mysterious illness his doctors were unable to identify.

I have never discovered whether or not the contents of the automatic scripts were correct or relevant, but later I received a thank you in the form of a beautiful papal medal bearing Paul VI's coat-of-arms, so I presume they were of help to someone. To this day the medal has a special place in my healing room.

Finally, it is worth noting that one of America's top mediums, John Edward, is a practising Catholic. He devotes a chapter of his book, *One Last Time*,[8] to the conflict that this created initially and how it was resolved when two sitters he had on the same day turned out to be a priest and a nun. The priest, who received spirit communications from several family members, has since become a good friend and has reassured him: 'I believe your gift is from God .... What you are doing is good – keep doing it, don't stop. And you are more than welcome in this church.'

Koran dictated by Angel Gabriel

Let me turn my attention briefly to another great world religion, Islam, which also displays evidence of spirit communication. A newer religion than Christianity, it was founded in AD 622 by Mohammed, an illiterate camel merchant, who was to become not only a prophet but also a military leader and legislator. This all came about through the appearance of 'Allah's messenger', the Angel Gabriel, resulting in Mohammed receiving the Koran. Mohammed made no claim to be divine; he was simply divinely chosen to receive what is the 'Bible' of the Muslim faith.

Mystery and controversy surround the Koran's origins, but if we take the book at face value it was either produced through Mohammed's automatic writing ability (he was said to be illiterate, so could not have written it himself) or dictated to others by Gabriel, speaking in trance through his medium. Gabriel, according to the Bible, has been a regular communicator over the centuries, for Daniel, Zacharias and Mary all reported visits from this divine messenger. In the case of Daniel, Gabriel was called upon to interpret a vision he could not understand. It was Gabriel who foretold the birth of John the Baptist to Zacharias. Mary learned from Gabriel that she was destined to give birth to Jesus.

Mohammed first saw or experienced Gabriel at the age of 40, and these visitations are said to have continued for 23 years. During this time many of the 'inspirations' were of a lengthy duration, enabling some of the longest chapters in the Koran to be revealed in a single sitting.

Spiritualism and religion generally

Evidence of spirit influence is to be found in many religions, of which there are a staggering number – as many as 4,000. Each believes it is following or offering the right spiritual path and we have to accept that there are, indeed, many paths to God. Spiritualists would argue, however, that there is more to gain from listening to the wisdom of spirits speaking to us in the twenty-first century, than to rely blindly on the guidance of spirits whose words were chosen to have meaning and relevance to people living a very different existence more than one or two millennia ago.

1 Christine Wicker, *Lily Dale,* HarperSanFrancisco (2003).
2 Allan Kardec, *The Spirits' Book*, Paris (1862).
3 Rev Maurice Elliott, *The Psychic Life of Jesus*, Gordon Press (1974).
4 Horace Leaf, *The World's Greatest Mediums*, Spiritualist Association of Great Britain.
5 Bishop James Pike, *The Other Side*, Doubleday, New York (1968).
6 Hugh Montefiore, *The Paranormal: A Bishop Investigates*, Upfront Publishing (2002).
7 Matthew Manning, *One Foot in the Stars*, Piatkus Books (2003).
8 John Edward, *One Last Time*, Piatkus Books (1999).

Chapter 13
Spirit Guides and Beyond

I travel overseas a lot and never leave home without researching the place I am visiting. As well as a passport, visa and local currency, I regard a good guidebook as an essential travelling companion. One day, we will all make that great journey to the next world, but very few of us will have taken the trouble to find out what it will be like or how best to prepare for it. Perhaps this is due to the widespread but erroneous view that the spirit world is a 'land from which no one returns', and therefore no guidebooks can have been produced. This is wrong. There are plenty of them.

So let us take a journey to the spirit world in the company of some spirit guides. First, however, I want to distinguish between such guides and the spirit 'controls' who play an important role in the mechanics of mediumship. Every medium needs an assistant in the next world; someone who has special talents that make spirit communication easier. With mental mediums, the spirit control may be barely sensed and only occasionally seen or heard.

With trance and physical mediums it is a very different matter, for the spirit control is usually an entertaining go-between or master of ceremonies whose job it is to ease the tension, make jokes, induce a happy and expectant atmosphere, and generally 'raise the vibrations' in order to enhance the phenomena. Frequently, such spirit controls exhibit contrasting personalities to the medium.

Do spirit controls really exist, or are they secondary personalities of the medium?

That question has been posed since Spiritualism's earliest days and I am not sure if we are any nearer to fully understanding the nature of these entities. There is compelling evidence that *in some cases* a supposed spirit control – a spirit whose role is to assist others in communicating with the living through the medium – has proved not to be who he or she claims to be, suggesting that the personality is an aspect of the medium's subconscious. Adding support to this theory is the fact that very few spirit controls are willing to provide details about themselves that allow a positive identification to be made with a historical person. So, the argument goes, they are simply a product of the medium's mind, invented subconsciously to enable spirit communication to occur more easily.

In his or her normal waking state, a medium may have trouble accepting that the voices heard or visions seen are emanating from the next world. But in a trance, allowing another part of the brain to take on a very different personality – one that believes it *can* communicate with the spirit world – spirits are able to pass their messages on to sitters without the obstacle of the medium's cautious, censoring mind. If that sounds unlikely, consider for a moment the changes that stage hypnotists can bring about with impressionable members of their audiences. A normally shy and retiring individual becomes an Elvis Presley impersonator, another is shocked to 'see' that everyone around him is naked, while another believes he receives an electric shock every time he sits on a chair. The mind can be an incredibly powerful instrument.

Multiple personalities

Another phenomenon that throws even more light on the spirit control debate is multiple personality disorder, in which several personalities appear to exist within a single individual, sometimes with remarkable results. A classic case involved a woman named Sybil Dorsett, through whom 16 very impressive personalities manifested, including a builder, a carpenter, a writer and a musician. The last two became friends and took turns at taking over Sybil's body in order to have long conversations.

More recently, in Oshkosh, Wisconsin, USA, a man was accused of raping a 27-year-old woman, Sarah, who had 46 separate personalities. They included 'Emily', aged six, and a man named 'Sam'. Mark Peterson was alleged to have exploited her mental disorder by coaxing one of her personalities, a flirtatious 20-year-old named Jennifer, to have sex with him, without Sarah's knowledge. The defence claimed that consent had been given. The case made legal history when the judge swore in two of the personalities and allowed them to testify. Peterson was convicted of second-degree sexual assault but the verdict was later overturned.

Even some mediums suspect that their spirit controls may be aspects of themselves, but that does not explain the evidential nature of the spirit messages that are conveyed by them.

One of the best examples of the complexity of spirit controls involved the exceptional American trance and automatic writing medium Mrs Leonore Piper. Her principal spirit control was a 'Dr Phinuit' at the time she was investigated by William James, an eminent professor of psychology at Harvard, and Richard Hodgson, a tough Society for Psychical Research investigator, both of whom became convinced of her paranormal powers.

Although remarkably 'Dr Phinuit' had a poor knowledge of his own language, French, he provided astonishingly accurate information about people known to the sitters and to which the medium's normal mind could have had no access. However, when researchers checked on 'Dr Phinuit', discovering that no such person had lived at the time and in the place he claimed to have done, the spirit control confessed that his name was not Phinuit but 'Scliville', though he seemed uncertain about that, too. Why he should claim to be someone he was not is difficult to understand, unless he was a fabrication of the medium's mind.

Having been 'exposed', Dr Phinuit went into retirement, being replaced as the main control of Leonore Piper by 'George Pelham', a real person whose actual name was Pellow and who was known personally to some of the sitters and researchers. What emerges from such episodes is that the reality of the control need have no bearing on the evidential nature of the spirit communications conveyed by them.

The spirit guides

Communicators commonly known as 'spirit guides' are usually very different from the controls. We all have one or more guides. Non-Spiritualists would call them 'guardian angels'. They watch over us and help us – if we let them. Some, however, have a wider role. They are spirit teachers who, as well as being the spirit guides of specific mediums, share their views on life and death with all who will listen. Here, again, there is some confusion about who they are – they sometimes explain that the persona they use to communicate with us is not their real identity because they insist it is *what* they say that is important, not who is saying it.

There is some intriguing evidence of the separateness of spirit guides from their mediums. In her autobiography[1] one of Britain's most outstanding twentieth-century mental and physical mediums, Estelle Roberts, refers to the experience of a well-known authority and lecturer on psychic matters, Brigadier Roy C. Firebrace, who had sat in on her direct voice seances.

At one of these seances, the medium's Native American spirit guide, Red Cloud, told the brigadier that he would have further evidence of direct voice mediumship 'at some other time at some other place'. Soon afterwards, Brigadier Firebrace – who was a translator when Churchill met Stalin – was sent to Latvia as military attaché. There, he and his wife met a Russian woman interested in spirit communication and the three formed a circle for psychic development in the Firebraces' flat.

Physical phenomena began to occur, a trumpet moved around the room and eventually the brigadier was astonished to hear mention of Red Cloud's name. The spirit voice explained that Red Cloud had come to help until the Russian medium's spirit guide had gained greater proficiency at using the trumpet. The chuckle that accompanied this statement was instantly recognised as Red Cloud's distinctive laugh. From then on, Red Cloud visited the circle until it was broken up by the Firebraces' return to England. On their first visit to an Estelle Roberts' direct voice seance after their return home, Red Cloud referred to their circle and its happenings in Latvia, about which they had made no mention to the medium.

Another spirit guide who furnished proof of his identity was Black Hawk, the medium of a powerful Welsh medium, Evan Powell. The Native American spirit informed his medium that a book had been written about him and a memorial to him had been erected in Illinois. Both statements were confirmed and a copy of the book – *Life of Ma-Ka-Tai-She-Kia-Kiak or Black Hawk* – was tracked down and presented to Powell.

Channelling

In the early days of Spiritualism, most of the communicators claimed to be the spirits of individuals who had lived on earth. Today, there is a growing number of channellers through whom a wide and confusing array of communicators give voice to their beliefs. They include a 35,000-year-old warrior spirit called Ramtha; the Apostle John; Merlin, King Arthur's wizard; the group consciousness of six dolphins, known collectively as Cajuba; and extraterrestrials such as Mars Sector Six.

Is there a difference between being a medium for a spirit guide and channelling some other entity? Yes, according to Tony Neate, who has done both. I first met him and saw him in trance when he belonged to a group known as the Atlanteans. Today, he is co-principal of the School of Channelling, a founder-tutor of the College of Healing at Runnings Park, West Malvern, Worcestershire, and an author.[2] 'I came into channelling through being a trance medium,' he explains, 'which involves someone making contact with a departed soul. A channeller, though, is often a person who is accessing through their higher self another level of conscious-ness.'

When Neate was a trance medium, spirit guides communicated with his sitters. Now it is 'Helio-Arcanophus' (known affection-ately as H-A), who claims he once lived on Atlantis, who takes over his entranced body and gives teachings designed 'to help people understand and adjust to the New Age which is now upon us'. Neate says he looks at H-A 'as being part of a group consciousness on a higher plane'.

Whereas Neate was conscious of what was being said through his entranced body when spirit guides were communicating, he is oblivious to H-A's teachings at the time they are spoken. Seth, another well-known entity channelled through Jane Roberts, has said: 'It should be apparent that my communications come through Jane's subconscious. But as a fish swims through water, but the fish is not the water, I am not Jane's subconscious.' Since this book is about spirit communication, I will not digress into channelling apart from saying that teachings must be judged on their merit, whatever the source.

The world inhabited by spirit guides

Let us now take a quick look at the world from which the spirit guides come and to which we will all travel one day. There are some differences in the accounts of the next world, but they are no greater than the differences you would find if you picked up a travel magazine and read reports on the latest holiday destinations. At one you can sunbathe all day. Another will offer you the chance to ski. Or maybe an ocean cruise is more appealing. The physical world is a place of astonishing variety and there is no reason to expect the spirit world to be less diverse. But the first thing most guidebooks tell you is that you cannot compare the spirit world, in a geographical sense, to the Earth.

Air Chief Marshal Lord Dowding, the man who led Fighter

Command during the Battle of Britain, wrote a book[3] in which he asked his readers to visualise the Earth as the centre of a series of hollow spheres each bigger than the last. 'Each of these spheres represents a state of spiritual development a little in advance of that below, and the soul's progress is steadily onward and outward once the restrictions of Earth are left behind.'

T.E. Lawrence (Lawrence of Arabia), communicating through the hand of automatic writing medium Jane Sherwood,[4] found shedding those restrictions difficult:

> There has been an unreal quality in my surroundings, and in myself a feeling of shadowy and unsubstantial being. I still miss the weight of my Earth body, I suppose, although I should be sorry now to have to drag it about... my present body, solid as it seems, is now really composed of a kind of matter which on Earth I thought of as 'emotion'.

Paul Beard, who for many years was president of the College of Psychic Studies, has pointed out:

> It is often considered necessary for the sake of clarity to describe post-mortem experiences as if they take place in separate areas or 'spheres', and as if these areas are sharply divided off from one another. The real difference, however, has to be seen in terms of expanding consciousness.[5]

Beard went on to explain that 'the key to understanding discarnate life is that we are concerned with a number of different levels of consciousness, and what is true at one level is not necessarily true in the same way at deeper levels.' After-death experiences represent an adventure in growth: 'These three stages can roughly be equated with (1) the illusory state known as the Summerland; (2) the judgement; (3) life in the First, Second and Third Heavens.'

The fact that the world around us, soon after we die, is largely illusory is a common theme in spirit communications.

'There are so many different reports and descriptions of the life to come, making it difficult to believe any of them,' comments one of the UK's top mediums, Gordon Smith.[6] He believes that each individual interpretation is relevant only to the person who experiences it and that each mind will gravitate to a level of understanding 'most suited to its concept of Heaven'.

Another high-profile medium, Rita Rogers, with whom Princess Diana and Dodi Fayed had sittings, admits:[7]

> I always find it difficult to describe the spirit world. It isn't a three-dimensional place. It has no geographical location. It is neither above us or below us. It just is. The spirit world is not made up of white clouds, nor is it a furnace of flames. The only way I can describe it is by likening it to a state of mind. I am not saying it is a construct of our imagination but that it is akin to a higher level of consciousness than any place we might have visited here on Earth. In many ways dying and entering the spirit world is very similar to what happens when we go to sleep at night and dream.

Paul Beard, on the other hand, suggests that:

> early discarnate life is not wholly dreamlike but partly resembles it; like dreams it contains rapidly changing imagery; unlike dreams this imagery sometimes becomes stable and anchored for considerable periods...; again, unlike dreams, the imagery is not created wholly by the dreamer, but also by others to help him.

The time of judgement

After a period of adjustment, we move into the 'judgement' phase, not to be judged by others but to judge ourselves and accept our selves as the people we have created. An astonishing example of this came through the hand of Geraldine Cummins[8] from 'Mrs Willett' (Mrs Winifred Coombe Tennant), whose story I told earlier (*see pages 40–41*). Soon after her passing, she began to have a *change of heart* and managed to convey this urgently to her son, by automatic writing, through a medium who had met neither of them:

> *My dear, dear Alexander,*
>
> *It is my urgent need to write to you on a private matter that concerns us two. I have a humiliating confession to make and must cast away all pride ... I have been a witness of the film of memory, the record of my life ... There are, as you may know, underground chambers of the mind ... I have ... had a dismaying revelation of one of them. I feel I must share it with you or in future I shall have no peace of mind...*
>
> *The year before you were born ... my little girl Daphne died. Then ... came the lovely hope of another baby-girl to replace Daphne. Oh I was so bitterly disappointed when I learnt this happy dream was a deluding fancy ... I repulsed my baby-son, visited my bitterness on his tiny innocent self. It was more in thought than in act...*

This remarkable message goes on, in similar vein, for some time, ending with these words:

> *So I beg of you to remove from your mind any cruel, false thing I wrote of you in a posthumous message ... Mine has been the initial offence all along. If you have felt a barrier between us, I created it not you. For the sake of my peace of mind I beg of you to forgive my grievous fault... Dear sons, I send you from the hither world my true love in equal shares.'*

How fortunate for Mrs Coombe Tennant that she knew about mediumship and was able to assuage her guilt by communicating to her son in this way.

Descending to lower realms

One of the most fascinating and graphic insights into conditions in the next world was given through the automatic writing mediumship of Anthony Borgia.[9] What makes this account particularly interesting is that it purports to come from Monsignor Robert Hugh Benson, a deceased friend of the medium. He was the fourth son of Edward White Benson, first Bishop of Truro, who became Archbishop of Canterbury in 1888. Robert converted to Roman Catholicism in 1903 and, eight years later, as a monsignor, he became privy chancellor to Pope Pius X. Among the books he wrote before his death in 1914 was *The Necromancers*, which dealt with spirit return.

Some years later, controlling the hand of Borgia, Benson said that one of the greatest regrets of his life was that this book had added to the general misconception of the next life, and he had returned to put the record straight. He told of the conducted tour he was given of the different realms in the spirit world, including one that is very bright and beautiful, and is often referred to by Spiritualists as the 'Summerland', and another that he said might be called 'Winterland' but for the fact that 'earthly winter possesses a grandeur all of its own while there is nothing but abomination about the lower realms of the spirit world'. Like an explorer on Earth, Benson said he had 'penetrated deeply into those regions' and it was not a pleasant experience. He had been advised, however, that the facts should be given:

not with the intention of frightening people ... but to show that such places exist solely by virtue of an inexorable law, the law of cause and effect, the spiritual reaping that succeeds the earthly sowing; to show that to escape moral justice upon the Earth-plane is to find strict and unrelenting justice in the spirit world.

The good news for those inhabiting those realms, according to Monsignor Benson, is that 'the golden opportunity of spiritual reclamation is ready and waiting'. They have only to show 'an earnest desire to move ... one fraction of an inch towards the realms of light that are above ... and [they] will find a host of unknown friends who will help....'

So, heaven and hell are not as they are commonly depicted in the traditions of most religions, and no one is destined to suffer eternal damnation, however evil, as long as they are prepared to change. It is also futile to compare accounts of the next world and make a judgement on which is right or wrong, since each is probably correct, however different it may be to another – just as explorers in the Amazon jungle and the Arctic wastes would also send back conflicting descriptions of their surroundings.

What impresses many people about the philosophy offered by spirit guides is that it is eminently sensible, compassionate and inspiring.

Silver Birch

One of the best-loved spirit guides is Silver Birch. His words of wisdom appeared in the columns of *Psychic News* for many years before it was revealed that the trance medium through whom he spoke was the newspaper's editor Maurice Barbanell.

Famous journalist and theatre critic Hannen Swaffer was one of the regular sitters in Barbanell's weekly home circle, where the teachings were recorded by a stenographer, and it was Swaffer who encouraged him to publish them anonymously. Compilations have since appeared in book form and his words are often quoted.

Very few people actually attended those seances and heard Silver Birch speaking. I did. During the eight years when I was Barbanell's assistant at *Psychic News*, I also heard the Spiritualist editor – who, as far as I know, could not type – dictate hundreds of stories to his secretary. It was fascinating to compare the difference in style. When Silver Birch entranced him, the language was simple, to the point and flowed virtually without hesitation. When Barbanell was in his normal waking state, dictating news stories or his editorial comments, he would frequently pause, marshall his thoughts and sometimes ask his secretary to read back what he had said so far. He was very professional, but his journalistic style was markedly different from that of the spirit guide who spoke through him and whose words could go straight into print without editing, apart from minor changes to the stenographer's punctuation.

Let me conclude this necessarily brief visit to the spirit world with a few well-chosen words from Silver Birch. There are other spirit guides I could quote – White Eagle, Red Cloud and Moon Trail among others – whose words would be just as meaningful and relevant, but I have selected Silver Birch's teachings because of my associations with him and his medium.

The next world

When asked if the spirit world is as natural and as material to the spiritual senses as the physical world is to our present senses, Silver Birch replied: 'Far more, for this is reality. You are at present prisoners. You are hampered by the material body by which you are restricted on all sides. You are only expressing a very small portion of your real selves.'

Religion

'We strive always to reveal the religious significance of spiritual truth for, when your world understands its spiritual import, there will be a revolution mightier than all the revolutions of war and blood. It will be a revolution of the soul and, all over the world, people will claim what is their due – the right to enjoy to the full the liberties of the spirit. Away will go every restriction which has put fetters on them. Our allegiance is not to a Creed, not to a Book, not to a Church, but to the Great Spirit of life and His eternal natural laws.'

Materialism

'Each soul that becomes an instrument for the Great Spirit, each soul that moves out of darkness into light, out of ignorance into knowledge, out of superstition into truth, is helping to advance the world, for each one of these is a nail into the coffin of the world's materialism.'

Service to others

'We are all channels of the Great Spirit. It is a privilege to serve. There is no religion higher than service. Service is the true coin of the spirit. It is noble to serve. To serve is to enrich the lives of others and your own. To serve is to bring comfort to those who think there is nothing left for them in your world. It is in service that we find inner peace, tranquillity and repose. It is in service that we find steadfastness that enables us to have complete confidence in the overruling power, to strive to get closer and closer to the Great Spirit.'

Love

'There is a great power in the universe which has never been subject to the analytical scrutiny of laboratories, which cannot be resolved by chemicals or by scalpels, yet it is so real that it transcends all other forces which have been measured and weighed and dissected.' This, Silver Birch explained, was the power of love, adding: 'That love is deathless because it is part of the great Spirit, the creative spirit of all life, part of the power that has fashioned life; it is indeed the very breath and the very essence of life. And wherever love exists, sooner or later those who are united by its willing bonds will find one another again despite all the handicaps and obstacles and impediments that may be in the way.'

1 Estelle Roberts, *Fifty Years as a Medium*, Herbert Jenkins (1959).

2 Tony Neate, *Channelling for Everyone*, Piatkus Books (1997).

3 Air Chief Marshal Lord Dowding, *Many Mansions*, Rider (1943).

4 Jane Sherwood, *Post Mortem Journal*, C.W. Daniel Company (1992).

5 Paul Beard, *Living On*, George Allen & Unwin (1980).

6 Gordon Smith, *Spirit Messenger*, Hay House (2003).

7 Rita Rogers, *Mysteries*, Pan Books (2003).

8 Geraldine Cummins, *Swan on a Black Sea* edited by Signe Toksvig, Routledge and Kegan Paul (1965).

9 Anthony Borgia, *Life in the World Unseen*, MBA Publishing (1993).

Chapter 14

Ghosts, Poltergeists and Exorcisms

Are ghosts spirits?

No examination of spirit communication and the next world would be complete without tackling the perplexing subjects of ghosts – often referred to as earthbound spirits – and poltergeists, a name that derives from the German for 'noisy spirit', and the even more vexed question of malevolent spirits and their possible influence on us. That will lead us naturally to a review of possession and exorcism. Spiritualists in general do not concern themselves with most of these subjects for the simple reason that they are, for the most part, spontaneous occurrences that are beyond the control of these who experience them. Ghosts are also rarely seen or felt by more than one person at a time, so even the best cases rest on the testimony of solitary witnesses, whose reliability and accuracy we have to take on trust.

Another reason why Spiritualists do not get excited by reports of ghostly goings-on is that the generally accepted view of ghosts' repeated behaviour – always walking through the same wall, or descending the same flight of stairs, dressed in the same costume of a previous period in history – suggests that what is being seen is not a spirit but a psychic repetition of some important or traumatic event in the life of that individual, like the repeat playback mode on a video recorder. When the right circumstances occur, maybe on the same date or hour of the day, and conditions are conducive, the event is played back in the mind of the beholder. What lends credence to this theory is the ability of many mediums to psychometrise objects. Just by holding an item they can often describe accurately the personality or events involving its owner. This suggests that in wearing our clothes or holding everyday inanimate objects we imprint information about ourselves on them, which enables sensitive individuals, such as mediums, to read us like a book, without even meeting us. Perhaps the same mechanism is involved in imprinting the dramas of the past on the fabric of the buildings in which they are played out today.

I have spoken to many people over the years who have unexpectedly encountered a phantom in their homes or while visiting other buildings, and they are adamant that their experiences were real and unforgettable. Yet there are parapsychologists who assure us that ghostly events are products of the mind that are triggered by very mundane causes, such as draughts in old buildings or even electromagnetic waves from electrical appliances. Just to complicate matters, however, we must also contend with 'phantasms of the living' for which there are also some very well attested cases. And there's also a classic case of a man-made 'ghost' who became a regular communicator at Toronto Society for Psychical Research seances held in the 1970s by Cambridge psychical researcher George Owen and Canadian parapsychologists. Their experiments were designed to verify the existence of psychokinesis – mind over matter – and focused on 'table-turning' in which the table moved around and rapped responses to questions. They invented a spirit called Philip, giving him a fictitious identity and personality – that of a seventeenth-century English aristocrat who lived at Diddington Manor, Warwickshire, was unhappily married and fell in love with a gypsy named Margo. His wife declared Margo to be a witch and she was burned at the stake, at which point Philip leapt to his death from the manor's roof. For a year the experimenters deliberately attempted to conjure up a 'shared hallucination' of 'Philip', without success. It was only when they turned to table-tilting and rapping, following the same procedures that three British researchers had used very successfully since 1964, that 'Philip' began manifesting. 'He' communicated by raps, confirming the fictitious story of his life. The researchers achieved impressive table movements in bright light and raps were heard not only from the table but also from walls and overhead pipes. The group made a movie, *Philip, the Imaginary Ghost*, about their research in 1974 and also took part in a live demonstration on Toronto City Television in which the table, surrounded by the researchers touching only its top, climbed three steps to the platform. One interpretation of these remarkable results is that the experimenters had produced a 'thought-form' of Philip, through their collective unconsciousness, which was able to interact with physical objects in order to communicate. If that is a correct interpretation of what occurred, then perhaps ghosts and other paranormal phenomena could also have a human as well as a spiritual origin. But another possibility is that a mischievous spirit took over the proceedings and masqueraded as 'Philip'. As far as I can tell, the experimental protocol of the Toronto sessions had no way of eliminating that possibility.

Mischievous spirits

Certainly, it is important to 'test the spirits' and not take what is said through mediums or other methods of spirit communication at face value if it offends our reason or is questionable. That was a lesson learned by British-born journalist and author Joe Fisher who wrote the bestselling *The Case for Reincarnation*[1] after taking up residence in Canada. The book received a lot of publicity and soon after Fisher made an appearance on Toronto radio in July 1984, his publisher forwarded a letter from a laboratory technician called Aviva Neumann. She explained that under hypnosis, which was an attempt to cure leukaemia, different voices began to speak and claimed to be spirits of the dead. Fisher investigated and found himself speaking to a nineteenth-century Yorkshire sheep farmer named Russell, an ex-RAF bomber pilot named Ernest Scott, a

Cockney named Harry Maddox who was a Great War veteran, and a Greek girl named Filipa Gavrilos. According to her she had been Fisher's lover three centuries earlier in a town named Theros, and was now his spirit guide.

Soon, Fisher began feeling as if Filipa was speaking to him in broken Greek, giving him advice on all manner of daily matters including nutrition and health. 'She possessed more love, compassion and perspicacity than I had ever known,' said Fisher. His obsession with Filipa led to the break-up of Fisher's relationship with his girlfriend and he declared: 'If Filipa could have assumed a physical body, I'm sure I would have married her.'

Impressed with the wealth of information provided by the different personalities speaking through the hypnotised Aviva Neumann, Fisher decided to write a book about them. To do so he needed to research their claims in detail, so he set off for England and Greece to talk to historians and check through official records in order to corroborate their accounts. They proved to be remarkably accurate. Flying Officer Ernest Scott, for example, told Fisher he had started his RAF career in 99 Squadron at Mildenhall in Suffolk, had then moved to Newmarket and on to Waterbeach in Cambridgeshire. He flew Wellingtons, had chased the German battleship Tirpitz and bombed Cologne and the Ruhr Valley. Fisher was able to confirm all the details about 99 Squadron at the Kew Record Office, including obscure facts like the squadron being billeted for a period in the grandstand at Newmarket racecourse.

Fisher appeared to have gathered impressive evidence for life after death but there was just one flaw. Flying Officer Ernest Scott did not exist. Nor, he discovered, did Yorkshireman Russell or war veteran Harry Maddox, even though the stories they told were correct. Fisher was certain, however, that a visit to Greece would confirm the reality of the love of his life: Filipa. His hopes were dashed. He was unable to find Theros, the village near the Turkish border where they were supposed to have been lovers, and the other place she mentioned – Alexandroupoli – was only two centuries old, so it had not existed at the time Filipa claimed to have lived with Fisher in a past life. All the spirits who spoke through Aviva Neumann were liars. It could be argued that Fisher was the victim of an elaborate hoax and that the hypnotised laboratory technician was consciously or subconsciously drawing upon information she had researched or been exposed to at some time. But if that were the case, why would all the details be correct except for the names of the communicators: the one piece of information that they would have the greatest likelihood of getting right?

As an accomplished writer, Fisher still had a good story to tell, but it had a very different theme. He concluded that he had been in touch with 'hungry ghosts' or 'earthbound spirits' who were either unaware that they had died or were so enamoured of their earthly existence that they craved to stay attached to it.[2] When Fisher returned to Canada he confronted the alleged spirit of Ernest Scott with his findings. The spirit denied he had lied, but his demeanour changed and his usual good humour was replaced with irritability before he abruptly ended the conversation.

Fisher, who believed in life after death and had a vast knowledge of the subject, should have been alerted by two worrying features of the sessions he attended. Aviva Neumann was not a medium and would therefore have had no training in controlling who spoke through her when she was hypnotised. Mediums usually rely on a 'doorkeeper' who is, in effect, a spiritual bouncer who prevents unwanted guests from gate-crashing seances. He should also have had greater suspicion of the fact that none of the communicators was known personally to him.

I had enjoyed a long correspondence with Fisher, by letter and email, over the years. His book on reincarnation was one I heartily recommended to people interested in the subject and he was very complimentary about my magazine, *Life and Soul*, using excerpts from it in the revised edition of *The Case for Reincarnation* published in 1998. We eventually met for a relaxing drink in London, during one of his flying visits to Britain, and found we had much in common. So it came as a shock, little more than a year later, to learn that Joe Fisher had committed suicide by throwing himself from a cliff. Fisher understood better than most that ending one's life was not a solution to life's problems, whatever they are. And it raises the possibility, suggested by author Colin Wilson, among others, that in his final hours he was either possessed or exhausted by earthbound spirits who feed off energy like vampires after blood, and so was less able to deal with the troubles of everyday life. In such a state of mind he may have acted in a way that was contrary to his dearest principles. Whatever the cause, Joe Fisher's death was a tragic waste of an inspiring life.

The story of Joe Fisher is a cautionary tale that is difficult to understand from many viewpoints. Why would spirits feel it is necessary to give false names? 'Ernest Scott' clearly had extensive knowledge of 99 Squadron and those in its service so, even if he were a mischievous spirit, why did he not use the name of a real squadron member? I am reminded of Dr Phinuit, the spirit guide of Leonore Piper (*see page 202*) who acted as master of ceremonies at the famous American medium's seances, providing researchers with a wealth of evidence of an afterlife. But when his own identity was checked, no such person could be found to have existed, and when challenged he took umbrage and gradually gave up his role as a spiritual go-between, to be replaced by the spirit of a man known to the researchers.

Poltergeists and spirit attachments

I have always wanted to experience poltergeist phenomena. The nearest I got to it was at a house in north London where most members of a family had fled because of alleged banging noises and other strange goings-on. These apparently paranormal happenings occurred only at night, after the elderly father and his son went to bed. Their respective wives and other female members of the family had refused to stay any longer. I joined a local newspaper reporter, a Society for Psychical Research parapsychologist and a few other interested parties, in a small crowded room next to the bedroom. Father and son said goodnight. The lights were turned out. And we waited for something to happen. Eventually there were two loud bangs and we responded with murmurs of approval. The poltergeist had apparently put in an appearance. Not so. 'That's just my father taking his boots off,' said one of his daughters, who had joined us during the observation period but had no intention of staying any longer. Before long, there was a rumbling sound and we were told to put our hands on the dividing wall between our room and the bedroom. It felt as if the wall was vibrating. Intriguing, but far from evidential. Were father and son fast asleep in their beds, or were they thumping the wall or holding a vibrating instrument against it? We were not given an opportunity to investigate. Eventually, I decided that I was wasting my time and I announced to the small gathering that I would soon be leaving. At that, something brushed against my left leg. I froze. It was as if the poltergeist had responded to my announcement and was encouraging me to stay. 'Something has just touched my leg,' I told the others, trying to conceal my excitement and nervousness. 'Oh, that'll be the cat. She's come through the flap,' said the matter-of-fact daughter. It was time to go. If the cat sensed nothing paranormal, I was sure I would not. This case displayed none of the classic ingredients of a poltergeist case and I concluded that it might have been contrived by the family in order to be rehoused by the local council.

My *Psychic News* colleague Chris Rider had better luck when he accompanied the Rev John Pearce-Higgins, vice-provost of Southwark, and medium Donald Page, to a home that was suffering with poltergeist-type phenomena. The canon and his bishop, Dr Mervyn Stockwood (*see page 8*), were keen to use mediums to communicate with troublesome spirits. They felt discussion with the spirit entity was usually a far more productive and effective method of clearing hauntings and poltergeists than using exorcism to drive the spirits out. So, after listening to the family's experiences, Donald Page made contact with the spirit and apparently persuaded it to leave. At that point, the entity should have been guided by spirit helpers, but it seems to have taken a liking to Chris Rider and accompanied him home. The young reporter spent a sleepless night listening to bangs, crashes and other disturbances, and it took a visit from the canon and the medium to rid Rider of the mischievous entity.

The difference between ghostly hauntings and poltergeist activity

This episode helps us understand a basic difference between ghostly hauntings and poltergeist activity. Ghosts, generally, are associated with places and similar descriptions of one or more ghosts may be reported in a house by successive occupants, often unaware of the previous reports. Poltergeists, on the other hand, seem to be focused on an individual and can accompany that person and manifest in different places. Their activity, however, is usually short-lived, lasting just a year or so. The commonly held view is that a poltergeist is a form of spirit attachment – something that can afflict susceptible individuals of all ages. When the attachment occurs during pre-pubescence or adolescence, the spirit entity appears to be able to harness the child's sexual energy and produce a range of physical phenomena, sometimes of a noisy and violent nature. These subside as the child matures into an adult.

One of the best known recent poltergeist cases in Britain concerned Matthew Manning, a student in whose home an incredible range of phenomena occurred. The poltergeist also followed him to boarding school and its activities were witnessed by pupils and staff. Heavy objects would be moved from one place to another, occasionally being seen as they lifted from the floor or floated through the air. Mysterious writing appeared on the walls of Manning's home in Essex. And soon he discovered that he had the same ability as Uri Geller to bend spoons. It seems that what started as poltergeist energy had been harnessed and controlled by Manning. Scientists in various countries tested his psychic abilities with positive results and he developed automatic writing skills, with one spirit communicator providing medical diagnoses that were frequently very accurate. Today, his psychic abilities are focused on healing the sick. He told his remarkable story in *The Link*, which sold over a million copies in 19 countries, helped by TV appearances on popular programmes like *The Frost Interview*. So, although Manning and his family were eager to be rid of the mischievous spirit at the outset, it has turned out to be a force for good in his life. But that is rare.

Those most at risk of attracting earthbound spirits

Unwanted spirit attachments may be more common than we imagine, which is why the British Association for Spirit Release (BASR) was founded in 1999 under the chairmanship of Dr Alan Sanderson, a retired NHS consultant psychiatrist. Similar bodies exist in other countries. Its members include mediums, healers, scientists, doctors and therapists from a wide variety of disciplines. The symptoms of those seeking help include depression, mood swings and even physical illness. 'Certain types of people are particularly prone to attracting earthbound spirits,' British medium Linda Williamson, a BASR member, explains. 'Those who are mentally disturbed or who are very open psychically are most at risk. Anyone who uses a ouija board for amusement is unwittingly issuing an open invitation to any mischievous spirit who happens to be around.'

It has even been suggested that the American soldiers who abused prisoners in Iraqi prisons – a scandal difficult to comprehend given that the coalition forces were meant to be liberating the Iraqis from similar abuse by Saddam Hussein – may have been influenced by the earthbound spirits of victims of the former regime. That is not a defence that would be accepted in a court of law, nor is it an explanation that most decent people would find acceptable, but the many cases of possession by malevolent spirits lend support to the theory.

BASR members tackle spirit attachment by either convincing the earthbound spirit that he is dead or urging him to get on with his new life, assuring him that help will be available when he decides to go towards the light. Says Linda Williamson: 'The sense of joy, as they are taken away by the guides, is wonderful to experience... for me this is one of the most satisfying aspects of my work.' That achieved, the next task for the association's members is to explore the psychic, psychological or emotional reasons for the spirit attachment with the victim to understand why it occurred and to prevent it happening in future.

Ancestral origins

A British clergyman, Dr Robert Kenneth McAll, believed that the origins of many earthbound attachments are ancestral. His ministry was based at the Holy Trinity Church in south-west London's Sloane Street and his approach was to explore an afflicted person's family history, looking for trauma over several generations – which he described as 'the wounds and needs of the unquiet dead' – that may need healing. So, lives that came to an end in the family when the relative concerned was unprepared for death, was a victim of accidental death, violence or unforeseen illnesses, or where his body was not found and therefore no proper burial took place, could all be having an effect on lives today, according to Kenneth McAll's ministry. Even the souls who suffered abortions, miscarriages and still births could be lingering around today's generations, looking for release from the pain they are suffering. Having identified the individual from a previous generation who was most likely to be earthbound and causing problems, McAll would hold a requiem mass for that person. He wrote a number of books about 'generational healing', the first being *Healing the Family Tree*[5] which continues to be a Christian best-seller and has been translated into 14 languages. He is credited with 'freeing many thousands from their ancestral bonds that have been ignored in the past by both the psychiatric community and the church', and other clergy are now continuing his work.

Possessions and exorcisms

It is difficult to classify many of the phenomena or the entities behind them. When does a mischievous spirit become a malevolent spirit, or even a demon or the Devil himself? And are the spirits that claim demonic powers as bogus as the 'hungry ghosts' encountered by Joe Fisher? It is difficult for those who are called upon to tackle such cases to know exactly what they are dealing with.

The Rev Tom Willis, one of 12 exorcists for the diocese of York, was a parish priest for 44 years before retiring. In a brief account of some of the cases he dealt with,[3] he said there are no strict procedures laid out by the church to deal with people who are possessed. His first exorcism was in a flat in Hull where three generations of a family had seen a black shadow of indefinable shape moving around. The Rev Willis did not feel a great sense of evil and suspected it was a case of hysteria. They all prayed together, when suddenly the older woman began shaking violently and cried, 'Get it off me; it's trying to choke me.' She began going red in the face, and the priest knew he needed to take action. He laid his hands on her and said, 'In the name of Jesus Christ I command you to be bound and go to that place appointed for you.' Once she had recovered, she said she had seen a doll with staring eyes coming towards her. 'It was trying to choke me and I was absolutely terrified,' she added. Later, the priest confessed to the curate that he had been totally bewildered by the experience and they both agreed it was more than a psychological disturbance.

It was 3 am when he got home, to find the light on in his bedroom and his wife sitting up in bed. 'Thank goodness you're back,' she said. 'I've been scared. I had a horrible dream that something you'd been dealing with was trying to get back at me and the children. In my dream I woke up and went downstairs to the sitting-room and it was there. I got hold of it and commanded it to depart in the name of the trinity. I smashed it against the wall and blue liquid came out. Then I really did wake up, with the feeling that it had been more than just a dream. I went round and blessed all five children and prayed over each one.'

The Rev Willis asked his wife what 'it' was that she dreamt was in the sitting-room. She replied: 'A doll.'

Evil, it seems, can take many forms and manifest in the most unexpected of circumstances. Stanislav Grof, a well-known Czech psychiatrist, has told of an experience he had in the 1960s when he was pioneering a psychotherapeutic technique involving the use of the drug LSD to enable patients to relive their past. A fellow doctor referred an apparently incurably suicidal patient named Flora to him, in the hope that his new method would change her behaviour. Grof's account was included in a three-part series on 'The Possessed' written by Colin Wilson specially for the *Daily Mail*[4]. The psychiatrist told Wilson that this patient had been involved in a robbery in which a man had been killed. When released on parole, she had become a violent drug addict who struggled with wild and dangerous impulses such as driving her car at top speed into other vehicles.

Grof agreed to try treating Flora and his first two sessions with her satisfied him that her difficulties were caused by problems she encountered as a baby in her mother's birth canal. But during the third session her face froze into what Grof described as 'a mask of evil' and she began speaking in a deep, male voice which introduced itself as the Devil. He said Flora was his and he commanded Grof to stop treating her, issuing threats of what would happen if he refused. What particularly frightened the psychiatrist was that this 'intruder' seemed to have insights into his personal life. He was convinced he had encountered a dangerous force of evil and said the next two hours were the worst in his life. Wilson continued:

But then he realised that the presence was feeding on his own fear and anger – the more he struggled, the stronger it became. The only answer was to stay calm and centred, and to starve the presence of the emotional energy that was making it strong. Gradually, Flora's hand – which had become contorted and clawlike – relaxed in his own, and the 'mask of evil' vanished from her face.

Flora recalled nothing of the session when she woke up and her behaviour improved dramatically. She ceased to be a drug addict and took a regular job. But triumphing over evil is not always so simple.

The true story behind the film The Exorcist

Hollywood has exploited the horror element of poltergeist cases with a string of movies whose special effects have ensured box office success. The best of these, undoubtedly, is *The Exorcist*. But few moviegoers will have realised that this work of fiction by William Peter Blatty about a young girl possessed by the Devil is based on an actual case of spirit possession involving a 13-year-old boy.

Douglass Deen

His possession and exorcism took place in Washington DC in 1949. At first, the sounds of scratching around his bed at night was blamed on vermin but a rat exterminator could find nothing. Then his bed began to vibrate, objects were propelled around the room and the bedclothes rose as if someone were standing up inside them.

A local Lutheran vicar agreed to let Douglass stay the night in his home but the moment the lights were switched off all manner of phenomena occurred. The boy's bed vibrated so he moved to an armchair. That turned upside down throwing Douglass onto the floor. The vicar made up a mattress but that began to move around the floor. Neither the boy nor the vicar got any sleep that night. Psychiatrists at Georgetown Medical Centre, run by Jesuits, recommended a Catholic priest carry out an exorcism but when that failed, Deen was sent to Father William Bowden, an expert on exorcism. For the next two months, during which he remained constantly with the boy and repeatedly pronounced the ceremony of exorcism, Deen reacted with obscenities and reciting Latin rapidly – which he had never learned – in a deep voice. It took some 60 exorcisms before the disturbances ended, but it could be argued that normality returned to Douglass Deen's life not because of the religious ceremonies but because, with his maturity, the spirit could no longer manipulate the sexual energy surrounding him.

In recent times, the Roman Catholic Church has tried to modernise its approach to evil and exorcism, arguing in favour of a 'more subtle and sophisticated' interpretation than that of a Devil with a tail and a pitchfork. In 1999, Cardinal Jorge Medina launched a new formula for exorcism which takes into account a modern understanding of evil. This rite is a revision of 21 exorcism rituals which were approved by Pope Paul V in 1614, and acknowledges that psychological disturbances and illnesses have often been misinterpreted as a diabolic possession.

But this seems to have been of little help to the present Pope who, in 2001, held an impromptu exorcism when a teenage girl began screaming insults 'in a cavernous voice' during an audience in the Vatican. Despite the efforts of Pope John Paul II and Father Gabriele Amorth, an exorcist from the Rome diocese, the girl remained possessed, according to *Il Messaggero* newspaper. It was said to be the Pope's third exorcism during his papacy.

Perhaps, after all, the Spiritualist method of communicating with such entities through mediums is by far the most effective way of tackling ghosts, poltergeists and possession.

1 Joe Fisher, *The Case for Reincarnation,* Somerville House (1998).
2 Joe Fisher, *Hungry Ghosts*, Grafton Books (1990).
3 *Sunday Telegraph Magazine*, 18 January 2004.
4 *Daily Mail*, 4, 6 and 7 August 2001.
5 Rev Robert Kenneth McAll, *Healing the Family Tree*, Sheldon Press (1982).

Chapter 15

Reincarnation

At the start of my investigation of mediumship and spirit communication, I met a number of Spiritualists who offered a very simple view of this world and the next. We are born. We die. And then we live for eternity in the next world where the sun constantly shines and the flowers are always in bloom. There, we can enjoy the Halls of Learning, attend grand concerts and listen to the wisdom of great teachers such as Jesus and Buddha.

I found this view unsatisfactory because it raised more questions about spiritual realities than it answered. If the next world had so much to offer, why did we need to be born into a physical world at all? And if a lifetime on Earth was important for our education, why was it assumed that one lifetime on Earth was all that was necessary before we ventured into the spiritual realms? Perhaps this was not our first life on Earth. Perhaps we would return many times in order to develop spiritually. The logic of the philosophy of reincarnation – which also offered a break from incessant sunshine in the 'Summerland' – appealed to me. When I began investigating it in some depth I was impressed with the evidence.

My interest in reincarnation was triggered in part by the conflicting views on the subject, not only of Spiritualists but also of spirit guides. Take the example of Silver Birch, whose spiritual teachings I have quoted previously (*see page 210*). Reincarnation plays an important role in the philosophy he expounds. Yet Maurice Barbanell, the medium he entranced in order to give us his teachings, refused to accept reincarnation – even though his guide assured him that they had both served together in previous lives. Barbanell argued that every case that purported to be evidence of reincarnation memories could just as easily be explained away as 'overshadowing' or possession by a spirit.

It always amused me that whenever reincarnation was mentioned in the columns of *Psychic News*, its correspondence columns would become a battleground between believers and sceptics, all holding to their beliefs with astonishing tenacity and sometimes a total disregard for the evidence.

In my opinion, the evidence for living more lives than one is compelling. I also believe that it complements spirit communication as evidence for life after death. After all, if we can prove just one case of an individual being reborn, then we have also proved the existence of a soul that is not inextricably linked to a physical body and condemned to die with that body, as materialists would have us believe. I have already written extensively on the subject,[1] so I will restrict myself here to a brief résumé of the best evidence, together with a few personal experiences.

If you are a European or South American Spiritualist, it is highly likely that you will believe in reincarnation – regardless of whether or not you have investigated the subject – because you are influenced by the teachings contained in Allan Kardec's books based on spirit communications.[2] But for much of the twentieth century, British and American Spiritualists rejected the idea. One reason for this, I am sure, is that Spiritualism offers the prospect of reunion with our loved ones in the next world. Imagine how you would feel when you arrive in the next world, only to find your partner had returned to Earth. Believers argue, however, that where true love exists, we will be reborn together over many lifetimes, perhaps in different relationships.

The prevailing view among Spiritualists has certainly changed in recent years, partly, I suspect, because of the huge upsurge of interest in hypnotic regression, because of the number of mediums who now declare their belief in it and because of the mounting evidence in favour of being reborn.

Hypnotic regression

Despite its impact on the public at large, I am not personally satisfied that most hypnotic regressions are real memories of past lives. The problem is that we are all exposed to such a wealth of information – from books, radio programmes, the media and films – that it is difficult to prove that a 'memory' we recall under hypnosis is not, in fact, based on something we have read or seen and then forgotten, but that has been retained by our subconscious and then regurgitated in the fictitious form of a past life. If this sounds complex or convoluted, I can assure you that there are cases that have such a cause. In these cases of cryptomnesia – or hidden memory – the names, places and incidents recalled were later shown to have been based on fiction: a long-forgotten novel read many years earlier.

Many therapists are discovering that past-life regression can be a very powerful tool in treating illnesses or problems in this life. So, for example, a person who has difficulty in maintaining relationships may recall a horrific experience in a previous existence that 'explains' his or her inability to trust a partner. Recalling that 'event' begins the healing process. Or perhaps a persistent pain in the back that no amount of medicine or massage can shift is magically healed by the affected person recalling being stabbed in the back during an earlier incarnation.

Having discussed such cases with the top therapists working in this field, I find that many of them are not concerned whether such memories are real past-life experiences or imagined scenarios invented by their patients' subconscious to explain the symptoms from which they are suffering and to dispose of them. Since digging deeper to find proof does not usually aid the healing process, the therapists and patients are happy to leave the memories' reality unexplored.

Mediums who accept rebirth

Among modern mediums who declare their belief in reincarnation are John Edward, Tony Stockwell, James Van Praagh, Stephen

O'Brien and Sylvia Browne, all of whom have had experiences that have convinced them of past lives. The first medium I met who offered evidence of this was Ena Twigg, whose mediumship has already been discussed (*see page 8*). Her story involved a sitter who was a stranger to her – he had booked an appointment by telephone and all she knew was his surname.

Normally, Ena Twigg remained conscious during a seance with a first-time sitter, but on this occasion she went immediately into trance. When she returned to her normal waking state she found she had been weeping profusely, and so had the man who had come in search of evidence for survival. It transpired that his daughter, who had polio, had died in an iron lung at the age of six. He was so overwhelmed by her spirit return that he asked if he could return at a future date and bring with him the clergyman who had conducted her funeral.

Some weeks later, just as she was drifting off to sleep, Ena Twigg saw the spirit of a young girl who asked her to find her daddy. She gave her name – which the medium recognised as that of the sitter – and at the spirit girl's insistence she wrote down the following message: 'Tonight I'm being born again.' The medium could not pass on the message because she did not have the man's phone number. Three weeks later, a parson arrived for a seance. When he said he should have been accompanied by someone else who could not come, Ena Twigg asked if it was the man whose daughter had died from polio. It was. She fetched her diary, in which she had recorded the message and the time it was written – two minutes past midnight. The vicar knew the man's wife had recently given birth to a daughter and when the dates and times were checked, they coincided.

This, I have to say, is an unverified anecdotal story, for Ena Twigg was not able to put me in touch with the sitter. However, I have no reason to doubt the account, which I included in my biography of her,[3] since in every other case where I was able to check the details with those involved, her versions were confirmed.

Past-life recall

We don't need to rely on spirit communications to verify reincarnation, since there are numerous well-researched cases of past-life recall that stand up to close scrutiny. In Britain, the best in recent years is certainly that of Jenny Cockell.

Jenny Cockell

Jenny Cockell, a Northamptonshire chiropodist and mother of two, had been troubled since childhood with recurring memories of a life in Ireland. Gradually, over the years, she was able to put together the remembered pieces of the jigsaw puzzle, discovering that she had lived in the village of Malahide, outside Dublin, and had died soon after giving birth to her eighth child.

What makes Jenny Cockell's story special is that her memories seem to have survived into this life because of a feeling of guilt due to the fact that following her previous-life death, her children would have been removed from the care of her alcoholic husband and put into care. Incredibly, Jenny was eventually able to identify her past life as that of Mary Sutton, and when she returned to Malahide – after a researcher had independently confirmed much of the information she had remembered – she reunited the surviving children from that past life. They had been placed in orphanages and some of them were unaware that they were living close to each other until Jenny Cockell's research located them. The only child who stayed with his father was the eldest boy, Sonny Sutton, and I have appeared a number of times on television programmes with him and Jenny.

Sonny says there are similarities in appearance between them. 'I can see my mother in her eyes,' he once told me. He also revealed that what convinced him beyond doubt was

Jenny recalling a couple of incidents in his life that occurred before his mother died. One involved her regularly waiting for him by a jetty to return in a boat. Jenny could 'see' that clearly in her memory, but could not understand its significance until it was explained to her by Sonny. She also recalled the time the children came running to her when they found a rabbit caught in a trap. Jenny Cockell remembered much more besides, but Sonny Sutton said there was no way anyone who was not there could have known about these incidents.

The evidence of birth defects

There are literally thousands of reincarnation cases that offer similar evidence, and the best have been investigated by the handful of researchers who are prepared to expend the time and effort on researching, corroborating and analysing such reports. The vast majority of cases occur in cultures that traditionally accept reincarnation – notably India and Sri Lanka – and the person who has investigated them more than anyone is undoubtedly Dr Ian Stevenson, Carlson Professor of Psychiatry at the University of Virginia, USA, where he was also director of the Division of Personality Studies of the Department of Behavioural Medicine and Psychiatry.

Stevenson, who died on 8th February 2007 at the age of eighty-eight, has published several impressive volumes on his studies which he says in suitably scientific language are 'suggestive of reincarnation'. But the pinnacle of his investigations is undoubtedly a collection of cases dealing with birthmarks and birth defects. What typically happens in the best cases of reincarnation is that a child will start claiming to be someone else from a very tender age, often insisting on being called by another name and demanding to be taken back 'home'. In some cases, this results in scolding and attempts to suppress the child's memories, but some families that have enough information try to help the child by seeking out the former life family.

Researchers often do not hear about these cases until after the two families have met, and this gives sceptics the opportunity to argue that the evidence has been contaminated and that the memories of the witnesses cannot be relied upon. However, Ian Stevenson has noted that in many of the cases, the children – for it is almost always very young children who have such memories, which they forget by the time they are around eight years old – also display birthmarks or birth defects. These appear to correspond with a disfigurement suffered in the previous life they have remembered, or are related to their cause of death.

The importance of this evidence cannot be underestimated, for it virtually removes the spirit overshadowing or spirit possession argument. Take the case of Ma Khin Mar Htoo, who was born in the town of Tatkon, Upper Burma, on 26 July 1967, the third of four children of a casual labourer and his wife, who sold water and food to passengers at Tatkon railway station.

At the age of three, Ma Khin began to say she was Kalamagyi, describing her life and a horrific accident at Tatkon station in which she died instantly. Ma Thein Nwe, whose nickname was Kalamagyi, had picked roses to sell to passengers on the train, but the points stuck and instead of diverting alongside the platform, the train took the central track, along which Kalamagyi was walking with her back to the train. She was hit and her body was badly mutilated as the train ran over her. One of her injuries, according to witnesses who saw her remains, was the severance of one of her legs just below the knee. Ma Khin Mar Htoo was born without a right leg from a point ten centimetres from her knee.

Sceptics really have only two explanations to offer – coincidence or the effect of the accident on her mother, who conceived just a few months after Kalamagyi's tragic death and who twice dreamed of Kalamagyi during the pregnancy. Neither explains Ma Khin's memories from a very early age, or the fact that she recognised her former mother in the street, shouting 'Ahmay (mother) Than Kyi' and followed her home. Later she identified other people, including pictures of individuals Kalamagyi had known but Ma Khin had never met. Moreover, if spirit possession or overshadowing is argued, then it must have begun soon after conception in order to have affected the growth of her leg.

During more than 30 years of studying cases suggestive of reincarnation, Ian Stevenson realised, in an examination of 895 case studies, that 35 per cent involved birthmarks, some of which were highly significant. He then isolated 49 cases where it was possible to locate adequate data to compare the positions of wounds on the body of the past-life person with birthmarks on the child claiming to remember that life. In 43 of the cases – 88 per cent – he found a concordance in their location.

So controversial were these findings that Ian Stevenson decided not to publish them immediately. Instead, he waited until he had numerous examples in his files at the University of Virginia, and his findings, together with 225 case studies, were published in a monumental, 2,000-page, two-volume, profusely illustrated academic work,[4] although a much briefer version has also been produced for a general readership in hardback and paperback.[5] Many of the cases discussed relate to violent deaths and involve birth defects that are very unusual and not attributable to the usual causes, such as drugs taken during pregnancy.

Cases involving death by shooting

Of particular interest are cases involving death by shooting, where an autopsy report shows the bullet's entry and departure wounds on a body. Stevenson has found that children with birthmarks who remember death by shooting invariably display similar marks. In the case of Dahham Farrici in Turkey, who claimed to be the reincarnation of a famous distant relative, a celebrated bandit who shot himself rather than surrender to police, there was a distinct mark on his neck where he remembered placing a rifle in that former life. On his birth, the wound bled and needed to be stitched.

As his study continued, Stevenson realised that Farrici ought to have a corresponding exit wound birthmark on the top of his head, where the bullet would have left his body, even though no one had ever referred to one and few people, when questioned, could remember ever seeing one. Investigation by Stevenson confirmed that it was there – hidden by a full head of hair and described by the investigator as 'a substantial linear area of alopecia in the left parietal area of the scalp'.

Stevenson writes that the influence of a deceased personality on an unborn child 'implies some kind of template that imprints the embryo or foetus with 'memories' of the wounds, marks, or other features of the other physical body,' adding: 'The template must have a vehicle that carries the memories of the physical body and also the cognitive and behavioural ones. I have suggested the word *psychophore* (which means 'mind-carrying') for this intermediate vehicle.' Although Stevenson was cautious about reaching conclusions, it is clear that his work, and that of other researchers, is providing us with evidence of survival of death unrelated to mediumship or the seance room.

The extraordinary Druze cases

Just how difficult it is to collect such evidence became apparent to me on two visits to Lebanon in 1997 to film a documentary, *Back from the Dead*, which was first screened in the UK on Channel 4 in May 1998 as part of the *To the Ends of the Earth* series and has since been shown around the world on cable and satellite channels.

Lebanon was one of the countries in which Dr Ian Stevenson was able to carry out extensive research until, because of hostage taking, America stopped issuing visas to its citizens. The focus of his and my interest in that country was the Druze community, who are largely unknown outside the Middle East and for whom a belief in reincarnation comes naturally. Not only is it embodied in their teachings, but the majority of people seem to have childhood memories of past lives.

The subject made a fascinating documentary as, together with sceptical psychologist Dr Chris French from Goldsmith College, London, and Jad Younis, a Jordanian Druze who helped organise the adventure, I encountered many extraordinary cases. Unlike

Stevenson and other researchers, we did not have the luxury of investigating deeply and, for the sake of good television, Chris French and I needed to be seen to be having intense discussions about the pros and cons, even though it was often too early to have reached definitive conclusions about individual cases.

I was impressed with the case of Haneen Al-Arum, who remembered her former life as Safa Eid, a schoolteacher who was killed when the US battleship *New Jersey* anchored off Beirut on 17 January 1983 and began shelling the Druze positions in the mountains. As a young child, Haneen recognised her daughter Shahira, and also identified and named Riad, her son in that life, and Layla his wife. Meeting her former husband again, she remarked – correctly – that he now had a beard, whereas he did not have one when she was still alive. Among the most extraordinary photographs in my album from that visit are those showing a young Haneen sitting affectionately by the side of her elderly husband.

I was equally impressed by Rabih Abu Dyab, who was then aged 12 and remembered being a famous Lebanese footballer, songwriter and singer, Saad Halawi, who was known as 'the Kevin Keegan of the Lebanon'. But he was not a playboy. Rabih told me as he recalled his past life that six months before he was killed he had become a Druze sheikh and had withdrawn all his records from the shops.

We must always be cautious when someone claims to have been a celebrity in a former life, but in Rabih's case there was corroboration from Halawi's family, notably a cousin of the player. Saad had died instantly in Beirut when he went into a building that was an ammunitions dump and there had been an explosion. Learning that Saad Halawi's sister Samar knew of Rabih's claims but had not met him, the TV production team staged a reunion for the cameras. It made compelling viewing but was not particularly evidential, since Rabih would almost certainly have been able to guess the identity of the mysterious woman he was introduced to and because Samar clearly wanted to believe the young boy was her reincarnated brother.

Among the other cases I encountered was that of Alleya, whose parents would not allow her to marry a teacher named Rifat Mlafat, who was later killed. Alleya is now a teacher and her former lover, reincarnated in the body of Sami Erayes, is one of her pupils.

Lebanese paediatrician Dr Abdel Abu Assi told me that among his patients is a girl he has treated in two consecutive lives, first as Dada, who died at the age of 11 during a picnic, from an accidental shot fired by a hunter, and now as Eclass. She insisted on being taken to Dr Abu Assi when she was sick, and told him who she was in her past life. He fetched Dada's medical records and started asking her questions. 'This child knew everything,' he told me. 'She even knew about her death: that she had been shot in the chest and what her father had done to fetch her to the hospital.'

The Druzes, incidentally, believe that at the moment of death the soul transfers to another body that is just being born. The religion does not accept an intermediary stage in which the soul waits for an appropriate body in which to be reborn. The evidence, however, suggests that Druze cases are largely similar to those in other communities – though there are always cultural influences – and it was rare to find a past-life recall that precisely fitted the death and birth dates of the two individuals involved.

The question of karma

Despite the scientific evidence, belief in reincarnation can be highly controversial, particularly if discussion of it involves karma and an attempt to explain life's inequalities and tragedies. Air Chief Marshal Lord Dowding, who directed the Battle of Britain, discovered that in 1945, when he spoke at a Theosophical Society meeting in London. 'I have some reason to suppose that those who sowed the seeds of abominable cruelty at the time of the Inquisition reaped their own harvest at Belsen and Buchenwald,' he proclaimed.

This statement caused an uproar, naturally, since it suggested that those who died in the concentration camps were not victims but sinners who were at last receiving the punishment they were due from past-life misdeeds. Among those who rebuked him was journalist Hannen Swaffer, who pointed out that if Dowding was right, 'Belsen and Buchenwald were brought into being by God, of whose purpose Hitler and Himmler were the instruments.' There were probably many who regarded Dowding's comments as anti-Semitic.

Over half a century later, however, very similar views were expressed by – of all people – Israel's leading political rabbi. Speaking in a sermon in August 2000, Rabbi Ovadia Yosef, aged 79, said Hitler's victims were 'reincarnations of the souls of sinners, people who transgressed and did all sorts of things which should not be done. They have been incarcerated in order to atone.'

Rabbi Ovadia was the spiritual leader of the Shas party, which represents Sephardic Jews and had 17 seats in parliament, and his weekly sermons were broadcast by radio all over Israel. The majority of Israelis condemned his views, but his defenders argued that he was simply giving a spiritual explanation for the Holocaust. He very quickly tried to repair the damage he had done, however, by claiming his words had been 'taken out of context'. In a later sermon he declared: 'Six million Jews, among them one million children, were killed by the wicked Nazis. All were holy and pure and complete saints.'

Glenn Hoddle, England's football coach in the 1990s, also got into hot water when he proclaimed his belief in reincarnation during an interview with a reporter from *The Times*: 'You and I have been physically given two hands and two legs and half decent brains,' he explained. 'Some people have not been born like that for a reason. The karma is working from another lifetime. I have nothing to hide about that. It is not only people with disabilities. What you sow you have to reap.'

Following this statement, many people took the view – which was perhaps influenced by the England football team's poor results – that Hoddle had vilified the disabled and it was time for him to go. The Football Association sacked him. But those who ridiculed his beliefs did not offer an alternative explanation for why a loving Creator allows some people to be born perfect and others to suffer a lifetime of pain or disability.

Although I personally accept the evidence for reincarnation, I have no real understanding of the spiritual laws that govern it, nor do I know whether we all reincarnate regularly, or whether it is only those with specials needs, such as individuals whose lives are cut short, who are required to return. On one point I am adamant: none of us is in a position to determine how the laws of cause and effect may have been applied to an individual. Someone born seriously disabled *could* be suffering punishment for a terrible past-life. But by the same token, inside that body *may* be a highly evolved soul who has agreed to return with those disabilities in order to give others a greater understanding of suffering and how to cope with it.

It is not for us to judge. But a British TV documentary screened in 2004 will certainly have made many viewers reconsider their lives and those of others in a very different light. The subject of the film, *The Boy Whose Skin Fell Off*, was Jonny Kennedy who, throughout his 36 years, had suffered from a painful genetic skin condition called dystrophic epidermolysis bullosa. A film crew began recording when it became apparent that he had only months to live. Despite the agony he suffered when the dressings that covered three-quarters of his body were changed, and the many limitations that his condition placed on him, he was astonishingly upbeat about life and its purpose, dedicating his time to raising money that would help other sufferers. The film opened with an image of Jonny slumped in his wheelchair. It was only after his pre-recorded voice began a commentary that it became clear that he had just died: 'I have come back in spirit. I will tell you the story of my life . . . and my death.'

His wicked sense of humour was always in evidence, even when preparing for his funeral and choosing his coffin. It eventually became clear that what helped sustain Jonny Kennedy was his

Spiritualist outlook on life. He had attended his local Spiritualist church in Alnwick, Northumberland, for many years and he observed: 'Earth is a classroom and I believe we are all sent here to learn lessons. I have learnt what it is like to be in severe discomfort all my life and feel frustrated. I know there is more to it than this mortal coil. We are just a shell, except I have got a dodgy shell. Death is a freedom to me, it's an escape. Everyone knows it's coming and that means having to say goodbye.'

Clearly, the lessons Jonny Kennedy learned during his difficult life included not being bitter and asking, 'Why me?' but being mischievously good-humoured and realistic about the life he had been given.

1 Roy Stemman, *Reincarnation: True Stories of Past Lives*, Piatkus Books (1997).

2 Allan Kardec, *The Spirits' Book*, Psychic Press (1975).

3 Roy Stemman, *Medium Rare: The Psychic Life of Ena Twigg*, Spiritualist Association of Great Britain (1971).

4 Ian Stevenson, *Reincarnation and Biology: A Contribution to the Etiology of Birthmarks and Birth Defects*, Praegar Publishers (1997).

5 Ian Stevenson, *Where Reincarnation and Biology Intersect*, Praegar Books (1997).

Chapter 16

Television Mediums

TV mediums reach out to millions

Mediumship was made for television. It offers all the ingredients on which powerful dramas depend: love and loss, grief and joy, despair and hope, separation and reunion. Having witnessed hundreds of public demonstrations by clairvoyants over the years, it came as no surprise to me when TV companies eventually stumbled on mediumship and realised its enormous potential. But I confess that I never expected it to become so popular, nor for the mediums involved to attain celebrity status around the world so quickly. Whether it can maintain the current level of popularity on television remains to be seen, but it has certainly introduced millions to Spiritualism's philosophy and the evidence for life after death.

Though mediums made brief appearances on US and British TV in the 1960s and 1970s, usually in documentaries or on talk shows, it was George Anderson who was the first to be given his own programme on American cable TV in 1982. *Psychic Channels* changed the way the public perceived spirit communication and it blazed a trail for other psychic shows to follow. Anderson's account of his work, *We Don't Die*, was also the first book by a medium to become a bestseller. He has since written an equally successful psychic sequel: *Lessons From the Light*. Anderson is an impressive demonstrator with the ability to obtain names, dates and other evidential material from his spirit communicators. According to his website, in 2001 he became the first medium to receive approval 'from network television Standards and Practices to appear on network primetime television in his own series of specials'. I am aware of only one ABC Special featuring George Anderson, but it made quite an impact because of the content and the celebrities who participated. Screened in April 2002 and called *Contact: Talking to the Dead*, it consisted of readings for high-profile individuals who had recently lost loved ones, though he received no advance information about them before the readings.

Among the spirits he appeared to make contact with was that of Bonny Lee Bakley, 44, wife of actor Robert Blake, the star of TV detective series *Baretta* and also *In Cold Blood*. Her murder, a year earlier, was one of the most sensational homicides in recent Hollywood history. The couple had dined together in Los Angeles on 4 May 2001, after which they walked a block and a half to their car. Blake's story is that he then realised he had left his gun in the restaurant and returned to collect it. On his return to the vehicle, he found his wife had been shot dead. Bonny Lee's mother, Margerry Bakley, and her sister Marjorie Carlyon, agreed to attempt spirit communication through George Anderson in the hope that Bonny Lee would shed light on the unsolved case. But the murder victim said she did not want to talk about the circumstances of her death, apart from saying it was terrifying at first and then, said George Anderson, 'a very strong calm came over her'. The medium added, 'She was not surprised at her fate. She does admit she contributes to ending her life but she doesn't want to say she committed suicide and it's very important you understand that.'

That last remark is puzzling, since there was never any suggestion that Bonny Lee Bakley had taken her own life. And it was perhaps just as well that her apparent spirit communication provided no clues about her killer, for the LA police arrested her husband Robert Blake, 68, on the very day that the George Anderson ABC Special was screened – 22 April 2003. Had the programme contained allegations about the murderer – even from the spirit world – it would not have been aired. Blake was charged with his wife's murder and the trial began at the beginning of December 2004.

Much that Bonny Lee Bakley communicated was enthusiastically accepted by her mother and sister. 'It's Bonny, out and out, word for word,' said Margerry Bakley. What particularly impressed her was Bonny Lee's statement: 'We'll always be bosom buddies.' Margerry exclaimed: 'We had breast reduction surgery together!'

Among the other participants in the George Anderson special were Vanna White, the *Wheel of Fortune* beauty, Mackenzie Phillips, daughter of Mamas and the Papas lead singer John Phillips, and world wrestling champion Bret 'The Hitman' Hart. They all heard from dead family members.

CNN's *Larry King Live* has introduced many mediums to the viewing public in recent years, and it was James Van Praagh who featured on the programme just a few days after the George Anderson ABC Special. The purpose was to promote a CBS mini-series titled *Living with the Dead*, a drama based on his 1998 bestselling book, *Talking to Heaven*. King reminded viewers that it was an appearance on his show that gave Van Praagh an early boost to his mediumistic career. Playing the part of the medium in the series was Ted Danson, two-time Emmy winner for his role in *Cheers*, who also appeared on *Larry King Live*, revealing that he had received a spirit communication through Van Praagh from his father, who had died six months earlier, even before the mini-series was mooted. Danson refused to go into detail, saying only, 'But they were things that no one else could know. And the essence, the spirit of the message was just the essence of my father.' Van Praagh, who gave brief readings to telephone callers during the live broadcast, was also promoting his most recent book, *Heaven and Earth: Making the Psychic Connection*, as well as announcing his own syndicated TV show, *Beyond*, which began in September 2002.

John Edward

It is undoubtedly John Edward who has made the biggest TV impact of recent times, both in the US and other countries, and it was Larry King, once again, whose interviews helped launch Edward's TV career. So when he wrote *After Life: Answers From the Other Side* – which shot straight into the *New York Times'* bestsellers list at No. 4 when published in 2003 – it was Larry King who contributed the foreword; an interesting choice, given that King does not declare himself to be a believer. But his words probably echo the feelings of a large majority of the television audience for whom *Crossing Over* and other televised demonstrations of spirit communication are essential viewing. King observes:

John Edward certainly is one of the most extraordinary people I've ever known or interviewed. He's appeared on my show many, many times, and to say the least, provides fascinating TV. I'm a pure agnostic. That is, I don't know if there's a God or not. I don't know if there are other universes or not. And I certainly don't know if there's some sort of life after death. I'll admit John often provides insights into the departed that are not explainable. I don't know if he's seeing or hearing from the departed or if he's tuning into the viewer's vision of the departed. I'm not even sure if there is such a thing as psychic phenomena. However, I cannot deny that John Edward often amazes me.

A quick trawl on the Internet will throw up a variety of websites, discussion groups and message boards which seek to dismiss spirit communication, mediumship and other paranormal phenomena as impossible and their exponents as fakes. Inevitably, because of their celebrity status, the TV mediums are usually the target of these attacks, which depend largely on sarcasm and offer little in the way of evidence for their claims, apart from generalisations. One of the exceptions is Michael Shermer, founding publisher of

Skeptic magazine, director of the Skeptics Society, a monthly columnist for *Scientific American* and the co-host and producer of the 13-hour Fox Family television series, *Exploring the Unknown*. In his book *How We Believe: The Search for God in an Age of Science*, he says that Leah Hanes, who was a producer and researcher for NBC's *The Other Sid*e, had explained to him in April 1998 how Van Praagh 'used her to get information on guests during his numerous appearances on the show'. She said:

> *I can't say I think James Van Praagh is a total fraud, because he came up with things I hadn't told him, but there were moments on the show when he appeared to be coming up with fresh information that he got from me and other researchers earlier on. For example, I recall him asking about the profession of the deceased loved one of one of our guests, and I told him he was a fireman. Then, when the show began, he said something to the effect, 'I see a uniform. Was he a policeman or fireman please?' Everyone was stunned, but he got that directly from me.*

If true, this reflects very badly on Van Praagh. But it reflects just as badly on Hanes and her NBC colleagues for providing information on request to a medium about the guests for whom they expected him to read. It underlines the reasons why we need to be cautious about televised mediumship, for we are given no guarantees about the conditions under which such demonstrations take place. We realise that the studio audience is there by appointment, that their identities are known to *someone* in the production team and that they have been selected because their stories are dramatic. But we assume this and other information is not shared with the medium. And we also understand that only the very best messages are shown, and are edited to be as entertaining as possible. Even so, it is impossible to dismiss all the TV mediums as cheats deriving their evidence from 'cold' or 'hot' reading techniques (*see page 168*).

Bestselling thriller writer Michael Prescott, formerly sceptical of the paranormal, has written very positive essays about John Edward and James Van Praagh on his entertaining website (www.michaelprescott.freeservers.com), tackling the thorny questions of scepticism and alleged trickery in great depth. Prescott tells visitors to his site that he spends part of each year in Arizona, and it was at the University of Arizona that psychology professor Gary Schwartz conducted research with mediums, which he discussed in his book *The Afterlife Experiments*. George Anderson and John Edward were among the mediums who participated and all scored way above chance according to the researchers' analyses. Having read the book and been intrigued by the results, Prescott tuned into Edward's *Crossing Over* programme on the Sci-Fi Channel – which is no longer being screened. His verdict? 'Though it astonishes me to say it, I have come to think this guy is for real. I think something genuinely spooky is happening. I cannot see any plausible prosaic explanation for the apparent faculty that John Edward possesses.'

Prescott points out that cold reading relies on offering recipients of messages generalisations to which they can respond. To demolish that argument he cites numerous examples from *Crossing Over* where the statements made were so unusual or obscure that they would apply to very few people. Like the woman who was asked by Edward if anyone in the family had been a shepherd. She replied: 'My dad used to joke about being a shepherd. He'd say that when he retired, he wanted to be a shepherd so he could say, "Get the flock outta here!"' On another show he said to a man in the audience: 'There was a neighbour's dog ... I don't want to use the word torture, but you ... abused this dog.' The man, shamefaced, acknowledged the accuracy of this statement.

In 2003, a year after posting his original essay on the medium, Prescott wrote a second titled, 'More Thoughts on John Edward' in which he stated:

Since then, I've learned a lot more about psychic phenomena and about the mentalist techniques that can simulate such effects. I've thought of ways that Edward could fool his audience, but so far I've seen no good evidence that he is actually making use of these techniques.

Prescott is equally supportive of James Van Praagh, whose *Beyond* show has been discontinued. When Van Praagh appeared on *Larry King Live* on 30 January 2004, he had to take calls at random from all over the world, in real time, Prescott explains:

He had no chance to prepare and, with only a minute or two for each caller, little opportunity to ask questions. Since he couldn't see the caller, he certainly couldn't be accused of reading the person's body language or facial expression. It seemed like a good test of mediumship on live TV — working without a net. Did Van Praagh pass the test? He did. With flying colours.

At its best, television can be a powerful advocate of spirit communication. Sadly, there are just as many programmes which are deliberately sensational, making no attempt to be level-headed and objective about the messages received or the quality of the psychics and mediums used. The nadir, for me, was the disgracefully tacky *The Spirit of Diana* which was shown on pay-per-view cable TV in the US on 9 March 2003. Excerpts were also shown on a UK channel. Under the guise of being an examination of the spiritual aspects of Princess Diana's life, the real, audience-grabbing motive was a seance attempt to contact her spirit. 'Now, for the first time on television, we will reach out to the spirit world and attempt to communicate with Princess Diana,' it declared.

My preference is always for research-based documentaries, which is why I enjoyed HBO's *Life Afterlife* about the mediumistic experiments of Gary Schwartz at the University of Arizona. Californian-born Laurie Campbell was one of the mediums it featured. She is now director of mediumship at the university's Human Energy Systems Laboratory as well as being a subject for numerous mediumistic experiments.

A Canadian journalist, Patricia Pearson, was suitably impressed when she had a reading with Campbell in 2002. In her feature for *National Post of Canada* (1 August 2002) she explains that Campbell is the least famous of the five mediums tested by Schwartz, she has no TV show and has not written a bestseller. What's more, there's no need to visit her for a reading: she does them over the telephone, which is becoming a popular method with many of the top mediums. The writer saw this as an advantage because it meant Campbell could not pick up visual clues. Pearson had to wait three months for the reading and it cost US$200 which, I have to say, is cheap compared with other top-flight mediums. Pearson made no complaint about the cost because Campbell certainly delivered. 'A spirit medium put me in touch with my deceased grandmother the other day,' she wrote. 'We talked for about an hour. I told the medium, "Thank you very much." Then I spent a week staggering around in a state of extreme cognitive dissonance.' The family connections she was told about were unusual and very specific. But it was information about the sister of a friend of hers that proved to be the most astonishingly accurate. This is how Pearson recorded what happened when the medium described a girl with auburn hair:

> I asked her to focus on it, and she took off like a shot. She established the last place that this young woman was seen, the era of her death (the late 1970s), the purse she was carrying, the fact she had books in her arms, the time of day, the clothes she wore, the 'tremendous confusion' surrounding her death, how her body was found. Her name. Campbell did not get one detail wrong. Not one.
>
> I came away from this extraordinary conversation knowing that psychic phenomena exist. The damn woman riffled through my head. I remain unconvinced that she was talking to living souls, but she was most certainly tuning into my brain in a way that was as mysterious to me as our telephone conversation would be to an 18th-century observer.

In the UK, three mediums have dominated television in the past few years: Derek Acorah, Colin Fry and Tony Stockwell. Acorah is a former Liverpool Football Club player, and his theatrical presentation of his mediumship makes him a natural choice for television productions, though it also provides ammunition for sceptics who regard it all as a charade. It doesn't help, perhaps, that the TV show on which he has regularly appeared, Living TV's *Most Haunted*, involves visiting haunted houses and communicating with the ghosts of long-dead individuals, all filmed in deliberately spooky conditions. *The Antiques Ghost Show* was a welcome departure, involving Acorah psychometrising objects and having experts in art, genealogy and history discuss the likely accuracy of his psychic impressions. But Acorah, who has demonstrated his mediumship in many countries, is also an able Spiritualist medium, as he proved when he appeared at the Labatt's Apollo, Hammersmith, London, together with Colin Fry and Tony Stockwell, in a sell-out one-night show called *The Three Mediums* which was filmed and broadcast at a later date.

Colin Fry, who first found fame in Spiritualism as a physical medium, using the name Lincoln, has followed in the footsteps of John Edward and James Van Praagh, giving spirit messages to a small, select audience in the intimacy of a TV studio for his record-breaking *6ixth Sense* series, during which he has also given one-to-one readings for celebrities.

But it is Tony Stockwell's approach that, in my opinion, has been the most refreshing and evidential. Introduced by Fry to Living TV when it was looking for another medium for a new series called *Street Psychic*, Stockwell is an East Ender with a down-to-earth and often cheeky approach to spirit communication. The *Street Psychic* producers required him to walk the streets of different towns and cities in the UK – as well as San Francisco in the US, for a special programme – stopping unsuspecting passers-by and inviting them to have an instant reading. The broadcasting code in the UK limits the way in which mediumship can be demonstrated, so Stockwell needed to focus on the characters and relationships of people who agreed to participate, rather than giving spirit messages. The broadcasting authorities also require such programmes – but not documentaries taking a 'serious' look at spirit communication – to include a disclaimer, describing the content as 'entertainment' and pointing out that there are other interpretations of the information given. Nevertheless, Stockwell's psychic abilities are beyond question.

All three mediums now tour the UK, filling some of the biggest theatres with enthusiastic audiences who have been captivated by their TV appearances and long for a spirit message from their psychic heroes. I attended one of Stockwell's demonstrations at the New Theatre in Oxford, in May 2004, and was impressed on several counts. Although there were more females than males in the audience – which is also typical of Spiritualist churches – their ages ranged from teens to eighties. Very few, I suspect, knew where the nearest Spiritualist church was or had even considered visiting it; but the prospect of communicating with the next world in the comfort of a modern theatre was irresistible. They were probably making the right choice – as an introduction to Spiritualism – because the promotions company behind Stockwell's demonstrations had borrowed television techniques and used them to great advantage for the show. Sharing the platform with him was a video camera pointed at the audience. When he singled out an individual to receive a spirit message, the camera zoomed in and the image it captured was displayed on a large screen behind the medium. The recipients were also handed a microphone so that everyone in the theatre could hear their responses. It made the demonstration far more exciting than usual. Colin Fry made a surprise appearance at the show I attended, joining Stockwell to give a few spirit messages. During the summer of 2004 they toured together, supported by the television production and development company that stages their shows and ensures a very professional result, complete with large posters, glossy programmes and items of merchandising.

It's a far cry from the early days of Spiritualism and it will not be to everyone's liking, but it is certainly breathing new life into the gift of mediumship and opening minds to the possibility of spirit communication. The crucial test, however, is to forget the packaging and to examine the content: how evidential are the messages that are communicated?

What struck me about Tony Stockwell's demonstration in Oxford was how very specific he was about the information he was conveying to most of the recipients, and how very unlikely it was that these details would be relevant to others in the audience. To one woman who had lost her son, he talked about her visits to his grave. 'I go every day,' she responded. Stockwell continued, 'I see a butterfly. Watch out for that symbol when you visit.' The grieving mother responded: 'He has a plastic butterfly on his grave.'

In an audience of several hundred, it is difficult to locate recipients of spirit messages once the show ends, the applause fades and people head for the nearest exit. But I was fortunate to recognise one of the lucky few – Tracey Gregory – in the long queue of fans who had formed an orderly queue to have their programmes autographed by Stockwell and Fry. Though she had seen Fry demonstrate at a public meeting many months earlier, she had not seen Stockwell, either in person or on television, before the Oxford meeting. She was sitting with a friend in the dress circle when Stockwell singled her out for a message from 'a child'. He then clarified that it was a boy.

'He would be three or four,' he continued. She knew a boy who fitted that description: the son of a friend who had died at the age of three-and-a-half.

'His death was a big shock, very sudden,' the medium continued, adding: 'There was something odd about the last couple of days of his life. He was in this world one moment and in the spirit world the next.'

The youngster, named Stephen, had been seriously burned in a house fire. But he appeared to be making a good recovery in hospital and there was no immediate fear for his life. His mother was at his bedside when Stephen opened his eyes, said, 'I love you,' and then closed them. Moments later, he passed away. Stockwell's description of the suddenness of his death was impressively accurate.

'He looked on you as his Mum,' the medium added.

It was a simple statement but one that was packed with meaning, as Mrs Gregory explained later. 'When he was born, I didn't have any children. My friend then became pregnant again and her next child was born very early, prematurely. When we went out together, she would push her new-born child in her pushchair and I would take care of Stephen. He called me his "second Mum". So his statement was spot-on.'

The evidence continued.

'You told his mother you were coming here today and that you'd let her know if you received a message from him.'

Again, Stockwell was correct. 'We're very open about these things,' Mrs Gregory told me when I interviewed her a few weeks later. 'Often, when I'm over at her house, strange things happen, like pictures falling off the wall, and we talk about who is responsible. I told her I would be seeing a medium demonstrating in Oxford, and she was delighted when I told her later that Stephen had communicated.'

After references to the way Stephen's mother's pregnancy had changed her life, Stockwell continued:

'There's a little girl, alive. It's his sister. He's showing me that she has a scar on her forehead. He's poking it with his finger.'

His sister, it transpires, was also badly burned in the same house fire that cost Stephen his life, and her face and body are badly scarred. The surgeons were concerned, at one time, that the damage to the skin on her forehead could not be adequately repaired, but they succeeded. That, Mrs Gregory believes, was the significance of Stephen pointing to that part of her body.

'He wore blue pyjamas on his last night,' the medium added. Such observations are often dismissed as trivial by the sceptics, but if they are accurate – as this was – then they add to the sum total of evidence provided. Mrs Gregory confirmed that he was wearing blue pyjamas not only on the day he died but also when the house was engulfed in flames.

'And I see him taking the cord out of his dressing gown and whipping people,' said Stockwell, with a mixture of surprise and amusement.

Mrs Gregory confirmed that he would never keep his dressing gown on to keep warm, preferring to remove the cord and playfully whip people with it.

'He tells me you bought him slippers with ladybirds on them.'

'Yes, that's right. And boots, too.'

Looking puzzled, the medium added: 'Now this is strange. He's showing me him putting his fingers into your mouth and you biting them.'

Laughing, Mrs Gregory replied that Stephen hated having his fingernails cut. But he would put his fingers into her mouth and allow her to chew the nails off. He wouldn't allow anyone else to do it.

'By the time you were told of his condition, he was dead,' Stockwell continued.

In fact, Mrs Gregory was close to having her own first child and was out of the country when Stephen and his sister were badly burned, and the news was kept from her so as not to upset her.

'I'm getting 2:30 and also 4:10,' Stockwell added. 'I don't know if it was 2.30 when he was taken ill and 4.10 when he died ...'

She understood perfectly and interrupted him to explain: '2.30 was when Stephen died and 4.10 was when my son was born, but not on the same day.' She explained to me later that Stephen's death, on 11 November, had taken place 17 years ago, as had the birth of her son, a month later. Until then, I had assumed that the medium was in communication with a young child and that the death was recent. But Stephen was discussing events of many years ago in order to bring comfort to those who still remember him and love him.

'He brings a little girl in the spirit world. I feel they play together.'

This spirit child, she believes, is her own daughter. And although Stephen passed on before her birth, he appears to be showing the same interest in family and friends as he would have done if he were still on earth.

Mrs Gregory realises that her own experience of spirit communication, however stunning its accuracy, will not persuade many sceptics. 'I think each person has to go to a medium and make up his or her own mind. But I know that Tony Stockwell told me things that no one else in the world could know. I've received a number of messages from mediums, but I couldn't *believe* some of the things he came out with. In fact, I couldn't sleep that night – I kept turning it over in my mind. It was amazing.'

Yet, had I not been at Oxford's New Theatre that night with my notebook, and subsequently met and interviewed the recipient of just one of the remarkable messages, it would be just another spirit communication that would by now be a distant and largely forgotten memory for most people present, except Tracey Gregory and those with her. The audience will have been impressed, but left with the feeling that they had eavesdropped on a private telephone conversation. Yet the communication was far more momentous than that. In the absence of a more compelling explanation, I believe that it – and the hundreds of similar messages that are conveyed by the top mediums every day of the year – provides us with remarkable evidence of an afterlife that is largely ignored by science. Since demonstrations by people like Stockwell and Fry, or John Edward and James Van Praagh, are routinely videoed, I hope it will not be long before funding can be found to carry out an in-depth study of this remarkable resource, providing us with an abundance of proof and a new perspective on life and death.

Chapter 17

The Best Evidence

One of the most frustrating aspects of spirit communication is that there is no universally accepted criterion on which the evidence for contact with the next world can be judged. Some of the most eminent scientists and philosophers of the past have spent years studying the subject and declared themselves totally satisfied that they have been in communication with spirits of the dead. Sir William Crookes, Sir Oliver Lodge and Alfred Russel Wallace were among them. But because their experiences were often personal and the mediums they sat with are no longer around to repeat the experiments, sceptics feel justified in dismissing their work as if they were deluded fools or – worse – willing collaborators in fraud.

Nevertheless, I believe that with every passing decade, and despite the changes that occur in the type of mediumship displayed, we are building up a body of evidence that will eventually be beyond doubt. In the meantime, any individual prepared to carry out an investigation of spirit communication can reach his or her own verdict long before science makes up its mind.

In this book, which has looked at a range of different types of communication methods and the evidence they provide, I have already shared with readers some of the best modern evidence for spirit communication. To draw this study to a close, therefore, I offer some additional comments on topics and phenomena that may throw additional light on a very complex subject.

One day, in the fullness of time, we will all know whether life continues after death. My own view is that certainty of survival based on evidence gives us a whole new perspective on life and since our time on Earth serves to develop our soul and prepare us for the afterlife, the sooner we expand our spiritual horizons to embrace that understanding and live our lives accordingly, the better.

Apports

An apport is said to be a materialised gift from the spirit. This description, however, is somewhat misleading, since apports are usually objects that arrive in the seance room not from the next world, but from some other place on Earth. One English medium, Mrs Everitt, refused to have anything to do with apports on the basis that 'they are usually stolen'. Some of them are quite extraordinary and, by their very nature, would appear to have been impossible to smuggle into the room undetected and undamaged by the medium.

One of the most extraordinary seance room apports was said to have been produced in 1880 by English materialisation medium Madame d'Esperance. Her spirit guide, Yolande, emerged from the cabinet at one seance, placed a glass carafe half filled with sand in the centre of the room, then draped a piece of material over it. The sitters were amazed to see the drapery rising. Yolande reappeared from the cabinet, removed the cloth and revealed a tall plant. After a few minutes of singing, the sitters discovered that the plant had burst into bloom.

Ten years later, the same medium produced a seven-foot high golden lily in full bloom and exuding overpowering perfume at another seance. The sitters were told they could not keep it, and Yolande became quite upset when she was unable to dematerialise it. The sitters had to keep it in a darkened room until the next session, when it was placed in the centre of the room and vanished as mysteriously as it had arrived.

Even more extraordinary are the accounts of seances held by Charles Bailey, an Australian bootmaker, at the beginning of the twentieth century. He became the personal medium of Thomas Welton Stanford, a Melbourne millionaire, whose collection of Bailey's apports is now preserved at Stanford University, California, to which he gave a $50,000 endowment for psychic research in 1911.

To rule out trickery, the medium allowed himself to be strip-searched. On occasion he was then placed in a bag, with holes for his head and hands, and tied up, or put in a cage covered with mosquito netting. Even the sitters were sometimes searched to rule out collaboration. Despite these precautions, apports of creatures occurred, including two nests with a live bird in each, a live, 18-inch, shovel-nosed shark and a crab.

Infrared photographs taken at a Jack Webber seance in the early 1940s are said to have captured the moment an apport of a brass bird materialised. It appears to be emerging from the body of the Welsh medium.

Cross-correspondences

In assessing the validity of claims of spirit communication, we need to evaluate the likely source of the information provided. Is it more likely that messages somehow manifest from the conscious minds of living people than from the surviving minds of the dead?

One of the strongest post-mortem cases concerns the so-called Cross-correspondences, in which a huge but largely meaningless collection of messages (conveyed by both trance and automatic writing) was received over a 31-year period from 1901 through a variety of women mediums in various parts of the world. They contained Greek and Latin references and it was only when they were pieced together like a jigsaw that they appeared to make sense.

Those who accept the Cross-correspondences as evidence of spirit communication say they were deliberately complex because they were part of an experiment in communication from the early pioneers of psychic research, including F.W.H. Myers, Henry Sidgwick and Edmund Gurney, all of whom had died before the messages started. This case is clearly too complicated to examine here, but it has succeeded in satisfying some sceptical researchers that the dead academics were in touch with the mediums concerned.

Clairvoyance

I have commented elsewhere on the way in which televised mediumship has opened up the minds of many people to spirit communication. In Britain, however, a strict broadcasting code requires the programme makers to treat the subject as 'entertainment', despite the often emotional content of the messages conveyed. Even so, there must be nagging doubts in the minds of many who view such programmes that some of the studio recordings are somehow stage managed.

A recent series called *Street Psychic*, featuring young London medium Tony Stockwell, has offered a refreshing change of pace, by sending him out into the community with a film crew, offering to give readings to passers-by. Their reactions are often amusing, but when he gets a positive response, the information he is able to give to complete strangers is impressive. In the UK he has to follow the production guidelines for giving general life readings, but for a programme he filmed in San Francisco he was free to demonstrate his mediumship and spirit communication, again without any previous arrangement with the people he met on the street.

Drop-in communicators

Every so often, a spirit communicator comes through at a seance and asks for a message to be given to someone other than those attending. These 'drop-in' communicators are comparatively rare and, I suspect, are not often reported because they seldom provide enough information or incentive for any of the sitters to verify their statements. A special study of them has been made by Cambridge psychical researcher Alan Gauld[1], and they are important from an evidential point of view on the one hand because their messages cannot be attributed to telepathy with anyone present, and on the other because they seem to demonstrate that a surviving personality with special reason is eager to communicate with *anyone* who will listen.

One of the most intriguing cases of this kind occurred at a seance in Reykjavik, Iceland, in 1937 with the medium Hafstein Bjornsson. A drop-in communicator came with a very strange request: he said he wanted his leg. He eventually identified himself as Runolfur Runolfsson (nicknamed Runki) who had been swept out to sea while walking home in a drunken state one night. His remains had been washed up on the shore, but according to him one of his legs was missing ... and he wanted it back.

It seemed like an impossible request to satisfy until a new member, Ludvik Gudmundsson, a fish merchant, joined the circle and Runki told him that his missing leg had been placed in the wall of his house in Sandgerdi. After making enquiries about his Sandgerdi home (he also had a house in Reykjavik), Ludvik discovered that a carpenter *had* placed a thighbone that had been found on the shore in one of the walls. The wall was opened up, the bone given a decent burial in a coffin and Runki returned at the next seance to describe the event and thank Ludvik for what he had done. Instead of then ceasing to communicate, as most drop-ins do, he became the medium's principal spirit control.

Materialisation

Recent reports of materialisation seances held in Britain by medium David Thompson are very entertaining. The medium is securely trussed up and gagged, but spirit voices are soon heard in the darkened room, people are touched by materialised figures and objects are moved.

Much of this occurs in total darkness and so far the spirit controls have not allowed the use of permanent red light or infrared photography to record what is happening. This raises more than a little scepticism, particularly as some of the communicators have been said to be celebrities and colourful characters such as comedians Peter Cook and Dudley Moore, as well as Quentin Crisp.

All of this led *Psychic News* editor Tony Ortzen to declare, without naming Thompson, in an editorial on 31 January 2004 headed 'Let There Be Light in Seance Room Dark...', that although other psychic publications may do so, 'we will not report any seances held in the pitch black at which alleged spirit visitors fail to offer any credible proof of identity and back that up with irrefutable evidence. Neither will we report seances of any kind of physical mediumship at which no form of illumination is present.' He later qualified this by saying that direct voice seances were an exception to this rule.

Was he asking too much by making such demands? Among those who supported the *Psychic News* policy was George Cranley, who ran the recently disbanded Noah's Ark Society. He told of attending a materialisation seance with Welsh medium Alec Harris (who later moved to South Africa) in a small room 'lit by red bulbs, which were not dimmed'. A man materialised with only half a face and was recognised immediately by his relatives: he had died after cancer had eaten away half his face.

The husband of a friend of Cranley materialised in his Royal Marines' uniform, walked over to her, kissed her and called her by a pet name, which was not even known to their children. 'That's what materialisation is all about,' he added.

Alec Harris passed away in 1974. A book about his mediumship[2] written by his wife Louie tells of seances at which materialised spirits conversed with sitters in up to six languages, including a Hindi dialect. The very reasonable point that *Psychic News* makes is that there is no point in spirits materialising if it is too dark to see them.

Mediumship

Every time a study of mediumship is published, sceptics raise objections, arguing that there might have been 'sensory leakage' or that controls were not sufficiently tight. Researchers involved in such experiments respond by introducing ever-more stringent conditions under which mediums are tested – and still get significant results.

A research team at the University of Arizona's Human Energy Systems Laboratory, Tucson, led by Professor Gary E.R. Schwartz and Linda G.S. Russek, have been investigating the ability of five top mediums – including John Edward and George Anderson – to provide evidential spirit communications. In order to prevent visual clues, the mediums were not allowed to see the sitters, and the recipients of the messages were permitted to give only 'yes' or 'no' answers to questions.

In fact, few questions were asked. In one test, the mediums scored an impressive 83 per cent accuracy overall. In another experiment, the score was 77 per cent. Then, to overcome possible criticism by sceptics that even 'yes' and 'no' responses might give the mediums too much feedback, a relocation and extension experiment was conducted with one of the sitters at a later date, in which no questions were allowed for the first ten minutes, and then a period for 'yes' and 'no' answers followed. The success rate was still 77 per cent.

'The data suggest that highly skilled mediums are able to obtain accurate and replicable information,' they conclude in a report published in the Society for Psychical Research's *Journal*.[3] 'Since all possible measures were taken to eliminate the factors of fraud, error and statistical coincidence, other possible mechanisms should be considered in future research. These include telepathy, super-psi and survival of consciousness after death.' The researchers add that their goal is to 'apply the gold standard of multi-centre, double-blind medicine experiments to mediumship science'.

Meanwhile in Scotland, researchers Professors Archie Roy and

Patricia Robertson have published an account[4] of a double-blind procedure they have developed for assessing the relevance of a medium's statement to a sitter. It requires not only that the medium and sitter are hidden from each other, but also that the sitter does not speak to the medium, does not even know that he or she is the recipient of a message, and that neither of the two researchers is involved in selecting the recipient. These complicated procedures are described in detail. Statements made by the medium during the session are then transcribed and given to *every* potential sitter present, and they are all asked to tick the statements they believe are relevant to them. Only when all the replies are in and assessed is it revealed which of the recipients the message was intended for.

One of Britain's top mediums, Gordon Smith, has participated in these experiments. In the third and latest paper on their work,[5] Roy and Robertson reveal that there is only a million-to-one possibility that their positive results are due to chance. The main conclusion of the second series of experiments, conducted over a two-and-a-half-year period, 'is that it shows in a highly significant manner, in circumstances that precluded the operation of normal factors, that *recipients* accepted a higher proportion of statements from mediums as relevant to their lives than did *non-recipients*'.

At the end of the day, it is normal and spontaneous spirit communication that is most meaningful for those who are bereaved. That was certainly the case for Veronica Keen, wife of one of the Society for Psychical Research's longest serving investigators, Montague Keen, whose particular interest was survival evidence. He collapsed and died while asking a question during a debate on the paranormal in January 2004, at the Royal Society in London. Within hours, his widow tells me, Monty was producing evidence of his survival. At his wake, just as a medium told the gathering that the researcher was present and enjoying the proceedings, a picture fell off the wall. Since then, spirit communications from him have been received from overseas as well as from English and Irish mediums, and Professor Gary Schwartz is planning to arrange proxy seances in the hope that Monty Keen will be able to provide outstanding evidence for spirit communication.

Survival codes

A variation on the spirit communication theme is for an individual not to convey some deep, meaningful wisdom or intimate details of his life on Earth from the spirit world, but instead to provide a secret code that only he knows, which will open a lock or decipher a message. The idea is that it would demonstrate telepathy between the deceased and the person who cracks the code.

Dr Robert Thouless was a pioneer in this field but did not succeed in transmitting the required information from the spirit world after his death. More recent attempts have also failed – sometimes when the code has been broken *before* the individual has passed over. But it is still a fruitful area for research and it is to be hoped that the late Susy Smith's Afterlife Code Project will be resurrected and encourage more participation from believers and sceptics alike.

Teleportation

Another form of physical mediumship, teleportation involves the instantaneous transfer of an object from one location to another. Presumably it is engineered by spirit entities and is a similar process to that involved in the production of apports. This phenomenon was reported by observers participating in both the recent Scole and SORRAT experiments (*see pages 95 and 98*).

Probably the most extraordinary account of teleportation involves a request made at the beginning of the last century by Ernesto Bozzano, a leading Italian psychical researcher, during a physical seance with a medium who was an intimate friend 'and with whom apports could be obtained at command'. Bozzano writes:

I begged the communicating spirit to bring me a small block of pyrites which was lying on my writing table about two kilometres away. The spirit replied (by the mouth of the entranced medium) that the power was almost exhausted, but all the same he would make the attempt.

The spirit eventually told the sitters that he had been able to disintegrate a small portion of the object and bring it into the room but there was not enough energy to reassemble it. He then told them to turn on the light.

We did so, and found, to our great surprise, that the table, clothes, and hair of the sitters, as well as the furniture and carpet of the room, were covered by the thinnest layer of brilliant impalpable pyrites. When I returned home after the sitting I found the little block of pyrites lying on my writing table from which a large fragment, about one third of the whole piece, was missing, this having been scooped out of the block.

Sceptics would argue that such an event is impossible. It is, however, worth recording that teleportation has now been witnessed in the laboratory – admittedly at a sub-atomic level. Anton Zeilinger of the Institute of Experimental Physics at Vienna University published a paper in *Scientific American* in April 2000 in which he stated: 'Teleportation has become a lab reality – for photons'. They have found a way of inducing instant change in particles by creating pairs of photons and changing the state of one. Through a phenomenon known as 'entanglement' the other photon also changes immediately.

Chinese and Japanese researchers, on the other hand, have witnessed and recorded astonishing teleportation of actual objects in the laboratory. Using 'super psychics' – often children – they have carried out controlled experiments in which small objects, such as pills, have been sealed in transparent containers and then transferred to other containers. The psychics were not allowed to touch the objects or containers and some of the Chinese research was witnessed by government observers.

The Chinese scientists used a four hundred shots-per-second high-speed camera to film the proceedings while a psychic teleported a pill from inside a sealed glass container. On one exposure the pill can be seen penetrating the glass wall, on the next it is half inside and half out, and on the third it is completely outside the container. (p.120). Neither the pills and glass containers were damaged, suggesting that, under the right conditions, solid materials can interpenetrate each other.

The Federation of American Scientists' website revealed in November 2004 that the US Air Force Research Lab has paid consultants US$ 25,000 for an 88-page *Teleportation Physics Report* which reviews experiments and concepts in the field, including the Chinese and Japanese research. The report's author, Eric Davis, has called for US $7.5 million funding for future teleportation experiments.

Trance

As I indicated in the chapter devoted to trance (*see page 16*), it can be one of the most evidential forms of mediumship. As an example of this, let me repeat the story of Emma Hardinge Britten, a pioneer of English and American Spiritualism.

A member of the crew of the mail steamer *Pacific*, which had sunk in the ocean, controlled young, entranced Emma and disclosed facts about the tragedy that were then unknown. (Many years later, as we have seen, Helen Duncan was to have a similar experience during the Second World War.) Because of the nature of the details given through her mediumship, Emma Hardinge – as she then was – was threatened with prosecution by the boat's owners when the story was made public. The action was not pursued, however, when all the details communicated from the spirit world were found to be true and accurate.

A spiritual transformation

It seems that those in the next world are as eager as we are to establish communication and are working with ingenuity to achieve that aim. We do not know what limits, spiritual or otherwise, might be placed on that endeavour, but it should be clear to the reader that every avenue is being explored from the next world to strengthen and enhance the lines of spirit communication. All it requires is a similar endeavour in the physical world and we might be able to look forward to a spiritual transformation that is beyond our wildest dreams.

It is appropriate that I should leave the final words to a spirit guide – Silver Birch – whose wisdom guides thousands of people, around the world, on their journey through this life:

Learn to be free. Do not imprison yourself. Do not hedge yourself around and refuse to allow new inspiration to come to you. Truth is a constant search. Its boundaries ever widening, for as the soul evolves the mind responds. You become free when you realise there is no limitation to knowledge, truth, wisdom and growth. You become free when you discard at once that which you know in your heart is false, that which reason rejects, because your intelligence cries out in revolt. You become free when you are not afraid to discard error in the face of new light.

1 Alan Gauld, *Mediumship And Survival*, David and Charles (1983).
2 Louie Harris, *They Walked Among Us*, Psychic Press (1980).
3 *Journal of the Society for Psychical Research*, No. 862, January 2001.
4 *Journal of the Society for Psychical Research*, No. 864, July 2001.
5 *Journal of the Society for Psychical Research*, No. 874, January 2004.

Bibliography

Beard, Paul, *Living On*, George Allen & Unwin (1980).

Borgia, Anthony, *Life in the World Unseen*, Anthony Borgia, MBA Publishing (1993).

Caillard, Lady Zoe, *A New Conception of Love*, Rider (1934).

Cassirer, Manfred, *Medium on Trial*, PN Publishing (1996).

Chapman, George and Stemman, Roy, *Surgeon from Another World: Extraordinary Encounters*, W.H. Allen (1978).

Cornell, Tony, *Investigating the Paranormal*, Helix Press, New York (2002).

Cummins, Geraldine, *Swan on a Black Sea* edited by Signe, Toksvig, Routledge and Kegan, Paul (1965).

Dixon-Smith, Roy, *New Light on Survival*, Rider (1952).

Dooley, Anne, *Every Wall a Door*, Abelard-Schuman (1973).

Dowding, Air Chief Marshal Lord, Many Mansions, Rider (1943).

Drewery Eileen, *Why Me?*, Hodder Headline (1997).

Edward, John, *One Last Time*, Piatkus Books (1999).

Edwards, Harry, *The Mediumship of Arnold Clare*, Rider (1941).

Edwards, Harry, *The Mediumship of Jack Webber*, Rider (1940).

Edwards, Harry, *Thirty Years a Spiritual Healer*, Herbert Jenkins (1968).

Elliott, Rev Maurice, *The Psychic Life of Jesus*, Gordon Press (1974).

Findlay, Arthur, On the Edge of the Etheric, Psychic Press (1931).

Findlay, Arthur, *Looking Back: The Autobiography of a Spiritualist*, SNU Publications (1955).

Fisher, Joe, *Hungry Ghosts*, Grafton Books (1990).

Fisher, Joe, *The Case for Reincarnation*, Somerville House (1998).

Flint, Leslie, *Voices in the Dark: My Life as a Medium*, Macmillan, London (1971).

Fuller, John, *Arigo: Surgeon of the Rusty Knife*, Thomas Y. Cromwell Company (1974).

Gauld, Alan, Mediumship and Survival, David and Charles (1983).

Harris, Louie, *They Walked Among Us*, Psychic Press (1980).

Harrison, Tom, *Visits by Our Friends From the Other Side*, Saturday Night Press Publications (1989).

Hutton. Joe Bernard, *Healing Hands*, W.H. Allen (1966).

Kardec, Allan, *The Spirits' Book*, Paris (1862).

Leaf, Horace, *The World's Greatest Mediums*, Spiritualist Association of Great Britain (1966).

McAll, rev Robert Kenneth, *Healing the Family Tree*, Sheldon Press (1982).

MacLaine, Shirley, *Going Within*, Bantam Press (1989).

Manning Matthew, *One Foot in the Stars*, Piatkus Books (2003).

Montefiore, Hugh, *The Paranormal: A Bishop Investigates*, Upfront Publishing (2002).

Neate, Tony, *Channelling for Everyone*, Piatkus Books (1997).

Nolen, Dr William, Healing: *A Doctor in Search of a Miracle*, Random House (1974).

Perriman, A. E., *Broadcasting from Beyond*, Psychic Book Club (1952).

Pike, Bishop James, *The Other Side*, Doubleday, New York (1968).

Radin, Dean, *The Conscious Universe: The Scientific Truth of Psychic Phenomena*, HarperSanFrancisco (1997).

Randi, James, *Flim-Flam*, Prometheus Books (1982).

Raudive, Konstantin, *Breakthrough*, Colin Smythe (1971).

Roberts, Estelle, *Fifty Years as a Medium*, Herbert Jenkins (1959).

Rogers, Rita, *Mysteries*, Pan Books (2003).

Rogo, D. Scott and Bayless, Raymond, *Phone Calls from the Dead*, Prentice Hall (1979).

Sherwood, Jane, *Post Mortem Journal*, C.W. Daniel Company (1992).

Smith, Gordon, *Spirit Messenger*, Hay House (2003).

Solomon, Grant and Jane, *The Scole Experiment*, Piatkus Books (1999).

Stemman, Roy, *Healers and Healing*, Piatkus Books (1999).

Stemman Roy, *Medium Rare: The Psychic Life of Ena Twigg*, Spiritualist Association of Great Britain (1971).

Stemman, Roy, *Reincarnation: True Stories of Past Lives*, Piatkus Books (1997).

Stevenson, Ian, *Reincarnation and Biology: A Contribution to the Etiology of Birthmarks and Birth Defects*, Praegar Books (1997).

Stevenson, Ian, *Where Reincarnation and Biology Intersect*, Praegar Books (1997).

Webster, Kenneth, *Vertical Plane*, Grafton Books (1989).

Wicker, Chruistine, *Lily Dale*, HarperSanFrancisco (2003).

Useful Websites

for more information about subjects discussed in this book

SPIRITUALIST ORGANISATIONS
UK
Spiritual Truth Foundation: www.silverbirchpublishing.co.uk
Spiritualists' National Union: www.snu.org.uk
Arthur Findlay College: www.arthurfindlaycollege.org
College of Psychic Studies: www.collegeofpsychicstudies.co.uk
Internationalist Spiritualist Federation: www.theisf.com
Great World Christian Spiritualist Association: www.greaterworld.com
London Spiritualist Mission: www.spiritualistmission.co.uk
Spiritualist Association of Great Britain:
    www.spiritualistassociation.org.uk
White Eagle Lodge: www.whiteagle.org
Allen Kardec Educational Society: www.allan-kardec.org
USA
National Spiritualist Association of Churches: www.nsac.org
Brazil
Advanced Study Group of Spiritism: www.geae.inf.br

MEDIUMS
Colin Fry: www.colinfry.co.uk
Derek Acorah: www.derekacorah.org
George Anderson: www.georgeanderson.com
James Van Praagh: www.vanpraagh.com
John Edward: www.johnedward.net
John Holland: www.johnholland.com
Keith Charles: www.keithcharles.biz
Leslie Flint: www.leslieflint.com
Stephen O'Brien: www.stephenobrien.co.uk
Sylvia Brown: www.sylvia.org
Tony Stockwell: www.tonystockwell.com

SPIRIT COMMUNICATION
The ADC Project: www.after-death.com
The Case for the Afterlife: www.victorzammit.com

HEALING ORGANISATIONS
National Federation of Spiritual Healers: www.nfsh.org.uk
UK Healers: www.ukhealers.info

PARAPSYCHOLOGY
Society for Psychical Research: www.spr.ac.uk
Parapsychology Foundation: www.parapsychology.org
Rhine Research Center: www.rhine.org
Consciousness Research Laboratory: www.deanradin.com
Gary Schwartz VERITAS Research Programme:
   www.veritas.arizona.edu

ELECTRONIC VOICE PHENOMENA RESEARCH
American Association: www.aaevp.com
German Association: www.vtf.de
World ITC: www.worlditc.org

PUBLICATIONS
Life & Soul: www.lifeandsoul.com
Psychic News: www.psychicnewsbookshop.co.uk

Index